The 'Poor Child'

The 'poor child' at the centre of development activity is often measured against and reformed towards an idealised and globalised child subject. This book examines why such normative discourses of childhood are in need of radical revision and explores how development research and practice can work to 'unsettle' the global child. It engages the cultural politics of childhood – a politics of equality, identity and representation – as a methodological and theoretical orientation to rethink the relationships between education, development, and poverty in children's lives.

This book brings multiple disciplinary perspectives, including cultural studies, sociology, and film studies, into conversation with development studies and development education in order to provide new ways of approaching and conceptualising the 'poor child'. The researchers draw on a range of methodological frames – such as poststructuralist discourse analysis, arts based research, ethnographic studies and textual analysis – to unpack the hidden assumptions about children within development discourses. Chapters in this book reveal the diverse ways in which the notion of childhood is understood and enacted in a range of national settings, including Kenya, India, Mexico and the United Kingdom. They explore the complex constitution of children's lives through cultural, policy, and educational practices. The volume's focus on children's experiences and voices shows how children themselves are challenging the representation and material conditions of their lives.

The 'Poor Child' will be of particular interest to postgraduate students and scholars working in the fields of childhood studies, international and comparative education, and development studies.

Lucy Hopkins is a lecturer in children and family studies at Edith Cowan University, Western Australia.

Arathi Sriprakash is a lecturer in sociology of education at the University of Cambridge, UK.

Education, Poverty and International Development Series

Series Editors
Madeleine Arnot and Christopher Colclough
Centre for Education and International Development, University of Cambridge, UK

This series of research-based monographs and edited collections contributes to global debates about how to achieve education for all. A major set of questions faced by national governments and education providers concerns how the contributions made by education to reducing global poverty, encouraging greater social stability and equity, and ensuring the development of individual capability and wellbeing can be strengthened. Focusing on the contributions that research can make to these global agendas, this series aims to provide new knowledge and new perspectives on the relationships between education, poverty and international development. It offers alternative theoretical and methodological frameworks for the study of developing-country education systems, in the context of national cultures and ambitious global agendas. It aims to identify the key policy challenges associated with addressing social inequalities, uneven social and economic development, and the opportunities to promote democratic and effective educational change.

The series brings together researchers from the fields of anthropology, economics, development studies, educational studies, politics, international relations and sociology. It includes work by some of the most distinguished writers in the fields of education and development, along with new authors working on important empirical projects. The series contributes significant insights on the linkages between education, economy and society, based on interdisciplinary, international and national studies.

Selected volumes will include critical syntheses of existing research and policy, work using innovative research methodologies, and in-depth evaluations of major policy developments. Some studies will address topics relevant to poverty alleviation, national and international policy-making and aid, while others will be anthropological or sociological investigations of how education functions within local communities, for households living in poverty or for particular socially marginalised groups. In particular, the series will feature sharp, critical studies that are intended to have a strategic influence on the thinking of academics and policy-makers.

Published titles:

Education Outcomes and Poverty
A reassessment
Edited by Christopher Colclough

Teacher Education and the Challenge of Development
A global analysis
Edited by Bob Moon

Education Quality and Social Justice in the Global South
Challenges for policy, practice and research
Edited by Leon Tikly and Angeline Barrett

Learner-centred Education in International Perspective
Whose pedagogy for whose development?
Michele Schweisfurth

Professional Education, Capabilities and the Public Good
The role of universities in promoting human development
Melanie Walker and Monica McLean

Livelihoods and Learning
Education For All and the marginalisation of mobile pastoralists
Caroline Dyer

Gender Violence in Poverty Contexts
The educational challenge
Edited by Jenny Parkes

The 'Poor Child'
The cultural politics of education, development and childhood
Edited by Lucy Hopkins and Arathi Sriprakash

Forthcoming titles:

Gender, Education and Poverty
The politics of policy implementation
Edited by Elaine Unterhalter, Jenni Karlsson and Amy North

The 'Poor Child'
The cultural politics of education, development and childhood

Edited by Lucy Hopkins and
Arathi Sriprakash

LONDON AND NEW YORK

First published 2016
by Routledge
2 Park Square, Milton Park, Abingdon, Oxon OX14 4RN

and by Routledge
711 Third Avenue, New York, NY 10017

Routledge is an imprint of the Taylor & Francis Group, an informa business

© 2016 L. Hopkins and A. Sriprakash

The right of the editors to be identified as the author of the editorial material, and of the authors for their individual chapters, has been asserted in accordance with sections 77 and 78 of the Copyright, Designs and Patents Act 1988.

All rights reserved. No part of this book may be reprinted or reproduced or utilised in any form or by any electronic, mechanical, or other means, now known or hereafter invented, including photocopying and recording, or in any information storage or retrieval system, without permission in writing from the publishers.

Trademark notice: Product or corporate names may be trademarks or registered trademarks, and are used only for identification and explanation without intent to infringe.

British Library Cataloguing in Publication Data
A catalogue record for this book is available from the British Library

Library of Congress Cataloging in Publication Data
The 'Poor Child' : the cultural politics of education, development and childhood / edited by Lucy Hopkins and Arathi Sriprakash
pages cm. — (Education, poverty and international development)
Includes bibliographical references and index.
1. Students with social disabilities. 2. Poor children—Education. 3. Poor children—Social conditions. 4. Educational sociology. I. Hopkins, Lucy. II. Sriprakash, Arathi.
LC4065.P66 2015
371.826'94—dc23
2015005692

ISBN: 978-0-415-74129-3 (hbk)
ISBN: 978-1-315-81533-6 (ebk)

Typeset in Galliard
by Swales & Willis Ltd, Exeter, Devon, UK

Contents

List of illustrations ix
Notes on contributors x
Acknowledgements xii

Introduction 1

1 Unsettling the global child: Rethinking child subjectivity
  in education and international development 3
  LUCY HOPKINS AND ARATHI SRIPRAKASH

PART I
Cultural representations of childhood and poverty 21

2 'It shouldn't happen here': Cultural and relational
  dynamics structured around the 'poor child' 23
  ERICA BURMAN

3 'Black kid burden': Cultural representations of Indigenous
  childhood and poverty in Australian cinema 43
  KRISTINA GOTTSCHALL

PART II
Contextualising the 'poor child': Children's voices as modes of resistance 63

4 Child labour, schooling and the reconstruction of
  childhood: A case study from Kenya 65
  ANGELA GITHITHO MURIITHI

5 Victims of what? Misunderstandings of anti-trafficking
  child protection policies in Benin 84
  SIMONA MORGANTI

6 The construction of resilience: Voices of poor children
  in Mexico 102
  LUZ MARÍA STELLA MORENO MEDRANO

PART III
Questioning the project of schooling and the politics of development 125

7 Policy constructions of childhoods: Impacts of multi-level
  education and development policy processes in Southeast
  Asia and the South Pacific 127
  ALEXANDRA MCCORMICK

8 Modernity and multiple childhoods: Interrogating the
  education of the rural poor in global India 151
  ARATHI SRIPRAKASH

9 Picturing education, poverty and childhood from the
  perspectives of yak herder children in Bhutan 168
  LUCY HOPKINS

Conclusion 191

10 Revisioning 'development': Towards a relational
   understanding of the 'poor child' 193
   ARATHI SRIPRAKASH AND LUCY HOPKINS

   Index 205

Illustrations

Figures

1.1	Advertising a preschool and childcare centre in Bangalore, India	4
6.1	Risk factors among participants associated with income, housing and parents' lack of educational opportunities in Jalisco, Mexico	107
6.2	Protective factors among participants associated with family, community, friends and school in Jalisco, Mexico	108
6.3	Developmental assets among participants associated with personal characteristics and adaptation skills in Jalisco, Mexico	109
9.1	Competition drawings of education and poverty	172
9.2	Tshering's view of what teachers think about yak herding	179
9.3	Tshering's depiction of what he thinks about yak herding	180
9.4	Tshering's view of what parents think about education: the story of the 'bad boy'	181
9.5	Tshering's view of what teachers think about education	184
9.6	Tshering's view of what parents think about yak herding and education	185
9.7	Tshering's depiction of what he thinks about education	186

Tables

4.1	Reconstructed understandings of childhood in Kiratu	79
6.1	Demographic information about the participants	110
7.1	Partial overview of a genre chain for *Education for All* (EFA)	131
7.2	EFANAP acknowledgement and inclusion of CSOs/NGOs against Dakar goals	136
7.3	Mechanisms for education policy deliberation	139

Contributors

Erica Burman is Professor of Education at the Manchester Institute of Education, School of Environment, Education and Development, University of Manchester, UK. She is the co-founder of the Discourse Unit (www.discourseunit.com), a transinstitutional, transdisciplinary network researching the reproduction and transformation of language and subjectivity. Erica works on critical developmental and educational psychology, feminist theory, childhood studies, and conceptualising and challenging state, structural and interpersonal violence in relation to minoritised women and children.

Angela Githitho Muriithi is the Research Manager for BBC Media Action, East Africa. She has a background in education and is deeply interested in the education of children from disadvantaged communities, especially child labourers.

Kristina Gottschall is a lecturer in the Centre for Indigenous Studies at Charles Sturt University, New South Wales, Australia. Her research areas include popular and public pedagogies, popular film culture, post-structural theories, social semiotics, subjectivities, gender, sexuality, indigeneity and discourses about youth-hood.

Lucy Hopkins is a researcher in cultural studies, literature and education, with a particular interest in social justice. She works on 'global' childhoods and issues of ethics and subjectivity in discourses of childhood, discourses of 'whiteness', and poststructuralist and feminist theories. She is currently undertaking research in Bhutan on childhood and youth-hood.

Alexandra McCormick is a postdoctoral fellow and lecturer in the Faculty of Education and Social Work at the University of Sydney. She teaches on a range of undergraduate and masters units in education, social policy and development studies, and on the Refugee Language Program. Her research interests include the normative transfer of education and development policies, critical discourse analysis and teaching for social justice. Alexandra is currently researching policy processes for post-2015 development agendas in the South Pacific.

Luz María Stella Moreno Medrano is the founder and director of Kórima Consultoría Educativa in Mexico, an organisation aimed at promoting spaces of personal and collective growth through educational projects of social transformation and participatory citizenship.

Simona Morganti is an anthropologist. She completed her PhD in anthropology at the University of Modena, Italy, after extensive fieldwork in Southern Benin on child fostering, child work migration and child trafficking. In Benin she also acted as a consultant for NGOs and international agencies engaged in child protection.

Arathi Sriprakash is a lecturer in the sociology of education at the University of Cambridge, UK. Her research focuses on the global politics of education and international development.

Acknowledgements

This book began as a conversation between two friends. We were sitting in a park in Sydney, talking about our work and our encounters with the troubling idea of a 'global' childhood in projects of education and international development. We came to this conversation from different disciplinary locations – Arathi from sociology and Lucy from cultural studies. But we were excited about how our ideas were bumping up against each other, stretched and reshaped in their meeting. We began to scribble down some of our thoughts and questions on some old paper found at the bottom of one of our bags. Suffice it to say, those initial notes would not have turned into this book without the help and support of many people.

First and foremost, we are indebted to all the authors who contributed to this volume: a set of brilliant women across the world who joined our conversation and made it all the more rich. It was an immensely rewarding experience to learn about new research, exchange ideas, and engage in debate with such a thoughtful and talented group of scholars. We hope we can all meet in person one day!

We would also like to thank Madeleine Arnot and Christopher Colclough for their incisive and patient feedback on early drafts, as well as Anna Clarkson and Clare Ashworth for their support. Deb Hayes helped us sharpen our ideas, as did Helen Proctor and Lekkie Hopkins, whose encouragement and careful reading of our work was always perfectly timed – right when we needed it most. We would also like to express our gratitude to Jing Qi for assisting with referencing, to Alissa Thiere for her sharp eyed copy-editing, to Jean-Francois Thiere for his help with formatting and to Sejuti Jha for traipsing through Bangalore traffic to get a perfect picture of the preschool advertisement we discuss in our opening chapter. Lucy would like to thank Matt Stretton, for his love and support, and for his research assistance in Bhutan. Arathi would like to thank Rahul Mukhopadhyay for his companionship in academia, and Scott Walter for his companionship in life.

Our daughters, Lily and Lekha, were born during the writing of this book. We dedicate our work to the hope that the world they share is respectful and just.

Lucy Hopkins and Arathi Sriprakash

Introduction

1 Unsettling the global child
Rethinking child subjectivity in education and international development

Lucy Hopkins and Arathi Sriprakash

Introduction

The 'poor child' at the centre of development activity is often measured against and reformed towards an idealised, globalised and normalised child subject. In this book we examine why such normative discourses of childhood are in need of radical revision and explore how development research and practice can work to 'unsettle' the global child.

We begin our discussions with an examination of an image, an advertisement for an elite, private preschool and childcare centre in Bangalore, India (see Figure 1.1). The billboard depicts a white child playing with a toy aeroplane. On his head is drawn a pilot's hat, an adult simulation of a child's drawing, in crayon. Beside him read the words, *Some see 'child's play'. We see 'star pilot'*. The boy looks at the camera, smiling, as if aware of the potential approval of the viewer. In our view this boy simultaneously represents the ideal child, the model student and the future citizen: his whiteness, his masculinity, his status as middle-class, as well as his 'inherent' childishness (signified by his playfulness) and his immanent adulthood (signified by being a future 'star pilot'), all work to position him within a normative discourse of childhood. We see this representation as highly significant and problematic. Here we take this child, this innocent, playful boy-child, to signify an abstracted and universalised child subject that is rehearsed and repeated across cultural and social spaces within development and development education discourses. In doing so, we introduce the normative child as a central figure under examination in this collection, and seek to elucidate how this child subject – and the dominant discourses of childhood that underpin it – circulate in problematic ways within international development and development education, simultaneously obscuring and 'Othering' the 'poor child'.

While this advertisement is for an elite, private preschool (and therefore not aimed at the 'poor child'), it reveals how a universal child subject plays out across global spaces; this child is Western, middle-class, male, and is situated as a global ideal. The use of the white child as the educational ideal in this advertisement is, within its location in the non-Western space of India, highly significant in terms of how it situates educational development. Indeed within the space of the advertisement, the boy *is* seen to represent the ideal student, and the ideal child,

Figure 1.1 Advertising a preschool and childcare centre in Bangalore, India

who, in the imagination of potential viewers, their own children will be(come) if they are sent to this preschool. In representing the white child as the model student within a space in which brown children – Indian children – not white ones, are the norm, the advertisement positions the desired subject as Western. Within development discourses, such a problematic conceptualisation is ubiquitous: as Olga Nieuwenhuys tells us, 'development agencies have decided [that] the highest possible goal [for non-Western childhood is] the emulation of a kind of childhood that the West has set as a global standard' (2009, 148). The use of this boy as the ideal works to position as 'Other' all those children who do not fit this cultural ideal.

The positioning of the boy on the billboard as the ideal child – and student – draws on normative discourses of childhood: as Henry Jenkins reminds us, 'the most persistent image . . . of the innocent child is that of the white, blond, blue-eyed boy . . . and the markers of middle-classness, whiteness and masculinity are read as standing in for all children' (1998a, 13). On the billboard, the boy's clothing foregrounds how the advertisement plays into such a positioning of the child subject and collapses it with the idea of the ideal or model student: he wears a chequered shirt, sleeves rolled up, with a blue vest over it, signifying his potential role as a student. But this is necessarily a middle-class, Western student, the blue vest reminiscent of the uniforms of elite schools in Britain and, in colonial 'mimicry', in India.[1] Ironically, in a double manoeuvre, this uniform recalls and replays the colonising of the Indian child/student within educational discourses – a practice which is perpetuated through the very educational development discourses under discussion in this volume.

Importantly, the advertisement's use of the white, male, middle-class child to represent the ideal student obscures the cultural location or origin of this child subject. The child's whiteness is constituted as a 'lack' of ethnicity or racial signifiers – an invisibility of context (Burman 2008). This is foregrounded in the advertisement by the boy's literal lack of context: he is placed against a white backdrop, removed from any locational specificity. The white child is unmarked by categories of difference or specificity – naturalised and normalised – and it is the very invisibility of cultural (racial, class-based and gender) markers, that allows the Western child subject to be considered a universal subject.

Placed in opposition to this invisible white child is the 'poor child'; she is positioned as a marked subject, whose differences from the norm make her the object of educational and development reform. The 'poor child' of our book's title, then, is excluded from dominant conceptualisations of what both childhood and education should be. This child, both marked as 'Other' and situated outside the space of the billboard, is constituted as lacking in relation to the normative child: not only economically poor, she is also seen as 'poor' in terms of cultural deficit, language, cultural support, and her inability to benefit from schooling and other opportunities.

The implications of the discursive dominance of the universal child – and thus the exclusion of the 'poor child' – for development and development education are many. While universalisms do not necessitate the homogenisation of the subject, the universal child's cultural dominance encourages and permits North–South transmission of epistemologies and ontologies, and in doing so, allows for a certain context-blindness in terms of how subjectivity is considered and constructed (Burman 2008). The naturalisation of the universal child subject in turn covers over its own Northern origins. In eschewing universalisms, we consider the work of Judith Butler (2005), who, with Adorno, suggests that abstract universalisms become ethically problematic – or in Adorno's terms, ethically violent – when they fail to take into consideration the context on which they are imposed. In being proposed as the norm, Butler argues, universalisms foreclose any debate on their own normativity. How the 'poor child' is constituted by, through and in relation to these normative discourses is frequently overlooked by development theory, policy and practice.

The driving aim of the collection, then, is to unsettle simplistic notions of the 'global' or 'universal' child. We do this by bringing multiple disciplinary perspectives into conversation with development and development education, to provide new ways of approaching and conceptualising children and childhoods. We highlight a range of theoretical and methodological approaches to the child, ranging from poststructuralist discourse analysis, through to arts-based research methodology and textual analysis, and to empirical studies that focus on listening to children's voices and putting children in context. Such an interdisciplinary approach calls on poverty theorists and policy makers to address the complex ways in which the 'poor child' is constituted. Indeed, in bringing these fields together, we call for the de-disciplining of the field of exploration surrounding the child.

The manoeuvre of engaging with multiple disciplinary and methodological forms of enquiry emerges from our multiply imbued understanding of the cultural politics of childhood; a perspective that has so far been marginalised within poverty and development studies. We understand the cultural politics of childhood as a politics of equality, involving the struggle for redistribution in the material lifeworlds of diverse communities. Ethnographic studies of communities of children living in devastating poverty, for example, reveal the complex nature of this struggle. We also see the cultural politics of childhood as a politics of identity, involving the struggle over recognition. This orients our inquiries to discursive analyses of the construction of children's subjectivities. Yet again, we understand the cultural politics of childhood as the exploration – and critique – of the political and educational interventions made in the name of the 'poor child', as a struggle over their representation.[2] We present 'cultural politics', then, within this collection, as a methodological and theoretical orientation through which to explore the multiple ways in which education, poverty and development bear upon the 'poor child'.

Not simply a critique of development, this book provides alternative scholarly perspectives which open up new ways of researching poverty and children's lives within poverty contexts. In what follows, we set the scene for this collection by unpacking those ideas that the volume seeks to challenge: we make use of the work of scholars from childhood studies, cultural studies, critical psychology and sociology who critically examine the idea of the universal child, and seek to uncover the obscuring of its Western origins. Then we sketch out potential new theoretical and methodological approaches to the 'poor child' and explicate how these are advanced in the chapters that follow.

Unsettling the universal child

As our discussion of the billboard illuminates, normative discourses of childhood frame the child as a universal subject; an abstracted subject who can be rehearsed and repeated across myriad social and cultural spaces. This child is a subject who is natural, and outside of culture; a subject who at once masquerades as fixed and coherent and works as a mobile signifier for a range of worldviews (Baird 2008). While the figure of the universal child and all its attendant problems have been widely critiqued within childhood studies (James *et al.* 1998; Lee 2001; Jenks 2005; Mannion 2007), education (Cannella and Viruru 2004), cultural studies (Jenkins 1998a; Holland 2004; Baird 2008; Robinson and Davies 2008) and critical psychology (Burman 2008, 2012), this normative discourse of childhood continues to circulate widely and informs much policy and practice in the fields of international development and development education (Cannella and Viruru 2004; Burman 2008; Nieuwenhuys 2010; Balagopalan 2002, 2008, 2011). Importantly, the figure's persistence within contemporary debates about children and childhood – its continued relevance to analysis of development and education – necessitates this collection's continued interrogation of the subject.

The universalism of the child subject is underpinned by its abstraction: this is a figure that exists everywhere and nowhere. It is emptied of specificity and consequently, the child is, as Barbara Baird points out, 'constituted as apolitical, ahistorical and naturalised' (2008, 296). The positioning of this child outside of culture and history and beyond the reach of politics is reproduced within development discourses and policy, and particularly in the United Nations Convention of the Rights of the Child (UNCRC). Arguably *the* major policy document shaping international development agencies' engagement with children (Burman and Stacey 2010; Balagopalan 2011), the UNCRC draws on a child subject that operates as 'the norm against which all the everyday, discrete lives of children in various parts of the world have now come to be measured and evaluated' (Balagopalan 2008, 268). This child is an essentialised figure who is universally applicable; the child is without a lived reality. As Olga Nieuwenhuys reminds us, 'the UNCRC speaks of an abstract child – *the child* – as if all children, irrespective of age, sex, culture and other particularities, share an essential set of immutable qualities' (2009, 5). This child is constituted as fixed and coherent, even though – as we shall see – its mobility is based on its ability to take on multiple signifiers.

This abstract child subject is figured in terms of a universal humanism which allows for the assumption of universal moral categories. As Kerry Robinson suggests, 'the child continues to be constituted as a "universal child" . . . in which understandings of what it means to be a child are viewed to be a shared "human" experience' (2008, 115). The essence of all children, this conceptualisation assumes, is the same. Crucially for our discussion of development discourses, if the normative conceptualisation of the child subject is seen to be representative of *the only possibility* for the child's ontology – one that is shared by all – then the values that underwrite dominant understandings of this subject are assumed to be universally applicable. This plays out in development discourses as imperatives that 'children should not be forced to do heavy work; to sleep on the streets; to carry arms; to undergo genital mutilations, and so on' (Nieuwenhuys 2008, 5). The decontextualisation of the child subject through its abstract universalism allows this child to be uncritically co-opted into myriad social, political and cultural spaces.[3] The chapters in this volume explore how this occurs through development and education policy and discursive representation. The collection, then, disrupts the unproblematised use of universalised norms, claiming instead, with Burman, that universalist discourses that underpin ideas of child rights (for example) are 'rendered cultural and culturally specific in every transaction and communication' (2012, 3).

The idea of the 'natural' is central here in creating the child subject as normative. The normative discourse of the child subject draws on the depoliticised and normalised space of nature in ways that work to produce an inevitable and incontestable subject. Despite comprehensive critique of such a notion within the field of childhood sociology, childhood scholar and human geographer, Affrica Taylor, highlights the continued insistence on the link between nature and childhood:

> Childhood and nature seem bound together as the essential and original raw materials of life itself . . . the compelling romance of this coupling is underpinned by the premise that childhood and nature constitute a pre-destined, wholesome and enduring match. Supported by the certitude and moral authority of its affiliation with nature, the naturalness of childhood is confidently reaffirmed on an everyday basis.
>
> (2011, xiii)

Nature, here, is put in the service of dominant notions of childhood, in order to normalise such a notion of childhood, to obscure the role of the political, cultural and social in the formation of the child subject. Citing Latour, Taylor reminds us of how 'nature' enacts such an obfuscation: 'the continuing uncritiqued deployment of capital N nature acts as a political foil. In this form, Nature functions as the final word – it reduces politically contentious "matters of concern" . . . to indisputable "matters of fact"' (Taylor 2011, xxi). For its use in development and education discourses, then, the child subject and the characteristics with which it is imbued, become irrefutable through its association with nature. This works to reinforce the moral authority of the values and ideas that are normalised through this positioning of the child as natural.

Not only does the normalising of childhood as a natural category work to naturalise views about children, the abstract child – as an absolute, impermeable and moral category – can be evoked in the defence of various cultural and political worldviews (Meyer 2007). As Meyer (2007, 99) argues, 'the child' becomes a shorthand for sacralisation and moral status; its meanings no longer have to be made explicit. This rhetoric is so powerful that in fact *any* opinion can be justified by simply referring to children, and without having to explain *why* and *how* children justify it. The figure of the child is then mobilised in the protection or justification of a range of other discourses, ideas and policies. Chapters in this book explore this, for example, in relation to laws on labour and mobility (see Morganti's chapter), agendas for education reform (see McCormick's contribution), and militarised interventions in Indigenous communities (see discussions by Gottschall).

The many critics of the abstract universalism of the child subject have pointed again and again to the very real cultural and historical origins of this seemingly decontextualised subject: the normative child's abstraction necessarily conceals, in Barbara Baird's words, how this child is 'laden with racialised, gendered, classed and sexualised cultural assumptions' (2008, 291). As we discuss, these assumptions emerge from a Western conception of childhood, which is covered over by the appeal to the universal (Burman 2010). As a discursive figure, rather than a contextualised subject, the universalised child is drawn on within myriad discourses – including international development and education – to give meaning 'over and above reference to real historical children' (Baird 2008, 291). Such a manoeuvre is permitted, as Erica Burman points out, because such assumptions – the markers of race, gender, class and culture – are 'normalised into absence' (2010, 3); they are obscured by the positioning of this child as natural.

Development discourses and the universal child

The use of the white child in the Indian preschool advertisement discussed above is clearly not a neutral manoeuvre. As childhood scholars regularly point out, the normative child subject who is positioned as 'global' and 'universal' emerges from a confluence of Western positionings: in particular, he is constituted within narratives of immanence and innocence, both of which emerge from Victorian (and other) historical narratives of the child. These narratives are scientised and normalised through child development discourses and shored up by the inherent 'naturalness' of the child subject. As Burman and Stacey point out, they are central in shaping the figuration of the child within development discourses:

> In the North, and globalised through international development policies ... the model of child development inscribes an ideal-typical white, middle-class childhood that is also culturally masculine – as indicated by the normative developmental trajectory from irrationality to rationality and from dependence to independence and autonomy.
>
> (2010, 230)

Here Burman and Stacey highlight how the taking up of the white child subject as ideal or normal engenders the adoption of a linear narrative trajectory between the (irrational, dependent) child and the (rational, autonomous) adult. This dichotomous positioning of child and adult hinges on the notion of the child as an immanent adult, while it naturalises and rehearses the positioning of this non-adult child as innocent. In what follows we examine the ways in which these Western philosophical underpinnings of the normative child subject intersect with dominant education and development discourses, and how they both conceal and 'Other' the 'poor child'.

Immanence, progress and development

The account of the child subject as natural is reinforced by biological and child development discourses, which rely on the natural development of children's bodies in order to constitute the child subject in terms of its immanence, its status as a *becoming*-adult. While such narratives have been largely challenged within childhood studies, they continue to powerfully inform the ways in which children and childhood are popularly constructed. The implications of this within development discourses are manifold: not only does this child allow for the naturalisation of ideas of progress, it also sets up childhood as a space of deficit, pinning the hopes for the child on the future adult subject.

The dominance of the idea of the child as an immanent adult – a subject in the making – relies on its positioning in negative relation to the complete, rational (male) adult subject – that fixed, autonomous being – that is figured within modernist discourses of subjectivity. The insistence on the dichotomous division of adult and child (an example of the dialectics which, as Alan Prout (2011) reminds us, underpin much of modernist sociological thinking) continues to constitute the child in terms of what the adult is not: the innocence of the child is juxtaposed with adult experience; the child's vulnerability is contrasted with the autonomy of this adult figure; the child's dependence is opposed to adult agency. Such a positioning of the child works to naturalise the opposition between adult power and children's dependency.

Within development discourses, this naturalisation of the oppositional relation between adult and child also works to make such binaries available for use in other cultural sites. As Jo-Ann Wallace suggests:

> the category of 'the child', a foundational product of the modern episteme, remains an unacknowledged and therefore unexamined organising principle . . . of the modern nation-state in its relations with many of its own citizens and those of the so-called developing world.
>
> (1995, 286)

The adult–child relationship works as a structuring metaphor for the ways in which hierarchies can be maintained or reproduced within society.

While the adult–child relationship sanctions the use of such hierarchies, the dominance of biological and child development discourses – through which the child is seen as being in a constant state of progress towards a fixed (ideal) adult state – naturalises and permits the use of this model of progress in other sites. Examining the multiple notions of 'development', Erica Burman (2008) suggests that the naturalisation of progress through the metaphor of the child's growth is dangerously repeated within the field of international development. The child's immanence and status as natural means that the model of progress from innocent child to autonomous adult can be rehearsed across cultural sites. She suggests that the rhetoric of child development finds an easy fit within international development:

> notions of progress, improvement, skill and adaptation emerge, words that might migrate or even flow easily between the specific and the general, or from individual to social allocation . . . Here we begin to see the political load carried by the discourse of development, and by children who are so often positioned as its bearers. Children thus provide the conceptual and emotional means by which contested social hierarchy can be perpetuated by being mapped onto an apparently natural asocial category.
>
> (2008, 95)

The naturalisation of this account of progress permits the imposition of such a model on developing countries and peoples; a slippage from child to nation, from child development to international development.

The implications of the ways in which the child is co-opted into the political and epistemological are crucial here: the naturalisation of hierarchies and ideas of 'progress' permit the reproduction of spurious notions of 'evolution' onto non-Western cultural spaces, setting up the West as a cultural and social ideal that is to be 'achieved' by the non-West (Castañeda 2002). The deficit model of the child – in relation to the fully formed adult – can be imposed on the nation. Postcolonial scholars have long pointed to the ways in which colonial powers characterised colonised nations in terms of their 'childish' or 'childlike' qualities, in opposition to the colonial adult power (see Nandy 2009), and this notion of the child continues to resonate within development discourses today.

The focus on the child's transformation into an adult that is implicit in the idea of immanence draws the focus away from the child subject *itself*, towards the future adult citizen. The child becomes a repository for future hopes: (re)enacting the slippage between child and nation, the future of the nation rests on the shoulders of the developing child. Not only does such an imagining of the child refute the legitimacy of the child's current subjectivity and reinforce outdated notions of the child as *becoming* (Prout 2011), it also positions the child in terms of a desired middle-class citizen subject who will 'save' the nation. Such a narrative is revealed within the billboard advertisement with which we began this chapter, as the child is inscribed as the future citizen through his positioning as a 'star pilot'. The text ('*we* see "star pilot"', our emphasis) positions the school as unique in being able to identify (and presumably shape) this future citizen: through the valuing of the child's 'inherent' self (that playful, innocent self which we elaborate below), the schooling environment will produce such a subject. The crayon-drawn pilot's hat signifies the future potential of this child, yet this is also done playfully, perhaps alerting us to the play-driven pedagogies through which the child will achieve such an adulthood. Importantly, this child's play is not discredited as (only ever) childish, rather it is embraced, but is simultaneously transposed into a potential future: a middle-class future.

Problematically, then, many discourses of development education draw on such ideas of the future citizen – almost uniformly a middle-class subject – in order to naturalise (formal) schooling as the producer of a 'better tomorrow' (Balagopalan 2008). Education is thus positioned as a site of liberation for both the child and the nation. Yet the focus on formal education sets up the middle-class subject as the end goal of schooling, a process which disenfranchises the 'poor child' – and repudiates their potential livelihoods – by claiming the only legitimate adult subject as a middle-class one.

Schooling and 'saving' the child

The positioning of the child as a future adult subject, and in direct opposition to the autonomous adult, reinscribes and normalises ideas of the child as innocent, vulnerable and in need of protection and separation from the adult world. Such a conceptualisation of childhood is central to the positioning of education and development in terms of a narrative of child-saving. As historian Linda Gordon argues, the very notion of children's 'best interests' – that underpins development policies such as the UNCRC and is intimately tied into discourses of child-saving – 'arises from the notion of childhood innocence, the idea that children should not have to bear the burdens of their parents' poverty; that children deserve opportunity precisely because of their youth' (2008, 335–336). The notion of children's innocence – both in terms of vulnerability and lack of responsibility – engenders such responses.

The school is constituted as one of the sites through which the child can be saved. As Balagopalan argues, 'the "school" signifies a "normal" childhood with its attendant emphasis on innocence, nurture and a clear separation of the roles of adult and child' (2008, 270). The ways in which development educational discourses draw on such ideas – emerging as they do from Victorian and Rousseau-ian notions of childhood – in the creation or negotiation of the 'schooled' subject is central here. While upholding the discourse of the normative child, the school becomes a repository for ideals about the future subject that is created within it.

The notion of childhood innocence is so compelling because it is based on a transposition of children's assumed biological vulnerability into the social realm. Indeed, Western biological and child development discourses work to naturalise this innocence through an insistence on an oppositional relationship between childhood and adulthood, in which innocence works to describe that which is not adult-like: qualities of vulnerability, incompetence and lack of knowledge work to differentiate the child subject from the adult as markers of innocence. This dichotomy between adult (power) and child (dependence) as it is reproduced through ideas of innocence permits and reinforces a kind of spatial, social distinction between adults and children. The cordoning off of children from the adult realm, as well as the capacity for adults to make decisions on behalf of children in the name of protectionism, are both caught up in this framework of childhood innocence.[4]

The trope of play – as a marker of childhood innocence – exemplifies how the separation of adults and children, both spatially and conceptually, is enacted within development and education discourses (Aitken 2001). Play, as *the* appropriate activity for children, is positioned in opposition to (adult) work; it is an activity to take place within the spaces of home or school, necessitating the repudiation of children's place on the streets; play forms the basis of 'appropriate' child-centred pedagogy, discounting or delegitimising other educational practices (Aitken 2001, 121). Such a notion of play is foregrounded in relation to the billboard advertising the private preschool: the ideal child is engaged in play, holding a toy aeroplane. The text, which says *Some see 'child's play'. We see 'star pilot'* foregrounds children's play as the normative activity of the child: play is naturalised for all viewers (apart from the exceptional eyes of the preschool, who view the child, as we have seen, in terms of his future subjecthood).

Children's capacity to play, contained within 'safe' and 'appropriate' sites, comes to stand in as a signifier for legitimate childhood to the exclusion of others. Indeed, as Burman suggests,

> Through the pedagogical dictum of 'learning through play', while Northern children's play is their work, since children of the South work, they are deemed robbed of their childhood, or at best their education (posing the spurious opposition between work and schooling).
>
> (2012, 6)

The formulation of play *as* work, and the implication that children's work is learning, privileges both the learning to be gained through formal education, and the normalised place of the child within the home or school, allowing for a kind of (negative) moral positioning of the child who works as outside of (normative) childhood. 'Play' and 'school' are placed in hierarchal opposition to 'work' just as the location of the child within the school or home is opposed to the child in the public space.

As the chapters in this volume elucidate, through the positioning of play and of schools as normative locations of childhood, the working child, or the child who exists within the public (adult) space, who is outside the space of education or the home, becomes a contender for discourses of 'child saving'. Balagopalan reminds us of the ways in which the 'poor child' – the street child or the working child – has been constituted as a 'child-at-risk'. She argues that this child is:

> framed in terms of a new moral discourse of 'saving childhoods'. This discourse produces certain images of reform aimed at normalising these poor Third World children, who it views as having 'lost their childhood', through locating them within the spaces of bourgeois childhood.
>
> (2008, 268)

This child becomes the subject of reform precisely because it is put in relationship to the normative childhood of innocence and play.

Yet these children's childhoods are also problematic precisely because they challenge the naturalisation of the dominant discourse of the child. As Stuart Aitken argues:

> Not only do children in the global South lack childhood as it is constituted in the North, but their economic savvy disrupts ideas of children as innocents and so they transgress the boundaries between constructions of adults and children.
>
> (2001, 124)

By co-opting these children into the (actual and conceptual) space of the normative child, by 'saving' them, the oppositional categories of adult and child, experience and innocence, and so on, are maintained.

The dominance of normative discourses of childhood play out across sites of development and development education, informing so much of how we see and read the child, and the developing nation. Yet this universal child subject operates in the exclusion of all others. So how do we reimagine the 'poor child' afresh?

Reimagining the 'poor child' and new insights into global development(s)

In critiquing the ways in which the dominance of the universal child subject simultaneously allows for the exclusion and reformation of the 'poor child', in this collection we call for a rethinking of the child subject in relation to ideas of development and development education. As social theorist Barbara Baird argues, the repudiation of an ahistorical and universalised figuration of the child involves:

allowing all that it disallows: the historical and political contingency of childhood and its variability; its gendered, classed and racialised nature; childhood desires and actions; and childhood excesses.

(2008, 296)

The chapters in the book explore not only the ways in which the figure of the child takes shape, but also the ways in which the construction of the child creates meanings within adult worlds.

Olga Nieuwenhuys (2008) argues that such a manoeuvre works to critique the paralysing dichotomy between universalism and cultural relativism by foregrounding them both as problematic abstract essentialisms, and advocating instead attention to ideas of children's agency. Critiquing the essentialisms that underpin relativism and universalism, Nieuwenhuys revisions this problem by foregounding children's subjectivity. She suggests that in being attentive to children's ways of being, 'culture and childhood are [considered] conceptual domains in flux: they are not "things" or natural phenomena, as in the essentialist approaches but practices that adults and children have the power to discard, adapt, transform' (2008, 8–9). Such a focus requires us to see 'children as subjects of their own history' (2008, 9) who have the capacity to act, to endorse and resist multiple discourses, and to take themselves up as subjects in myriad ways.

While ideas of agency that emerge in opposition to the universal child subject's vulnerability are reductive at best and problematic at worst, here we conceptualise agency – along poststructuralist lines – as necessarily contingent, unstable, relational and momentary. This is not the autonomous agency of the rational adult subject, but one that occurs only within the possibilities available to the subject within the context of the power relations in which the subject is engaged. This idea sees agency as a move into temporary power, rather than a reformulation of the self (Davies 2004).

In conceptualising the child afresh, we are attentive to the need to examine children's contexts and voices and the ways in which children's subjectivities are constituted. This involves a move away from modernist thinking about the subject as fixed, towards more contingent, fluid ideas of subjectivity. Each of the chapters brings different theoretical insights to the child subject – from social constructionist models to poststructuralist ideas of the subject as partial and strategic – and in doing so we seek to unsettle the boundaries of the normative child and its attendant subjective positioning. Crucially we are not suggesting a move from a modernist agenda to a new hegemonic understanding, but rather we seek to allow multiple ways of knowing to emerge and intersect. The book's exploration of the locational politics of poverty is important here: the focus on context attempts to move beyond liberal ideas of multiple childhoods (see Sriprakash, this volume) in order to investigate the ways in which complex politics of equality, recognition and representation bear upon the 'poor child'.

The book employs a range of epistemological strategies to unhook the universal child from discussions of development. We bring together different disciplinary insights and approaches to the child subject in order to initiate a dialogue about development and education across the fields of sociology, childhood studies and cultural studies. In sitting on the disciplinary fence in this way, we are responding to Burman's exhortation that 'views from the margins are what are needed to generate the critical crossings of theory and practice necessary to challenge the hegemony of dominant formulations of development [and we add, childhood]', (2008, 7). Central to this collection, then, is a desire to de-discipline the child, to view the child from the margins.

By engaging with the cultural politics of equality, recognition and representation in relation to the 'poor child', the book critically examines the ethics and impact of child-focused policies in contexts of poverty – both in 'advanced' nations such as the UK or Australia, and in 'developing countries' such as India, Kenya, Bhutan or Benin. It looks at the ways the constitution of childhood affects children's lives either materially (such as the conditions of children's work, mobility and schooling as the chapters by Githitho Muriithi, Morganti and Medrano explore), culturally (through specific types of representation, as examined by Burman and Gottschall) or educationally (through particular interventions by government or others, as explored by Hopkins, McCormick and Sriprakash). Significantly, the book also sheds light on the ways in which children themselves are challenging the representation, discursive construction, and material conditions of their lives.

The book opens in Part I, entitled 'Cultural representations of childhood and poverty', with contributions from Erica Burman and Kristina Gottschall, whose analyses of a charity campaign in the UK and Australian Indigenous film, respectively, illustrate the ways in which the 'poor child' is constructed and contested in and through these cultural representations. Importantly, the discussions in these two opening chapters raise debates about the locational politics and relationality of poverty by highlighting issues of childhood poverty and 'development' in the wealthy nations of the UK and Australia. Burman and Gottschall show how insights from cultural studies bring a rich and diverse way of thinking about discourses and texts of childhood within the setting of development and education. The analysis of films, images and text is based in an understanding that the reading of these texts is a political act: texts are seen as sites through which dominant discourses can be both created and contested. As Erica Burman has previously argued, the textual analyses of dominant discourses reveal the ways in which these discourses are normalised:

> texts that are in wider circulation are worthy of attention precisely because of their banality. They provide clues about the shaping of assumptions that quickly become normalised into absence, or what might be considered as the contours of the contemporary Euro-U.S. cultural unconscious. Like banal nationalism and racism . . . banal developmentalism needs to be identified and analysed, rather than overlooked or excused.
>
> (2010, 14)

In examining the representational politics of the 'poor child', these chapters insist on the importance of textual representations as *constitutive* of subjectivity, not simply reflective of how subjectivity is created. Therefore in drawing attention to the ways in which texts rehearse and reinforce dominant discourses, the methodological focus of cultural studies in these contributions opens up new avenues for unpacking the hidden assumptions of development discourses.

Part II, 'Contextualising the "poor child": children's voices as modes of resistance', explores how representations of children such as those discussed in Part I are being worked through and resisted by children themselves, who are in many ways engaging in a politics of recognition. In doing so, the chapters by Angela Githitho Muriithi, Luz Medrano and Simona Morganti bring to the centre the experiences and voices of children, reporting on rich historical and ethnographic research conducted in Kenya, Mexico and Benin, respectively. Through sociological and historical inquiry, Githitho Muriithi examines the changing constructions of childhoods in Kenya, from a socialised child, to a labouring child, and a schooled child. Her socio-historical analysis interrogates assumptions about children's vulnerability and the separation between labour and schooling. Relatedly, Medrano's chapter draws on participatory voice-centred research with poor children in Mexico to illuminate the ways in which these children develop strategies of resilience to negotiate the conditions of inequality in their social and school worlds. Building on this theme, Morganti's chapter explores the perspectives and experiences of children negotiating their mobility in Benin against the backdrop of 'child-trafficking'. Together, these chapters offer valuable insights for both development studies and childhood studies. Their centring of the child subject and attention to socio-historical contexts exposes the inadequacy and danger of top-down and decontextualised approaches to development and education. Importantly, the rich detail offered in these chapters points to the ways education development research can move towards a more complex, contextually situated interrogation of the child subject.

Part III, 'Questioning the project of schooling and the politics of development', examines the political agendas of education (more specifically, formal schooling) and international development. Chapters by Alexandra McCormick, Arathi Sriprakash and Lucy Hopkins show how the 'poor child' is constituted within these political projects in problematic ways and interrogate the specious notion of education as 'politics free', as a neutral or unquestionable space for children. McCormick's analysis of education development policy in South East Asia and the South Pacific 'denaturalises' dominant discourses of development by showing how they are formed through social and political contestations. By tracing these contestations, McCormick's analysis asks us to consider how universal discourses can be kept open to challenge and change. Sriprakash's chapter interrogates the 'deficit' model of the poor rural child in Indian education reforms. Drawing on ethnographic research with teachers in rural Indian schools, she demonstrates the ways development-as-modernisation is reinscribing a deficit notion of rural livelihoods and childhoods. This critique is expanded on by Hopkins in her chapter on schooling and childhoods in Bhutan and the limits of binaries such as education/poverty and tradition/modernity in dominant development discourse. Sharing a cultural analysis of Bhutanese yak-herder children's drawings and interviews, and building on earlier chapters that explore children's voices as modes of resistance, Hopkins illustrates how these children are rendering more complex notions of education, poverty and modernity than permitted through binary thinking in development discourses.

Together, the chapters in this volume point to the ways in which 'development' itself is much more complex and contingent than the linear trajectory or game of 'catch-up' that dominant theories assume. The concluding chapter of the book reflects on the ways a relational understanding of the 'poor child', as demonstrated through each of the contributions, can help rethink and revise projects of education and development. We consider the post-2015 education development agenda in light of the arguments put forward in each of the chapters, to end with a set of approaches for future development research, policy and practice.

Notes

1 Our use of the term 'mimicry' here is particularly loaded, drawing on Homi Bhabha's (1984, 126) reading of the colonised subject as 'almost the same but not quite; [a]lmost the same but not white'. Within this postcolonial conception, mimicry can be seen as both a capitulation and a resistance. See also Hopkins (2013).
2 Here we draw on Nancy Fraser's (2012) ideas on redistribution, recognition and representation in feminist politics to consider the multiple vectors of analysis that can be brought to studies of childhood and poverty.
3 Such a notion of the child is justified through a rejection of cultural relativism, a problematic dialectic that we begin to unpick later in this introduction. In no way are we suggesting throughout this volume that abstract universalism be replaced by culturally relative possibilities; rather we argue for a more nuanced approach, which takes into account children's agency and voices (see also Nieuwenhuys 2008).
4 While the narrative of the child as innocent is present in many conceptualisations of childhood (for example, within Hindu conceptualisations; see Uberoi 2006 for more), our focus here is particularly on those Western narratives from which international development discourses have emerged.

References

Aitken, Stuart C. 2001. 'Global Crises of Childhood: Rights, Justice and the Unchildlike Child.' *Area* 33 (2): 119–127. doi: 10.1111/1475-4762.00015.
Baird, Barbara. 2008. 'Child Politics, Feminist Analyses.' *Australian Feminist Studies* 23 (57): 291–305. doi: 10.1080/08164640802263440.
Balagopalan, Sarada. 2002. 'Constructing Indigenous Childhoods: Colonialism, Vocational Education and the Working Child.' *Childhood* 9 (1): 19–34. doi: 10.1177/0907568202009001002.
Balagopalan, Sarada. 2008. 'Memories of Tomorrow: Children, Labour, and the Panacea of Formal Schooling.' *Journal of the History of Childhood and Youth* 1 (2): 267–285. doi: 10.1353/hcy.0.0005.
Balagopalan, Sarada. 2011. 'Introduction: Children's Lives and the Indian Context.' *Childhood* 18 (3): 291–297. doi: 10.1177/0907568211413369.
Bhabha, Homi. 1984. 'Of Mimicry and Man: The Ambivalence of Colonial Discourse,' *October* 28: 125–133.

Burman, Erica. 2008. *Developments: Child, Image, Nation*. Hove, East Sussex: Routledge.
Burman, Erica. 2010. 'Un/thinking Children in Development: A Contribution from Northern Antidevelopmental Psychology.' In *Childhoods, A Handbook*, edited by Gaile S. Canella and Lourdes Diaz Soto, 9–26. New York: Peter Lang.
Burman, Erica. 2012. 'Deconstructing Neoliberal Childhood: Towards a Feminist, Antipsychological Approach.' *Childhood* 19 (4): 423–438. doi: 10.1177/0907568211430767.
Burman, Erica, and Jackie Stacey. 2010. 'The Child and Childhood in Feminist Theory.' *Feminist Theory* 11 (3): 227–240. doi: 10.1177/1464700110376288.
Butler, Judith. 2005. *Giving an Account of Oneself*. New York: Fordham University Press.
Cannella, Gaile S., and Radhika Viruru. 2004. *Childhood and Postcolonization: Power, Education, and Contemporary Practice*. New York: RoutledgeFalmer.
Castañeda, Claudia. 2002. *Figurations: Child, Bodies, Worlds*. Durham: Duke UniversityPress.
Davies, Bronwyn. 2004. 'Introduction: Poststructuralist Lines of Flight in Australia.' *International Journal of Qualitative Studies in Education* 17 (1): 3–9. doi: 10.1080/0951839032000150194.
Fraser, Nancy. 2012 'Feminism, Capitalism, and the Cunning of History: An Introduction.' Working paper. *Fondation Maison des Sciences de l'Homme*. August 2012.
Gordon, Linda. 2008. 'The Perils of Innocence, or What's Wrong with Putting Children First.' *Journal of the History of Childhood and Youth* 1(3): 331–350. doi: 10.1353/hcy.0.0021.
Holland, Patricia. 2004. *Picturing Childhood: The Myth of the Child in Popular Imagery*. New York: I.B. Tauris.
Hopkins, Lucy. 2013. '*Infinnate Joy*: The Politics of Childhood in Arundhati Roy's *The God of Small Things*.' In *Nationalism(s) and Cultural Memory in Texts of Childhood*, edited by Heather Snell and Lorna Hutcheson, 163–178. New York: Routledge.
James, Allison, Chris Jenks, and Alan Prout. 1998. *Theorizing Childhood*. Cambridge: Polity Press.
Jenkins, Henry. 1998a. 'Introduction: Childhood Innocence and Other Modern Myths.' In *The Children's Culture Reader*, edited by Henry Jenkins, 1–37. New York: New York University Press.
Jenkins, Henry, ed. 1998b. *The Children's Culture Reader*. New York: New York University Press.
Jenks, Chris. 2005. *Childhood*. London: Routledge.
Lee, Nick. 2001. *Childhood and Society: Growing up in an Age of Uncertainty*. Buckingham: Open University Press.
Mannion, Greg. 2007. 'Going Spatial, Going Relational: Why 'Listening to Children' and Children's Participation Needs Reframing.' *Discourse: Studies in the Cultural Politics of Education* 28 (3): 405–20. doi: 10.1080/01596300701458970.
Meyer, Anneke. 2007. 'The Moral Rhetoric of Childhood.' *Childhood* 14 (1): 85–104. doi: 10.1177/0907568207072532.
Nandy, Ashis. 2009. *The Intimate Enemy: Loss and Recovery of Self under Colonialism*. 2nd edn. Oxford: Oxford University Press.
Nieuwenhuys, Olga. 2008. 'Editorial: The Ethics of Children's Rights.' *Childhood* 15 (4): 4–11. doi: 10.1177/0907568207086941.
Nieuwenhuys, Olga. 2009. 'Editorial: Is There an Indian Childhood?' *Childhood* 16 (2): 147–153. doi: 10.1177/0907568209104398.

Nieuwenhuys, Olga. 2010. 'Keep Asking: Why Childhood? Why Children? Why Global?' *Childhood* 17 (3): 291–296. doi: 10.1177/0907568210369323.

Prout, Alan. 2011. 'Taking a Step Away from Modernity: Reconsidering the New Sociology of Childhood.' *Global Studies of Childhood* 1 (1): 4–14. doi: 10.2304/gsch.2011.1.1.4.

Robinson, Kerry H. 2008. 'In the Name of 'Childhood Innocence': A Discursive Exploration of the Moral Panic Associated with Childhood and Sexuality.' *Cultural Studies Review* 14 (2): 113–129. http://search.proquest.com/docview/635809492?accountid=36155.

Robinson, Kerry H., and Cristyn Davies. 2008. 'She's Kickin' Ass, That's What She's Doing!': Deconstructing Childhood 'Innocence' in Media Representations.' *Australian Feminist Studies* 23 (57): 343–357. doi: 10.1080/08164640802233294.

Taylor, Affrica. 2011. 'Reconceptualizing the 'Nature' of Childhood.' *Childhood* 18 (4): 420–33. doi: 10.1177/0907568211404951.

Uberoi, Patricia. 2006. *Freedom and Destiny: Gender, Family, and Popular Culture in India*. Oxford: Oxford University Press.

Wallace, Jo-Ann. 1995. 'Technologies of 'the Child': Towards a Theory of the Child Subject.' *Textual Practice* 9 (2): 285–302. doi: 10.1080/09502369508582221.

Part I
Cultural representations of childhood and poverty

2 'It shouldn't happen here'
Cultural and relational dynamics structured around the 'poor child'

Erica Burman

In September 2012, Save The Children UK launched a UK campaign on child poverty with the by-line 'It shouldn't happen here' to publicise increasing child poverty and neglect in Britain as a result of economic recession. This was the first time the organisation had launched a campaign in the UK linked to fundraising to support its UK programme work, and so made an impact as a major departure for an organisation that was largely known for its focus on child welfare and rights internationally – primarily via bilateral and local partnerships.[1] The slogan made topical the exceptional character of this focus, thereby also asserting the avoidable and ameliorable status of child poverty and neglect.[2] In this chapter I discuss this slogan, the campaign and selected media reception of this campaign, alongside other recent publicity material mobilised to publicise child welfare concerns, to explore some key tensions and dilemmas navigated by child-focused agencies. I do so not to criticise their campaigns but rather to identify the wider discourses of childhood the organisation necessarily engages with and their relations with broader cultural and economic debates. In particular I will suggest how such specific textual consideration illustrates not only how poverty and childhood are discursively framed (and framed in particular ways in relation to each other), but also how this incites further critical reflections including on 'our' own positionings as readers and writers of such texts ,with clear relevance for policy as well as academic analysis.

A key starting point for this chapter is the widespread acknowledgement of how the incipient abstraction that surrounds the notion of 'the child'/'childhood'/'children' within dominant cultural representational practices – as individual, separate, alone, distinct, and devoid of class, cultural community, 'race' and gender markers – belies a crucial dynamic of mutual configuration: 'child' implies 'adult' with a corresponding allocation and distribution of culturally loaded qualities. Failure to acknowledge and challenge this relationality and contingency is widely heralded as working to reproduce prevailing binaries of stigmatisation, as well as differential visibility and seriousness accorded to key issues such as poverty and material and social deprivation via a focus on children. Equally, 'the poor child' evokes specific imaginaries that – notwithstanding the widely noted abstraction from context as well as community that surrounds 'child' (Holland 1992; Castañeda 2002) – imply particular locations (Valentine 1996; Moss and Petrie 2002). Since this is a point that is largely assumed by current childhood researchers I will not labour it further. However, precisely because of this, what is of particular interest is the way child-focused organisations (such as Save the Children UK) narrate the relations between specific child-welfare or rights concerns and those of their families or communities and, beyond these, national economic policies.

Framing the analysis

The approach taken in this analysis draws on critical theories from deconstruction (Burman 2008a; Burman and Maclure 2011), postcolonial educational theory (Cannella and Viruru 2004), Foucauldian analyses (Rose 1990; Parker 1992, 2002; MacNaughton 2005) and feminist theory (Burman and Stacey 2010) to inform a discursive analysis of the Save the Children campaign. Consistent with methodological debates in discourse analysis (Burman and Parker 1993), it includes analysis of the cultural conditions of and for, and reception of, the campaign. Discourses are here understood as systems of statements that form subjects and objects (Parker 1992, 2002), that is, they are socially shared frameworks which have material effects, and whose contests over competing representations in fact occupy much of our daily policies and debates. As such, they are material practices whose explanatory powers are performed in each (re)capitulation of them, and whose conditions of intelligibility are correspondingly reinforced or reformulated.

Indeed, the material taken for analysis here is itself treated as a pre-text or indicative corpus that opens up wider discourses of local and global childhoods for critical scrutiny, alongside debates about the nature (origins, causes and contexts) of poverty (c.f. Penn 2005, 2011; Burman 1994, 1996a, 1996b). The text is written and visual from print media, ranging from newspaper coverage, publicly available reports, to media comment. The campaign was also launched via television advertisements, and I will comment later on its imagery, as well as the pictures that accompany the reports. While focusing in some detail on the campaign slogan, I also draw upon the report on child poverty and the working poor it aimed to publicise (Whitham 2012) and analyse, by way of indicative contrast, aspects of its media reception. My discussion here has benefitted from consultation with people from Save the Children who were involved in devising the campaign.[3] The analysis below is therefore less an exhaustive cataloguing of all its available repertoires, but rather motivates a particular set of readings which sees its text as a significant diagnostic intervention within its surrounding context. Thus I am less concerned with specific or systematic application of linguistic or discursive techniques than exploring how these inform ethical-political analysis of what is at stake in representations of childhood – in this case child poverty.

Why this text?

While there is no shortage of relevant material, this text (the campaign, its publicity and reception) was taken for analysis as it clearly signalled a specific departure from mainstream aid and child-saving campaign materials.[4] The conventional child charity genre of the global North usually focuses on some specific humanitarian disaster or acute emergency, soliciting funds for 'other' children and communities (e.g. Black 1992; Wells 2007). In this sense the Save the Children campaign was clearly successful in drawing attention to the limits of the normative genre, whose assumptions it disrupts.

My first reading of this text, which reflects others' reactions to it and, as we shall see, some of the wider media reception partakes of this, suggested a rather more negative reading: 'It shouldn't happen here' as implying the acceptability of 'it happen[ing]' elsewhere. Reflecting a methodological approach that attends to temporality and shifts of narrative positions (Doucet and Mauthner 2008), the text drew me into successive readings that worked to throw the unity of the subjective reading position into question. So this chapter traces a shift in interpretation and orientation from highly critical to more appreciative evaluation. Once I started to read the surrounding context, I arrived at a different interpretation of its claims and possible arenas of intervention. The implications of taking this reflexive account seriously at the very least highlights both the significance of attending to processes of temporal engagement and the importance of being open to the ambiguity of the text. Finally, this is obviously not the only – or possibly not the most relevant – reading of this text; rather, the reading here is motivated by and through a particular sensitivity to the framing of childhoods as a privileged and canonical mode of discoursing North–South relations, as power relations between rich and poor countries.

In this sense my critical comments about discourses of childhood mobilised by this and other texts should not be read as criticising individuals or organisations, and especially not the organisation that produced it (Save the Children) – who have led the way in formulating ethical-political debates on how children should be represented (see Save the Children 1992). Rather such text, through its skilled engagement with and subversion of prevailing discourses reveals not only the conditions of its own possibility within broader cultural and institutional discourses, policies and institutional practices, but perhaps hints at what would be necessary for its demise; that is, what wider cultural-political and economic changes would be necessary to make such representational practices redundant.

To highlight this double move, of mobilising but also disrupting subject positions, I draw on Butler's (1997) notion of 'turning' and 'turning around' (developed further by Macherey 2012) to move the focus from text to reader. In previous work I have discussed aid, development and marketing campaign materials involving depictions of children in terms of how the affective relations mobilised by and in relation to children and (individual and cultural-societal) models of childhood reflect and inform wider economic relations – including how both structure what development has come to mean (Burman 2008a, 2008b, 2012). Here I build on such analyses to attend more specifically to the processes of contextual engagement and political debate prompted by a specific campaign. Indeed, as a particular reflexive twist, what emerges as crucial to the reception of this campaign precisely revolves around questions of representation, of evidence, and specifically turns upon the question of who or what its topic is, and to whom it should be addressed. Far from being (only) about the condition of 'poor children' in Britain who unsurprisingly are found to be in a similar condition to poor children elsewhere, this text turns around to evaluate the reader and/or position it presumes and produces. Deconstructing the popular/academic and policy/expert binaries, both aid agencies and their media critics turn out to be preoccupied with similar concerns to those of academic childhood and education researchers: the ethics and politics of claims to and around childhood within national and international policy discourse.

In what follows I indicate the socioeconomic context for the campaign text and offer an account of its reception, before moving on to look more closely at its construction (drawing technical inspiration from some of the early work associated with social semiotics (Kress and Hodge 1979; Hodge and Kress 1988). Focusing in particular on criticisms made by one newspaper, I turn the campaign slogan text around to evaluate what it tells us about the canonical reader and the conditions of, and for, discourses of poor children and child poverty as they (in this rather prosaic way) engage the field of national and international relations.

The context

While I will return to these later, it is necessary to highlight some key events that form the conditions of possibility for this text. While the global market crash of 2007 onwards brought about worldwide recession, the United Kingdom under a Coalition government of Conservatives and Liberal Democrats has seen the post-1945 welfare state steadily rolled back, with severe cuts in public spending impacting significantly on all welfare provision including housing, social care and health services, and with major impacts on education (Tunstall *et al.* 2011; Hammett 2014). The government slogan 'we're all in it together' belies how the measures disproportionately target the poorest sectors of the population, and so – like other countries hit by the raft of measures associated with 'austerity' – there has been a deterioration in the conditions of children's lives. This is in a country where children have consistently emerged in annual UNICEF reports as among the least happy and healthy of all European countries. Moreover, just before the 2010 election (which brought in a Conservative and Liberal Democrat administration), the Labour government passed the Child Poverty Act. This committed the government to achieving four income-based child poverty targets by 2020.[5] Significantly, all major political parties supported the Bill as it went through Parliament but the current Coalition government has been particularly keen to criticise the relative measure of child poverty (often seen as the 'headline' measure). This suggests that, whilst reiterating their support for tackling child poverty, they did not feel held to account on needing to meet the 2020 targets (so that child poverty is expected to rise by over 1 million between 2014 and 2020) (see Social Mobility and Child Poverty Commission 2014; Sparrow 2014).

It was in September 2012 that Save the Children launched their campaign 'Child poverty: It shouldn't happen here' (across print and social media, and with television advertising) to publicise their research on child poverty in the

UK (Whitham 2012) and to draw attention to the ways the wider climate of public sector cuts were affecting children and their families and communities – even as the further and deeper swathes had not yet been announced or enacted (but are now well underway). While the previous Labour administration had pledged to end child poverty by 2020 (Cooke et al. 2008), there was a perceived need to hold the new administration to this commitment (or else expose how they were reneging on it). Other relevant conditions include concurrent policy repositioning around international aid which promoted a climate of popular opinion about Britain as needing help rather than being a provider of it, alongside a challenge to its imperial/colonial (self-)representation. The political climate had seen the rise and political promotion of anti-immigrant feeling, promulgating the view that foreigners are taking jobs, houses and consuming services that leave British citizens short-changed. Amid the Eurozone crisis, racism towards eastern European 'economic' migrants has increased, with mounting concern about the impact of citizens of other newer entries to the EU (especially Bulgaria and Romania) becoming eligible to migrate to the UK. Such issues have fuelled questions about British membership of the European Economic Union – also indicated by the surprise return of the UK Independence Party (a rightwing populist party) as a political force in the May 2013 local elections.

Save The Children's 2012 campaign: 'It shouldn't happen here'

This section offers a detailed semiotic analysis of the campaign slogan, 'It shouldn't happen here'. A first reading highlights the 'here' of 'It shouldn't happen here'. This makes topical child poverty in the UK; a first, minority, world context which – so the campaign suggests – should have surpassed such issues and so evokes the moral as well as economic repertoire inscribing discourses of development and underdevelopment. This invites reflection on what kind of 'here' is envisaged, alongside which kinds of children are (and are not) depicted. This reading focuses on what kind of relationship with the 'there' is implied where 'it should' or 'could' 'happen'. Let us take a closer look at the key slogan 'It shouldn't happen here'.

'It'

From a linguistic perspective, the use of the impersonal article 'it' offers an ambiguous constitution of the topic/problem: we do not know what 'it' is, and, conventionally, we would expect 'it' to refer to an already specified topic or referent (whereas 'this' would indicate topicalisation or focus) (Brown and Yule 1983; Levinson 1984). Hence the reader is invited into an evaluation of something from whose indefinite form and lack of topicalisation it is assumed to be known or familiar without declaring what exactly this is. This turns out to be very useful as it sets up a puzzle about what is at issue in the question of accounting for who is responsible for the pressures and stresses generated by child and family poverty. Hence, as it turns out, 'it' relates to the question of poverty, but also opens up the question of whether this is indeed a singular or plural 'thing', or a constellation of circumstances, or indeed an event which 'happens'. Who it *happens to* is left unqualified – it could be the child, the parent(s) (or caregivers) or family; or both the child *and* family. Or indeed the whole society, the 'we' who already (seem to) know about this and therefore have let this happen, and made it into an 'it'. This reading generates the involvement and complicity of the reader. It implies a common, singular referent that gathers together or even – drawing on Althusser's (1971) notion of 'interpellation' as the hailing into being of the subject – constitutes a common perspective from which to see 'it'.

'shouldn't'

This is a negative form of a modal verb ('should') and, as Kress and Hodge (1979) noted, modal verbs form a class that combine orientation (in this case obligation or moral evaluation) as well as markers of futurity/possibility: 'It [modality] indicates the mode within which an utterance is presented as true, reliable, and authoritative' (85), such that: 'Modal auxiliaries encode probabilities and hearer–speaker relations, but blur precise distinctions of past, present and future, knowledge and power, *is* and *ought* ' (126). Other modal verbs include 'could' and 'might' and all three combine notions of permission (and so power) and prescription (and so normativity), as well as possibility. Conventionally, 'should' implies strong exhortation on moral grounds, rather than merely describing hypothetical, if unlikely, future possible outcomes. ('Could' would imply greater likelihood, or in its negative form, 'couldn't' a stronger statement of presumed impossibility.) Its negative form ('shouldn't') suggests an acknowledgement of occurrence alongside an unqualified rejection, including some kind of repugnance that has the affective force of repudiation. The impersonal formulation ('It shouldn't') does not require specification of who is doing the evaluation but rather implicitly aligns or attunes the reader to it (or aims to do so). So, combined with the impersonal form but presumed previously specified 'it', this has the effect of exhorting the readership in the sense of demanding that they should share this view.

The assertive character of the formulation suggests that this is a state of affairs whose presence demands comment and declaration of a position. Contrast this with 'it shouldn't happen, but it does', which in fact is underscored by the discourse of disbelief or even shock. However, the Save the Children formulation does invite a possible reading that, while it 'shouldn't happen here', it 'should' (or could or does) happen elsewhere. This therefore acknowledges the normalised perspective of child and family poverty in other countries/contexts. Indeed we know Save the Children usually works in those contexts, not these/ 'ours'; hence what remains crucially at issue, as set in play by the text, is whether this is a descriptive or prescriptive normalised statement.

'happen'

'Happen' offers a description of a state or event which blurs the question of causality, that is, of *how* 'it happens' (or has come to 'happen'), including – crucially – who or what is responsible, since the action is expressed as indirect and without personal form. The focus on event, rather than process, names the topic but leaves the reader without a commitment to a particular view of why or how this has come about (as seen also in 'shit happens', which typically communicates a sense of helplessness or resignation). Rather than dragooning the reader into a particular explanatory framework, this can be seen to offer the possibility of a spontaneous joint response without commitment to particular interpretive frameworks or models of causality. Clearly this is politically astute for an organisation which – as a charity – is not 'allowed' to adopt explicitly 'political' positions. Moreover, the framing is problem-focused, rather than policy-focused, so avoiding the invitation to usher in party-political bickering. While the vagueness of causality, process and outcome expressed by 'it shouldn't happen' appear to make the statement lack content, the generalised sense of ambiguity of both topic and process work fruitfully to foreground a general moral orientation (that might be obscured with more information or detail), and also exert a narrative requirement for reference to other contextual information (elsewhere in the written text or images) to resolve the lack of determination (of what is happening, and to whom).

'here'

'Here' is a deictic term (Levinson 1984), whose meaning is tied to a specific place but – significantly – a place which is not specified in the text (as a particular location) or personally identified with (as in 'it happened *to me*'). Within English language conventions of reading and writing, 'here' could be anywhere whose specification is clarified by the (con)text. By enforcing a set of moves to resolve the indeterminacy, it invites a common, shared understanding of where 'here' is, which does the double work of constituting a shared viewing *point* (or what the Lacanians call anamorphosis) as well as perspective on *what* is viewed (De Kesel 2009). 'Here' is also relational since it is the contrastive opposite of 'there'. 'There' is the 'not-here', in the same way as 'them'/'other' is the 'not-us' or normative self/subject.

Thus 'here' works to suggest an answer to all the indeterminacies set up earlier (about what or where something occurs), although, as I have already indicated, this sets in train a rather uncomfortable resolution to the problem (that if 'it shouldn't happen here', it 'should' happen 'there'). The 'here' also draws the reader/viewer to look at what 'here' is, and the image accompanying the text depicts a white girl with blonde/light brown hair. Given how questions of poverty are so easily racialised as well as perceived to be associated with non-European/non-UK/'other' contexts, this visual specification of 'here' works to inform the reader that 'it' is 'happening' to 'us' (not 'there' or to 'them'). So we have an image of a pre-teen white girl-child (the stock material for generalised subjective identification within the modern European historical imaginary (Steedman 1995)) to whom something – that is shortly qualified as poverty – is happening.

Several moves are accomplished here that are worthy of comment. First, there is an avoidance of the iconography associated with being an 'immigrant' – as (shamefully) a black child would probably be assumed to signify – to drive its key point home; that this is home-grown poverty, not imported or even produced by the selective, racist, treatment of migrants in terms of housing and social support. However, while it may be understood as an intervention to destabilise this canonical index of privileged selfhood, this could also be understood as marking as the only worthy subjects those who are white. In the report many examples are drawn from Wales and Scotland as well as the de-industrialised north of England, highlighting the predicament of the (white and black) working class and working poor – that also emphasises regional diversity and works to unpack or disaggregate the monolith of whiteness to show how this is fractured by class, gender and geographical location.

Thus the slogan could be understood as confirming the very binary between 'us'/'them' and its alignment with other associated binaries of white/black, European/non-European, and even citizen/non-citizen, that have long structured discourses of inclusion and exclusion within British popular (and policy) discourse, and insidiously connects questions of economic security deeply with those of national security (Ahmed 2004; while for a specifically gendered analysis see Shepherd 2009). But in this last reading, the subject of the statement (in the sense of the one who speaks it) is claiming a privileged position. They are presuming the authority to include or exclude that is more focused on claiming agency around the 'should' rather than an affiliative, engaged position of being willing to attend to the 'what' or situation that is 'happen'ing. Thus the different readings of this by-line reflect specifications of subjective and affiliative orientations that are already available, rather than constituting them. The risks of such ambiguous formulations are always that previous knowledge and orientations come into play to disambiguate them. Thus what is set in circulation is the reader's own prior conceptions that are evoked, but not directly specified, by the text.

The 'Balkan' war of the 1990s was discoursed in Britain as 'war in Europe', to emphasise its immediacy and intensify the moral imperative to act. Just as this could be read as implying a lesser moral responsibility to care about or discretionary status accorded other, less proximal, regional contexts of political violence, 'it shouldn't happen here' can be read either as implying that something shouldn't happen here that should (could, does and so ought to?) happen elsewhere. Or, alternatively, drawing on its reputation as a leading international child-focused aid agency, the slogan could be read as working to inform and reproach the reader that something we (and Save the Children in particular) know happens elsewhere is also happening here; that we need to acknowledge it in order to stop it.

The campaign

The campaign was launched in early September 2012 and ran across mainstream and social media and was widely reported in the mainstream press. It publicised research done by Save the Children (Whitham 2012) that documented increasing levels of deprivation and in particular challenged prevailing mythology by focusing on the *working* poor, that is, children living in families where the parent or parents were working but still unable to provide adequate material circumstances. This clearly transgressed the widely held view (as we see in the *Daily Mail* reception below) that only children whose parents were not able to work or were in a situation of being out of work are experiencing poverty. The campaign documented accounts from parents as facing major deprivations, such as having to 'choose' between heating their accommodation or providing hot food.[6]

A second key feature of the campaign was its focus on relative, rather than absolute, poverty; that is, highlighting its relational character, such that economic position is not simply tied to concretely specified amounts of income (or equivalent) but is related to other national indices of economic distribution. This means that being in poverty in the UK can look rather different from being in poverty in countries that are less industrialised and with lower living standards. Thus what is evoked here is the question of the relativity of 'needs', as socially defined within particular cultural-historical contexts, that also challenges the sense of difference or relative superiority of living conditions in rich, so-called developed, countries.

A third key intervention was to draw attention to the felt impact and effects of poverty in terms of relayed stress and distress. Following the UNICEF emphasis on child well-being (with the UK's plummeting record noted earlier), survey results were cited as highlighting how many children were aware of their parents' financial worries and the ways this was impacting on family relationships and well-being, including worrying the children themselves. This focus on the mental health aspects of poverty corresponds to a much wider view of its limiting and distorting effects, beyond immediate concrete material indicators, that suggests a more subtle and sustained analysis, including broader future impacts on health and educational aspiration and success (c.f. 'Save the Children works in more than 120 countries. We save children's lives. We fight for their rights. We help them fulfill their potential' (Whitham 2012, 2)).

The campaign based its claims on research undertaken that was summarised in its report, based on interviews and focus groups with parents and young people. Typically child-focused agencies such as Save the Children advertise to generate funds to support humanitarian emergencies, or to draw attention to particular forms of child abuse. In such contexts there are usually clear aims (to solicit money) and outcomes (to spend that money on effective interventions to relieve suffering). In this case, just as the slogan's meaning is ambiguous, so there is less clarity about what it aims to achieve. What emerges is that this intervention was aimed not only at public awareness but also as an attempt to re-orientate policy, including government policy, around child and family welfare and child poverty.

This was in a context where attainable targets for the abolition of child poverty agreed to by the Labour administration were tumbling out of reach. So it would seem that, rather than being a more conventional fundraising campaign (although it was also this), the organisation was drawing on its position as a significant voice in the field of child welfare to draw attention to child and family poverty, to engage in debate about what this is, and so to offer a broader understanding of poverty, how it is experienced, and what its impacts are.

The reception

The campaign was reported widely across the British press. For example, the *Guardian* (the liberal left national newspaper) offered largely descriptive coverage that was respectful and echoing of the primary messages; it supplemented these with a case study generated by its own reporters that also exemplified the campaign's main arguments.[7]

By contrast, the *Daily Mail* (a right wing national populist newspaper) reacted with characteristic indignation and hostility, describing the designation of these situations as poverty as an 'obscene comparison'.[8] Effectively, it argued not only that it shouldn't, but that it doesn't, happen here and ended with the claim that Save the Children was 'misusing facts, playing on emotions and devising political stunts'. It therefore rejected the premises of the campaign's rationale (focusing on poverty as relative and its systematic causes), and articulated the widely held commitment to longstanding representations of poverty as absolute and life-threatening (rather than also life-limiting) and far away 'in Africa', presuming/ performing the constitution of an ethnocentric reader. The 'in Africa' evokes the stock image of a whole continent in distress, infantilised and incapable of self-government, in relation to whom aid or charity works to confirm the power of the donor as benefactor and moral saviour (Gronemeyer 1993; Mehmet 1995). Thus the starving child is figured as 'heart-rending' (and the article supplied an image of exactly this as a contrast with what it claimed as being fake images of British child poverty provided by Save the Children). But it would seem this affect is elicited only if the deprivation is kept at a safe distance rather than being home-grown poverty.

The bulk of the *Daily Mail* response was devoted to discrediting the campaign. The four principle objections were: first, that the advertising campaign used actors, so this is not true/real poverty; second, that language was being manipulated to change the meaning of poverty; third, a rejection of the accuracy of the claims made about child poverty in Britain; and, fourth, disputing the evidence on which these claims were generated.

First, the article criticised how the advertising campaign used actors in its online images and video, claiming that this meant that what was depicted was not true or real poverty: 'so this is not like those campaigns to tackle child-poverty in Africa, in which a real child who is actually starving makes you realise you have to put your hand in your pocket' (Murray 2012). Apart from the grotesque implication that it is only if/when one is confronted face to face with 'a real child who is actually starving' that the situation can be thought about and/or financial support is warranted, this overlooks wider debates about the politics of representation of humanitarian emergencies and disasters (Middleton and O'Keefe 1998; Glennie 2008; MacLachlan *et al.* 2010). There has been widespread concern about how the genre of disaster reporting can inadvertently contribute to further dehumanisation in attempting to convey the desperation and level of need via portrayal of the abject conditions people face. There is a well-known repertoire of famine reporting that has attracted claims of being 'disaster pornography' (Reeves and Hammond 1988) and exploitation, that has given rise to extensive discussion among aid agencies alongside recommendations to journalists to ensure responsible reporting and consent to their pictures. These concerns have been particularly acute in relation to the representation of child neglect, poverty and hunger, precisely because of the ways the dominant discourses of childhood (as supposedly signifying some universal idiom of innocence, need and unconditional call upon our support) works to abstract children from their families, communities, cultures and material-political contexts. Such discourses elide child with country in ways that confirm the childlike status of the aid-receiving country (Holland 1992; Burman 1994, 2008a; Hutnyk 2004).

The second charge levelled by the *Daily Mail* was that 'poverty charities [are] changing the meaning of the language we use'. At a trivial level presumably what this was supposed to mean was that the language used did not correspond with the kinds of descriptions the *Daily Mail* would recognise as poverty. The claim is that the conditions described as poverty within the campaign are nothing compared to real poverty, so that 'Poverty [is] redefined to mean not somebody who is literally starving but somebody who is in want'. It would seem this criticism is close to the mark, for Save the Children's intervention was precisely to open up for discussion what is meant by poverty in Britain today, and how poverty (in Britain, as elsewhere) is not merely about starving or surviving, but about limits to individual and social development, and ultimately about larger questions of inequality and distribution (so intervening in discussions about relative as well as absolute poverty).

The third complaint from the *Daily Mail* emerged from a complete rejection of the campaign's claims, arguing that if cases of poverty do exist (with the repeated example of parents choosing between food or heating), this could only come about through the abuse of the welfare system ('unless parents are grossly misusing their handouts'); that is, through individual failures and not any systemic insufficiencies. Here the *Daily Mail* was rehearsing its general rightwing individualist position that people in bad situations must be there through their own failings, as indicated in recent government discourse that associates social mobility (of lack of it – poverty) with 'character and resilience' (see the all-party manifesto launched on 11 February 2014, http://www.appg-socialmobility.org/). What this gives rise to is a direct repudiation of the central claim asserted by the campaign, that poverty affects the working poor as well as those who are 'workless', and that current levels of income along with various types of available social support are still grossly inadequate to give many children the conditions in which they can thrive – all of which perhaps precisely indicates why this campaign was needed.⁹

The final dispute concerned the status of the evidence on which the claims for the campaign were based. The *Daily Mail* claimed that the sample was not large enough. (This was despite being based on interviews with 1,500 children, and 5,000 parents, which clearly is a commendably large corpus on the basis of which statistical analyses of considerable power can be made.) This argument was striking in its lack of comprehension over what research is – that a sample always is precisely that, a sample, a selection.¹⁰ It illustrates rather graphically the widespread misunderstanding of research design practice, as well as how rumour can damage research claims.

At issue seemed to be the desire to locate any 'worry' either in the realm of the imagination or as ideological constructions manufactured by the campaign. But paradoxically, in the name of warding off the sense of passivity arising from being designated as being in poverty, the article reinforced many of the campaign's general arguments about the widespread effects of welfare cuts and the worsening economic climate:

> [M]any families in Britain worry about . . . pay[ing] the bills. It is a strain that affects us all . . . But worrying about [this] . . . does not mean we are stuck in 'poverty' . . . [M]any parents – indeed, nearly all, give things up to ensure that their children do not go without the necessities . . .
> (Murray 2012)

It was as if the need to maintain a position of not being a victim, alongside the generalised character of the predicament ('affects us all'), requires a voluntarist model of the subject as agentic and so responsible. This is what underlies the definition between real and fabricated poverty, and indeed between 'us' and 'them'. Hence – in what was in fact a covert exemplification of precisely the tropes being problematised by the campaign – both the traditional subject and object of charity were reiterated, therefore revealing what is at stake in warding off as 'obscene' the idea that 'the situation here in Britain [is] in any way analogous with the situation of starving children in Africa'. Agentic subjects cannot be in abject states, and it would seem better to deny the generalised and specific hardships, and their widespread effects, than reconsider what is understood as poverty. Ideas about relative poverty were bowdlerised and ridiculed ('Compared to a Russian oligarch, we are all in poverty' (Murray 2012)), and the reader invited to repudiate an understanding of social and material deprivation as poverty, perhaps precisely because this poses questions of distribution and justice ('Like the word "inequality", the word "poverty" has come to mean almost anything.' (Murray 2012)).

Arguably, such responses highlighted the success of the campaign. Save the Children's response to these criticisms can perhaps be determined from its semi-official blog 'Uncounted'¹¹ on 6 September 2012. It tackled head on two key criticisms: of political bias and the 'affront' of attending to domestic poverty. It presented the argument that development NGOs are necessarily political via their commitment to a theory of change, and therefore inevitably engage with and challenge prevailing power relations. Not only did this collapse the distinction between 'there' and 'here', between 'the starving children of Africa' and deprived British children and families, but also precisely attempted to highlight the double standards at play. Alongside measures of 'poverty', what is 'political' seems to be relative, as 'Uncounted' pointed out:

> Why then should addressing UK child poverty be any more political? Somehow it's ok, more or less, to challenge policy thinking on international development, but not so much when it comes to domestic policy. In that sense, it really shouldn't happen here (sorry).
>
> (ibid.)

Yet along with such pointed comments, it is also worth noting that all over the world, in so-called 'developing' contexts, development NGOs do campaign on domestic poverty. So paradoxically even asking the question 'should "development" NGOs campaign on domestic poverty?' can be read as actually reinscribing the very us/them binary of 'developed/developing' that Uncounted/Save The Children is apparently trying to destabilise. At issue here, therefore, is the very identity or subject status of those for whom this is 'here', not 'there'; i.e. 'us', the reader, and also perhaps Save the Children too.

To what ends?

Posing the question of the relativity of poverty, as the 'It shouldn't happen here' campaign did, alongside situating children's conditions within their family and community contexts, is both an urgent and unsurprisingly challenging project, since this throws into question wider systems of distribution. The relativity at issue is both that between rich and poor within one national context (Britain), and of course also between rich and poor countries ('here' vs. 'there').

Paradoxically, and as if despite themselves, the *Daily Mail*'s evaluation was accurate: 'what Save The Children is doing is what "poverty" charities here have been doing for years – comprehensively changing the meaning of the language we use'. It would appear that this was indeed what they were doing, in the sense of trying to intervene in what counts as common sense and as everyday discourse, and hence the hostile responses. The *Daily Mail*'s claims that 'Save The Children has redefined "poverty" to mean not somebody who is literally starving but somebody who is in "want"' correctly bring the focus onto two key issues: not only how poverty is defined and measured (absolutely ('literally'?) or relatively, as Save the Children is proposing), but also how 'needs' are understood and interpreted; and, alongside these, the discretionary (racialised, classed and national) basis on which they are differentially acknowledged. The campaign and its responses indicated not only the tensions structured by, but also the overt struggle at issue in, highlighting both the subjectivity of need and the inevitability of its relative evaluation. But what marked this campaign out as distinct was not only its 'domestic' character but its emphasis on relative poverty, participation and the working poor. For beyond this were its efforts to foreground the less apparently material, but still potent, wider effects of living in poverty; and above all the psychosocial character of economic conditions – as constitutive, as constraining, and as foreclosing of developmental possibilities.

Such heated debate stands in stark contrast with the World Bank's complacent claims of ending extreme poverty by 2030[12] – whose definition of 'extreme' is pegged to an 'absolute' monetary measure – in much the way that the *Daily Mail* equated poverty with 'literal' starvation. So what was played out in this debate are central questions around which claims about children, children's welfare, education and development and, crucially, their relations with those of their families and communities, turn.

The *Daily Mail*'s hostile reception focused on three key questions that I have argued resonate more widely as at stake in claims to or about the poor child. First, questions of representation, in the sense of both the ethics and politics of images of children, the political economy of images of childhood and, second, how this conjugates – in a very mundane sense – contests over what counts as truth (reconstructed tableaux of documented contexts or the naïve realist demand for unmediated image, even if or when this demeans and dehumanises in the act of performing 'truth'). Third, not only did this overlook the widely recognised staging of poverty in reporting (see www.imaging-famine.org), more significantly it also obscured the political character of so-called natural disasters, especially the role of war and conflict and the role of international actors (both state and non-state) in disrupting food production and distribution (Gill 1986), and the viewer/reader's own role as contributing to this through their cultural-political affiliations and inscriptions. So the question of 'evidence' was really not only about how much is enough (as media coverage – including the *Daily Mail* – claimed). Indeed such preoccupations appeared to work as a distraction from the content to focus instead on technologies of data gathering (just as watching a horror movie invites the viewer to focus on how they create the special effects as a way of dealing with or avoiding the shock, fear or distress generated by what is depicted) (Creed 1987; Taylor 1998; Burman 2008a).

The further issue posed by the campaign's question about the legitimacy of an international aid and welfare organisation campaigning on domestic issues was whether, as the saying goes, charity begins at home, or not. Until recently it would appear it does not, for significant reasons – not least to do with colonial legacies and responsibilities. While post-development analyses have argued for the need not to rush in, on the grounds that intervention almost always makes things worse (Escobar 1997), this call to attend to the local is not without risks either, as recent British shifts in aid policy indicate. At the very least this highlights the double standards at work in recent cuts to Department for International Development aid, first to India and now South Africa, on the grounds that, as emerging economies, they can look after their own poor. Once this us/them binary is (re)instated, the obvious question this invites is: so why can't we? And, further, the question of who 'we' are.

Two decades ago, Gronemeyer (1993) highlighted the covert demand structured within the discourse of 'helping' that the subject of charity should adopt the moral-political framework of the donor. In the *Daily Mail* treatment, the conditionality of welfare entitlements in terms of who and what constitutes 'misusing their handouts' is seen, while the no-longer-working classes are no longer allowed to buy 'ciggies or booze' (as people on benefits have sometimes been found to do[13]). Such examples highlight the contempt and violence of the British class system meted out by the rich to the poor, amid conditions that have only worsened since the Save the Children campaign was launched. In April 2013, the Coalition budget announced further measures to enact a major retraction of the welfare state, while on the very same day (presumably in the hope this would pass unnoticed), the chief executives of banks and companies published information on their bonuses totalling tens of millions of pounds. Efforts were by made by the current Chancellor of the Exchequer to create political capital even from the tragic case of the deaths of six children who died in a fire set by their father, with claims of his living on welfare benefits as 'a lifestyle choice',[14] while the emergence of the United Kingdom Independence Party (UKIP – an anti-Europe, anti-immigration, right-of-Conservative party) as a significant political force in the May 2013 local elections clearly owes much to the promotion within even mainstream politics of discourses of immigrants taking jobs and houses, and filling hospital beds and primary school places, such that the debate over immigration now (conveniently) displaces wider discussion of cuts/austerity.

Perhaps the most politically subversive move within Save the Children's 'It shouldn't happen here' campaign (among others), was drawing attention to the *working* poor who cannot thereby be subject to such moral character assassination. Their intervention highlights how the responsibility for children's welfare, education and future life prospects has to be seen as more than individual, beyond the efforts and resources of particular parents or families. This consideration is one that transcends NGO campaign publicity and is at least as relevant for wider poverty alleviation strategies. Indeed the focus on the working poor precisely challenges neoliberal discourses of individualism, adaptability and employability to show that no amount of individual effort may be enough to weather national and international economic pressures. This campaign also illustrates the many local norths and souths within the global North and South.[15] Hence inequality cannot be adequately represented by overall national measures, but rather the poor and dispossessed are everywhere, but represented nowhere.

Rather than reinstate such binaries, the real challenge posed by the campaign was its call to overcome the division between 'here' and 'there' in working to end poverty and inequality. So, yes, the *Daily Mail* was right – there *is* a need to change the language we use, to re-evaluate our criteria for evidence and reassess the 'political' status of poverty/development. But even on that score, at higher levels there is and has always been politicisation of aid and development, as indicated by the debate around the appointment of David Miliband to head Human Rescue International (Hofman 2013). So 'it shouldn't happen *here*', not because it should happen *there*, but because it shouldn't happen anywhere.

Nor because Britain is – as right wing discourse has it – becoming a 'third world' country and so now is in as much need of aid as one. Rather, bringing the problem of poverty so uncomfortably close to home necessarily imports an attention to questions of equity of distribution that muddies up what may have appeared to be clearcut distinctions between rich and poor, undeserving and deserving poor, and even donors and recipients. The focus on relative poverty in developed nations is clearly a reflection that, broadly speaking, certain types of acute or absolute poverty have largely been eradicated. However, the growth of food banks and homelessness across 'austerity'-struck Europe indicates the return (on a large scale at least, given that certain problems were never fully 'eradicated') of an experience of poverty that is about very basic material needs and therefore absolute. Above all, perhaps, what such debate brings to the fore is the need to go beyond easy polarisations of objective, real ('true') versus subjective (biased) to show how we all implicitly have, and so have explicitly to take, an explicit position relative to discourse and practice.

Post-script

On 5 March 2014, Save the Children UK launched a further campaign, via a video uploaded to YouTube entitled 'Most shocking second a day' (http://www.youtube.com/watch?v=RBQ-IoHfimQ). This juxtaposes two parallel alternative days in the life of a little girl, one where she has her birthday party and another where she is in the midst of a warzone. Without saying so explicitly, this refers to the situation of children caught in the Syrian conflict. The final slogan reads: 'Just because it isn't happening here, doesn't mean it isn't happening'. Interestingly, this appears to have received a much more sympathetic reception than 'It shouldn't happen here'.

Notes

1 While in the UK Save the Children is associated with international child-focused aid work, it has in fact campaigned on child poverty in Britain for many years.
2 As is the case of course for all (child and family) poverty.
3 I am grateful in particular to Graham Whitham and Alexon Westlake for their interest and openness to critical debate and, beyond this, to Graham's enthusiastic response and further comments which I have – with permission – drawn upon in this text. I also want to thank the editors of this book for their engaged and sympathetic editing.
4 It should be noted that this shift was not taken by Save the Children alone, but rather reflects broader concern among child-focused and other aid agencies – for example, a few months earlier (in June 2012) the UK-based poverty relief organisation Oxfam released a report highlighting how the UK government deficit reduction strategy was creating a 'perfect storm' of increased unemployment, falling incomes and rising living costs that disproportionately affect the most vulnerable and economically deprived (see http://www.oxfam.org.uk/media-centre/press-releases/2012/06/work-no-longer-pays-for-britons-caught-in-perfect-storm-of-falling-incomes-and-rising-costs).
5 These targets were: relative child poverty to affect 10 per cent or less of all children, absolute poverty 5 per cent or less of all children, low income and material

deprivation combined 5 per cent or less of all children and persistent poverty 5 per cent or less of all children) (all before housing costs).
6 In this sense the campaign was clearly not about 'exceptional' states of destitution, but rather was drawing attention to how ordinary working people are facing conditions of unacceptable deprivation.
7 See http://www.guardian.co.uk/society/2012/sep/05/save-the-children-uk-campaign.
8 See http://www.dailymail.co.uk/news/article-2198927/It-s-obscene-political-stunt-Save-The-Children-equate-British-families-starving-poor-Africa.html.
9 Universal access to child benefit was withdrawn in Britain in 2012, while at the time of writing this the most recent Department for Work and Pensions (DWP) Household Below Average Income dataset showed that 66 per cent of all children in poverty in 2011/12 were in households where at least one parent worked (data published 14 June 2013, https://www.gov.uk/government/organisations/department-for-work-pensions/series/households-below-average-income-hbai-2).
10 The author of the report for Save the Children, Graham Whitham, told me how when he was about to be interviewed on local television to launch the campaign, he was warned off air he would be challenged over the small numbers, but the reporter then backed down when Graham pointed out how large the sample actually was.
11 'Uncounted' is a blog that is described on its website as 'about inequality and development and those who are uncounted. It is written and maintained by the staff in Save the Children's policy and research department. Uncounted aims to stimulate debate but is not a reflection of Save the Children policy (http://www.uncounted.org.uk/2012-/it-shouldn't-happen-here?, accessed 5 April 2013).
12 http://www.worldbank.org/en/news/video/2013/04/02/jim-kim-world-can-end-extreme-poverty.
13 As also depicted in the reception of a Channel 4 television series 'Benefits Street', screened in early 2014.
14 'George Osborne insists linking Mick Philpott to welfare reform was right', Nicholas Watt, chief political correspondent, *Guardian*, Sunday 7 April 2013, http://www.guardian.co.uk/politics/2013/apr/07/osborne-philpott-welfare-benefits-reform (accessed 9 June 2013).
15 Indeed in Britain such geographical descriptors of privilege are reversed, such that the North is overwhelmingly poorer with all the conventional markers of deprivation such as lower life expectancy, than the South (as was confirmed yet again as recently as June 2013).

References

Ahmed, Sara. 2004. *The Cultural Politics of Emotions*. Edinburgh: Edinburgh University Press.
Althusser, Louis. 1971. *Lenin and Philosophy and Other Essays*. London: New Left Books.
Black, Maggie. 1992. *A Cause for Our Times: Oxfam – the First 50 Years*. Oxford: Oxfam.
Brown, Gillian, and George Yule. 1983. *Discourse Analysis*. Cambridge: Cambridge University Press.
Burman, Erica. 1994. 'Innocents Abroad: Projecting Western Fantasies of Childhood onto the Iconography of Emergencies.' *Disasters: Journal of Disaster Studies and Management* 18 (3): 238–253. doi:10.1111/j.1467-7717.1994.tb00310.x.

Burman, Erica. 1996a. 'Local, Global or Globalized: Child Development and International Child Rights Legislation.' *Childhood: A Global Journal of Child Research* 3 (1): 45–66. doi: 10.1177/0907568296003001004.
Burman, Erica. 1996b. 'Constructing and Deconstructing Childhood: Images of Children and Charity Appeals.' In *Psychological Research: Innovative Methods and Strategies*, edited by John Haworth, 170–184. London: Routledge.
Burman, Erica. 2008a. *Developments: Child, Image, Nation*. London and New York: Brunner-Routledge.
Burman, Erica. 2008b. *Deconstructing Developmental Psychology*. 2nd edn. London and New York: Brunner-Routledge.
Burman, Erica. 2012. 'Between Identification and Subjectification: Affective Technologies of Expertise and Temporality in the Contemporary Cultural Representation of Gendered Childhoods.' *Pedagogy, Culture and Society* 20 (2): 295–315. doi:10.1080/14681366.2012.688767.
Burman, Erica, and Maggie Maclure. 2011. 'Deconstruction as a Method of Research: Stories from the Field.' In *Theory and Methods in the Social Sciences, Second Edition*, edited by Bridget Somekh and Cathy Lewin, 286–294. London: Sage.
Burman, Erica, and Ian Parker, eds. 1993. *Discourse Analytic Research: Repertoires and Readings of Texts in Action*. London: Routledge.
Burman, Erica, and Jackie Stacey. 2010. 'The Child and Childhood in Feminist Theory.' *Feminist Theory* 11 (3): 227–240. doi:10.1177/1464700110376288.
Butler, Judith. 1997. *The Psychic Life of Power*. New York: Routledge.
Cannella, Gaile, and Radhika Viruru. 2004. *Childhood and Postcolonization*. New York: RoutledgeFalmer.
Castañeda, Claudia. 2002. *Figurations: Child, Bodies, Worlds*. Durham and London: Duke University Press.
Cooke, Graeme, Paul Gregg, Donald Hirsch, Naomi Jones, and Anne Power. 2008. *Ending Child Poverty: 'Thinking 2020'. A Report and Think-pieces from the Child Poverty Unit Conference*. Department for Work and Pensions, Working Paper No. 56. London: HMSO.
Creed, Barbara. 1987. 'Horror and the Monstrous Feminine: An Imaginary Abjection.' *Screen* 28 (1): 44–70. doi: 10.1093/screen/27.1.44.
De Kesel, Marc. 2009. *Eros and Ethics*. New York: SUNY.
Doucet, Andrea, and Natasha S. Mauthner. 2008. 'What Can Be Known and How? Narrated Subjects and the Listening Guide.' *Qualitative Research* 8 (3): 399–409. doi: 10.1177/1468794106093636.
Escobar, Arturo. 1997. 'The Making and Unmaking of the Third World through Development.' In *The Post-Development Reader*, edited by Majid Rahnema with Victoria Bawtree, 85–93. London: Zed Books.
Gill, Peter. 1986. *A Year in the Death of Africa*. London: Paladin.
Glennie, Jonathan. 2008. *The Trouble with Aid: Why Less Could Mean More for Africa*. London: Zed Press.
Gronemeyer, Marianne. 1993. 'Helping.' In *The Development Dictionary*, edited by Wolfgang Sachs, 53–69. London: Verso.
Hammett, Chris. 2014 'Shrinking the Welfare State: The Structure, Geography and Impact of British Government Benefit Cuts.' *Transactions* 39: 490–503.
Hodge, Robert, and Gunther Kress. 1988. *Social Semiotics*. Bristol: Policy Press.

Hofman, Michiel. 2013. 'David Miliband's new role will only hinder our aid work.' *Guardian*, 28 March. http://www.theguardian.com/commentisfree/2013/mar/28/david-miliband-new-role-aid-work.

Holland, Patricia. 1992. *What is a Child? Popular Images of Childhood*. London: Virago.

Hutnyk, John. 2004. 'Photogenic Poverty: Souvenirs and Infantilism.' *Journal of Visual Culture* 3 (1): 77–94. doi: 10.1177/1470412904042266.

Kress, Gunther, and Robert Hodge. 1979. *Language as Ideology*. London: Routledge and Kegan Paul.

Levinson, Stephen C. 1984. *Pragmatics*. Cambridge: Cambridge University Press.

Macherey, Pierre. 2012. 'Figures of Interpellation in Althusser and Fanon.' *Radical Philosophy* 173: 9–20.

MacLachlan, Malcolm, Eilish McAuliffe, and Stuart C. Carr. 2010. *The Aid Triangle: Recognising the Human Dynamics of Dominance, Justice and Identity*. London: Zed Press.

MacNaughton, Glenda. 2005. *Doing Foucault in Early Childhood Studies: Applying Poststructural Ideas*. Abingdon and New York: Routledge.

Mehmet, O. 1995. *Westernizing the Third World*. London and New York: Zed Press.

Middleton, Neil, and O'Keefe, Phil. 1998. *The Politics of Humanitarian Aid*. London: Pluto.

Moss, Peter, and Pat Petrie. 2002. *From Children's Services to Children's Spaces*. London: RoutledgeFalmer.

Murray, Douglas. 2012 'It's an obscene political stunt for Save The Children to equate British families with the starving poor of Africa.' *Daily Mail*, 6 September. http://www.dailymail.co.uk/news/article-2198927/It-s-obscene-political-stunt-Save-The-Children-equate-British-families-starving-poor-Africa.html.

Parker, Ian. 1992. *Discourse Dynamics*. London and New York: Routledge. http://www.discourseunit.com.

Parker, Ian. 2002. *Critical Discursive Psychology*. London: Palgrave.

Penn, Helen. 2005. *Unequal Childhoods: Children's Lives in Poor Countries*. London: RoutledgeFalmer.

Penn, Helen. 2011. 'Travelling Policies and Global Buzzwords: How International Non-Governmental Organizations and Charities Spread the Word about Early Childhood in the Global South.' *Childhood* 18 (1): 94–113. doi: 10.1177/0907568210369846.

Reeves, Michelle, and Jenny Hammond, eds. 1988. *Looking Beyond the Frame: Racism, Representation and Resistance*. Oxford: Third World First.

Rose, Nikolas S. 1990. *Governing the Soul*. London: Routledge.

Save the Children. 1992. *Focus on Children*. London: The Save the Children Fund.

Shepherd, Laura J. 2009. *Gender, Violence and Security*. London: Zed Press.

Social Mobility and Child Poverty Commission. 2014. *Meeting the 2020 Child Poverty Targets*. UK Government. https://www.gov.uk/government/publications/meeting-the-2020-child-poverty-targets.

Sparrow, Andrew. 2014. 'UK's child poverty goals unattainable, says report.' *Guardian*, 9 June. http://www.theguardian.com/society/2014/jun/09/child-poverty-goals-unattainable-report.

Steedman, Carolyn. 1995. *Strange Dislocations: Childhood and the Idea of Human Interiority 1780–1930*. London: Virago.

Taylor, John. 1998. *Body Horror: Photojournalism, Catastrophe and War*. Manchester: Manchester University Press.

Tunstall, Rebecca, Ruth Lupton, Dylan Kneale, and Andrew Jenkins. 2011. *Growing up in Social Housing in the New Millennium: Housing, Neighbourhoods, and Early Outcomes for Children Born in 2000.* CASE/143. London: Centre for Analysis of Social Exclusion, London School of Economics.

Valentine, Gill. 1996. 'Angels and Devils: Moral Landscapes of Childhood.' *Environment and Planning D: Society and Space,* 14 (5): 581–599.

Wells, Karen. 2007. 'Narratives of Liberation and Narratives of Innocent Suffering: Images of Iraqi Children in the British Press.' *Journal of Visual Communication,* 6 (1): 55–71. doi: 10.1177/1470357207071465.

Whitham, Graham. 2012. *Child Poverty in 2012: It Shouldn't Happen Here.* London: The Save the Children Fund. http://www.savethechildren.org.uk/sites/default/files/documents/child_poverty_2012.pdf.

Websites cited

http://www.savethechildren.org.uk/news-and-comment/news/2012-09/uks-poorest-children-bearing-greatest-burden-recession

http://www.dailymail.co.uk/news/article-2198927/It-s-obscene-political-stunt-Save-The-Children-equate-British-families-starving-poor-Africa.html

http://www.guardian.co.uk/society/2012/sep/05/save-the-children-uk-campaign

http://www.uncounted.org.uk/2012/09/it-shouldnt-happen-here/ (accessed 1 July 2013)

http://www.savethechildren.org.uk/sites/default/files/docs/The_importance_of_income_Summary.pdf

http://www.oxfam.org.uk/media-centre/press-releases/2012/06/work-no-longer-pays-for-britons-caught-in-perfect-storm-of-falling-incomes-and-rising-costs

http://www.unicef.org.uk/Latest/Publications/Child-well-being/

http://www.if.org.uk/archives/3648/britains-children-fare-worse-says-unicef

http://news.sky.com/story/1076033/unicef-austerity-risks-childrens-prospects

http://www.appg-socialmobility.org

3 'Black kid burden'
Cultural representations of Indigenous childhood and poverty in Australian cinema

Kristina Gottschall

Introduction

Despite the 'affluence' of Australia, deep poverty marks the lives of many Australians, especially in rural and remote Indigenous communities. Poverty in 'first world' countries like Australia might look relatively different from poverty in countries that are less industrialised and with lower 'living standards'; however, issues of poverty and development *are* very much relevant to these 'affluent' nations. For example, Burman in this volume discusses cycles of disadvantage, inter-generational unemployment and a growing class of working poor in the United Kingdom. While the circumstances described in Burman's work on the UK correspond to the lives of many Australians, some Indigenous Australians in isolated rural and remote locations are living in circumstances of poverty that actually looks a lot like 'third world' poverty, including inadequate housing, no electricity, no running water, no sanitation and little to no access to quality healthcare, education, related services and infrastructure (Young 2002; Altman 2007).

A recent report from the Australian Council of Social Service (2013), *Poverty in Australia 2012*, found that 12.8 per cent of Australians were living below the poverty line.[1] The report also found that Indigenous Australians were living below the poverty line at the much higher rate of 19.3 per cent. Living the effects of marginalisation as a result of colonialism and government neglect, and with the economic decline of many rural towns, Indigenous people are often caught in cycles of disadvantage. The *Poverty in Australia 2012* report shows that the gap between Indigenous and non-Indigenous life expectancy is 12 years for males and 10 years for females, and the mortality rates for Indigenous infants and young children remain two to three times higher than for all infants and young children. Clearly, disadvantage and poverty greatly impact on the lives of some Indigenous Australians, despite living in a country also characterised by great wealth.

For many urban Australians (and international audiences more broadly), popular films are often the only way the lives of Indigenous Australian children in isolated rural and remote communities are seen. This chapter focuses on the politics of childhood, particularly the politics of Indigenous Australian childhoods, by considering the representations of Indigenous children in a selection of popular Australian films. Popular film texts are powerful means by which societies construct, maintain, protect and challenge concepts of childhood. Engagement with films opens spaces to think about the complexities of childhood, poverty and development. For example, popular films can orientate audiences toward the burdens placed on the Indigenous child as a 'poor child', forced to grow up in contexts marked by racism, poverty and injustice. They can also illuminate how the Indigenous child can be an agent creating meaning within adult worlds, making his/her own subjecitvities. Popular Australian film is a space where society makes meaning around wider debates about poverty, childhood and development in the Australian context, and can thus serve as a form of pedagogy or learning around these issues (Lusted 1986; Ellsworth 1997, 2005). This kind of analysis, focused around cultural politics, is a framework that is potentially of great value to poverty and development studies, not least since it exposes, challenges, worries about and changes the discourses being used in national narratives and contained within mass media imagery and stories. The marginalisation of Indigenous Australian childhoods in the narrative of a 'modern', 'developed' nation, has been redressed to some degree in the last decade in Australia through several key feature films about Indigenous children by Indigenous filmmakers. Indigenous films about Indigenous childhood are cultural stories and representations that aim, in one way or another, to engage and teach viewers. However, the learning that occurs and the meanings that are made are far from straightforward or simple. The discursive formations that function together to tell these stories articulate a complexity of 'fiction and fantasy, regulation and persuasion' (Gonick 2006, 3), framing the way audiences can know the Indigenous child and the contexts of their worlds.

The films under analysis in this chapter are written and directed by two Indigenous Australian men: *Beneath Clouds* (2002) and *Toomelah* (2011) by Ivan Sen, and *Samson and Delilah* (2009) by Warwick Thornton. The films are mobilised here to examine Western/non-Western understandings of race, gender, age, poverty and place as they intersect in the formation of Indigenous childhoods. Of particular interest are the different gendered demands placed on boy and girl subjects, and how childhood (and particularly adolescence) is plagued with anxieties about young Indigenous people being at risk, vulnerable and sick, and simultaneously as capable, good, and agents of social cohesion. First, I discuss the politics of interpretation and popular film as a pedagogic device to argue for the usefulness of cultural analysis. I then analyse the discourses of childhood which have circulated and gained traction in the Australian public sphere via a high-profile government intervention in the Northern Territory of Australia. Linking this to childhood discourses on the screen, representations of Indigenous childhood in the Australian cinema are considered through familiar narrative and thematic tropes such as the 'lost child' and the child 'coming-of-age'. Finally, I isolate key scenes from *Beneath Clouds*, *Toomelah* and *Samson and Delilah* to offer some insights into formations of filmic Indigenous Australian childhoods and the Indigenous Australian child subject.

Calling into question the dominant idea of the universal child as 'not adult', as individual or separate and devoid of cultural and social markers, this chapter will consider how class, race, gender, age, poverty and place demarcate Indigenous child subjects, and how racial, gendered and age-based experiences, identities and power relations shape the young black subject. Through a semiotic, discursive and affective analysis framed by feminist, post-structuralist and postcolonialist theories, I consider how these films constitute and govern the child subject as 'not adult', as lost and vulnerable and/or as autonomous subjects on the road to adulthood. There is a key question for those of us in the field, that is, for development theorists, sociologists, educationalists and cultural scholars, and those who are concerned with issues of childhood poverty and racial poverty: How do discourses around race and age-based subjectivity enable and constrain our thinking? Cultural artefacts such as popular films are implicated here in that they influence societal and individual thinking, and this is precisely why the study of making meaning around popular films is of importance.

The politics of interpretation and film as pedagogy

Cultural analysis, including the critical engagement with, and analysis of, popular films is a useful way to learn about childhood and poverty. It is in popular texts that we can see what societies think about childhood and poverty and how societies account for the existence and meaning of such issues. Further, when audiences or spectators engage with films, they are entering a complex 'public' domain or forum that is focused on making meaning around these issues. Popular film incites learning about culture, subjectivity and being, and the inequalities around subjecthood in specific contexts.

Questions that can potentially arise through cultural analysis and engagement, and specifically within the films in question here include: How might learning/meaning emerge through the cultural practices of making Indigenous childhood? How are we invited by the film text to learn about intersecting formations of 'black'/'white', 'child'/'adult', 'masculinity', 'girlhood', 'rurality' and 'poverty'? How might these practices form and govern concepts of childhood, making meanings around the costs or benefits of being particular subjects in particular times and places?

The 'learning' that takes place through popular texts is a process of interpretation that is in itself a political process. In this sense, learning or 'the politics of interpretation' is a complex and ambiguous process. What meaning is made, how it is made and by whom, are multifaceted questions due to the nature of mode of address and spectator positioning. The film spectator is implicated in the labour of meaning-making in that while texts aim to engage spectators around meanings, meaning can only be 'activated' by spectators in the act of interrogation (McKee 1997a, 161). Assigning the spectator significant control over the production of meaning is not to threaten the conceptual integrity of the text itself, nor is it unfettered licence over meaning or a 'utopian dream of consumer freedom' (McKee 1997b, 118). This is because texts will still 'encourage certain acts of meaning-making and discourage others' (McKee, 1997b, 118). There are socially sanctioned ways of consuming a text and specific learned skills in spectating that frame the meaning that can be had. Through genre, for instance, 'horizons of expectation' (Jauss 1982 as cited in McKee 1997b, 118) are established where certain modes of meaning-making are taken up by the spectator, where certain expectations arise about how the story should materialise on the screen. Films 'restate and rehearse' stories about childhood, gender, race, place and culture all the time – ideas that have 'prevailed over time and that have been mythologised and ideologised by the discursive practices of institutions like the government . . . the media and the family' (Crilly 2001, 38). Characters, plots and imaginaries become verified and legitimated through repetition of key visual, aural and verbal discursive metaphors. Such filmic metaphors work as compulsive retellings of the 'same old stories' with the same set of 'stereotypes' (Bhabha 1992, 23). Given this, it is possible to talk about the ways in which meaning is 'closed down in particular texts at particular times, in particular cultures' but, importantly, without 'insisting on single, stable unified interpretation' (McKee 1997b, 118).

In complex and powerful ways, popular film texts construct, maintain, protect and challenge concepts of Indigeneity and childhood. Indigeneity is 'remade over and over again in a process of dialogue, imagination, representation and interpretation' (Langton 1993, 81). Both Indigenous and non-Indigenous people create Indigenous identities but clearly, the power to do so has historically not been evenly distributed. Popular films from Western contexts have long been implicated in making and remaking subjects around norms – racial, gendered, age-based – and around class and place. In this sense, cinema is a colonial medium with the power to look, the means to silence the other, and the will to produce the colonised as if fixed and knowable (McKee 1997a). Evidently, then, not all meanings or acts of meaning-making are equally available to all, and some may be impossible altogether. Taking this into account, film engagement and analysis needs to go beyond considerations of the accuracy or inaccuracy of representations, the negative or positive images presented, and whether the film is racist or not (McKee 1997a). Rather, the more pertinent or challenging question is, how is 'racial difference' inscribed within the textual features and key visual, aural and verbal discursive metaphors of film? Such textual features need to be analysed 'alongside the ways in which audiences are positioned in relation to these' (Jennings 1993, 6). Thus, modes of address and spectator positioning within filmic discourses on race and childhood, for instance, are vital aspects of cultural discourses that are 'formed by, and contribute to, the power relationships within which they are embedded' (Jennings 1993, 11). What the 'white' spectator sees or fails to see, what the 'adult' viewer brings to their reading of films about children, what the audience knows about poverty, can potentially make a significant difference to the meanings that are made and the discursive frames employed.

As feminist, post-structural and postcolonial studies remind us, contemporary cinema is located in a decolonising or postcolonising moment marked by contested and multiple meanings. Postcolonis*ing* because 'Indigenous and non-Indigenous peoples are situated in relation to (post)colonisation in radically different ways – ways that cannot be made into sameness' (Moreton-Robinson

2003, 31). Meaning, identity, the imperial gaze – all are destabilised in contemporary cinema (Huijser and Collins-Gearing 2007; Knopf 2013). For instance, relationships to places/land/country are potentially re-visioned in the light of Indigenous Australian land rights[2] (Collins and Davis 2004). Importantly though, looking at and relating to land, history, government policy, cultural practice and identity are moves that highlight cultural difference and potentially even conflict (Cain 2004; Huijser and Collins-Gearing 2007). Contemporary Indigenous filmmakers are located in this moment, using an arguably 'colonial' medium to tell their postcolonial stories, with the potential to re-vision race, gender, class and place norms. The ambivalence that marks many of these stories arguably destabilises white colonial security and the privileged position of the white viewer (Palmer and Gillard 2002, 2004).

This 'indeterminate space' or the politics of interpretation has long been the focus of media and cultural studies research (see McKee 1997a). In education research, such inquiry occurs in the popular or public pedagogy fields (Giroux 1994, 2000). In the former, spectators are recognised not as passive receptors but as key to representation and meaning-making processes. In the latter, students/spectators are seen not as passive receptors but key to meaning-making, to learning. Even though Giroux coined the term 'public pedagogy', feminist and poststructural scholars in the field more fully articulated meaning-making and the role of the audience as a complex and relational act. Close to 30 years ago, media scholar David Lusted acknowledged that the act of learning occurs through relational and contextual processes, a consciousness-changing experience between the text or the 'teacher', the learner and 'the knowledge they together produce' (1986, 3). Knowledge formation in this regard becomes 'interactive productivity' as opposed to 'merely a transmissive act' (Lather 1991, 15). The text or teacher 'invites learning' and the text or pedagogy may be designed in such a way so that learning can occur (Ellsworth 1997, 1). Yet, 'the structures within which we encourage people to engage in them' are equally significant (Simon 1992, 39). Acts of teaching and learning in this sense are profoundly discursive, semiotic and affective cultural and identity work, where in complex ways we learn our culture and our place within it (Chouinard 2009). We also learn about the limits and inequalities around subjecthood and ways of being in the world. This is why cultural analysis around popular films and critical thinking about the politics of interpretation are so important to understandings of the 'black child' or the 'poor child'. Such thinking highlights the discursive frames of societies' and individuals' thinking, while ideally enabling a space for that discourse to be challenged and for new possibilities to emerge. Without such a public forum or critical engagement, challenging the bounds of dominant discourse would most likely not occur.

The politics of Indigenous childhoods in Australia

It has long been argued that the normative understandings of childhood or the 'universal child' are synonymous with an individual, white, male, asexual, Western and middle-class subject (Walkerdine 1997; Lesko 2001). Positioned as a time of disorder, childhood is synonymous with incompleteness, a 'becoming' personhood, supposedly very separate from adulthood, which is understood as full, finished personhood (Kenway and Bullen 2001; Lesko 2001; Blatterer 2007, 2010). It is not always the case that discourses and stories around non-white, non-male, non-Western, non-middle-class subjects necessarily overturn the discursive norms, because these discourses, too, are often a part of colonial or paternal thinking. 'White' only means 'white' in its relation to 'black', 'adulthood' only means what it means in relation to 'childhood', and so on. It is this normative discourse that media and popular culture mobilise in their representations of childhood, and in Australia, these representations predominantly show the child as essentially naïve, vulnerable and at risk (Jenks 1996; Meyer 2007). The black child is not only seemingly at risk as a result of their 'childhood' status, but also because of their 'blackness', marked in a doubly risky way due to what they 'lack' as a result of their supposed cultural 'difference'.

When Australian media reports focus on Indigenous children, they generally do so in ways that portray them as poor subjects marked by disadvantage and thus in need of (paternalistic, authoritarian, white) protection. These were precisely the kind of discourses that were employed in the 2007 Northern Territory Emergency Response (also known as the Intervention) by the conservative Howard government in response to reports of rampant child sex abuse in the Northern Territory (NT) government's the *Little Children are Sacred* report (2007). The report concluded that sexual abuse of children in Indigenous communities in the NT had reached 'crisis levels' and needed urgent state and federal government response. Suspending the country's Racial Discrimination Act (1975), 600 soldiers from the Australian Defence Forces entered specified Indigenous communities that by law could only be entered by permit at the invitation of Indigenous Australian elders. A raft of reforms were enacted including a ban on alcohol and pornography, and the quarantining of a proportion of welfare benefits of those who were judged to have neglected or 'endangered' their children.

Discourses of the innocent child were mobilised here to construct Indigenous Australian children as inherently naïve, vulnerable and weak, and thus defenceless, at risk, and in need of urgent protection. Defining children as lacking sexual knowledge and experience, or lacking a sexuality altogether, defines the child as pure or sacred (Meyer 2007). In addition to this, the Howard government used a discourse of failure and problematic culture to represent these Indigenous communities as dysfunctional and unsafe for children and thus the justification for illegally entering these communities (Altman and Russell 2012). Childhood, and a particularly 'vulnerable' form of childhood – 'black childhood' – became a 'moral rhetoric' that worked to 'legitimize anything without actually having to explain it' (Meyer 2007, 98). In other words, the children themselves became the moral reason for the government to 'intervene' as if the only moral and right action that could be taken by the government in their sovereign position as paternal 'protectors'. Despite much criticism, the Intervention received bipartisan support from the Australian Labor Party at the time, and rebadged as

'Stronger Futures', was passed into law and locked in by the Labor Rudd/Gillard government for a 10-year period from 2012 to 2022.[3] It was, perhaps, the obligatory workings of this 'moral rhetoric' that prevented any real opposition to the Intervention, for to be opposed to such an intervention would seemingly give the impression that the alleged abuse and neglect was condoned. In spite of the actions of consecutive conservative and liberal Australian governments, it should be noted that in the 7 years since the initiation of the Intervention, not one prosecution for child abuse has come from the exercise (Pazzano 2012).

The discourses here that justify certain actions and make certain realities and subjectivities for Indigenous Australian childhood possible or impossible are the same kind of discourses circulating in the wider public sphere of popular culture. In this sense, discursive constructions of the (black) child have enacted influence, impact and significance in the policy/practice world and vice versa. In her study of the NT Intervention, Kelada (2008, 1) draws parallels between a well-known children's book[4] about a young boy conquering a wild land, and the imperialist actions of the Australian government. She argues that such stories may be dismissed as children's fantasies but 'what often goes unrealised is the extent to which fantasy can infiltrate adult realms and national identities with highly detrimental consequences'. Going one step further, I argue that such 'adult realms' and 'national identities' are already so inextricably bound and based on 'fantasy' as to throw into question the real and the fantastical. This is precisely why cultural analysis is so important and useful to the contexts we are concerned with here, as it ideally rethinks the basis of what we think we know and how we think we know it (Threadgold 2000). I now turn to the Indigenous Australian child of Australian cinema to explore the discursive territory of this cultural realm and its possible implications for broader societal conceptions of the Indigenous child.

The Indigenous Australian child of Australian cinema

Historically, Australian filmmaking has been marked by the conspicuous absence of Indigenous children and the silence of Indigenous Australian characters more broadly. This absence and denial of the right to speak has long been critiqued as a strategic part of the colonial project (Said 1985; Spivak 1988). In spite of this absence, however, there are approximately 24 feature films about Indigenous Australian childhoods.[5] With the possible exception of *Rabbit Proof Fence* (2002), all focus on a time in the Indigenous child's life *as if* key – their coming-of-age – as a marker of the end of their childhood. The coming-of-age trope in the Australian cinema has a long tradition, particularly since the 1970s 'revival' (Dermody and Jacka 1988). As well as being historically contingent and embodying social issues relevant at the time (Hamilton 2012; May 2012), many themes in coming-of-age films stay constant. Australian films have frequently reprised the story of the child protagonist obsessed with fitting in, being 'normal' and belonging (Caputo 1993; Moran 2006; Speed 2006). It is often said that the Australian film industry is obsessed with coming-of-age films because 'stories about tentative children, unstable and struggling over their identity, are metaphors for our national film industry and, indeed, the [Australian] nation itself' (Gottschall 2010, 177). Mirroring dominant ideas of childhood/adulthood dichotomies in the public sphere, the child protagonists in these films are apparently on a transitional journey from childhood as dependence, to adulthood seen as independence, as if a metaphor of the shift from 'colonial dependence' to 'postcolonial independence' (May 2012).

In his comprehensive work on Australian national cinema, Tom O'Regan (1996) argues that films concerned with 'generational cleavages' are popular because they raise less controversial issues, and certainly, many of the funny and tender coming-of-age comedies do. Yet many of these films explore 'weightier, grown-up issues' and are quite hard-hitting (Marsh 2013). In fact, many coming-of-age films in the Australian context have child protagonists embodying a set of contradictory discourses, as young, naïve and vulnerable, *and* also intelligent, independent and strong. Thus they are anxious and anxiety-inducing subjects, and can thus be understood as a way age-based subjectivity is practiced and functions as a cultural dynamic (Gottschall 2011). For Collins and Davis (2004) the past nostalgia of some Australian films about childhood[6] has all but been displaced by films about young people that emphasise the 'immediacy of moment'. In such films the child protagonists are mobile and are both physically and metaphorically trying to escape a traumatic history as subjects of shame, marginalisation and prejudice.[7] For Marsh (2013) though, nostalgia can still be found in contemporary Australian films about childhood.[8] Here the belief endures that childhood is a 'golden age' (Marsh 2013, 2), and the child is moral, good and a 'promise of better things to come for the nation' (Caputo 1993, 13). For Gonick (2010) it is the girl subject in particular who embodies gendered and age-based concepts of 'innocence and experience' while at the same time signifying 'transition and transcendence' as the 'future girl' of affirmative action. Gonick also observes that it is the Indigenous girl who must carry the additional burden of her people's cultural survival on her small shoulders. I explore the ambiguity of these discourses in the following film analyses and also this idea about Indigenous girlhood more specifically.

What needs further examination is the significance of the presence of an Indigenous child as the protagonist in the coming-of-age trope. In particular, we need to examine how filmic Indigenous children are often positioned as at risk, vulnerable and sick, and simultaneously as capable, good and agents of social cohesion. For Palmer and Gillard (2002, 2004) contemporary films about young Indigenous people produce ambivalence and the conditions to 'unsettle and disrupt' (2004, 76). By creating a space for the marginalised, these films use Indigenous childhoods 'to problematise neo-colonial discourse and taken-for-granted ideas' (75). For instance, the 'far from straight-forward' treatments by Sen and Thornton arguably disrupt (white, masculine) authority, while raising and leaving uncertainties, unresolved questions and ambiguous endings. Sen and Thornton's films differentiate themselves from the coming-of-age 'pack' in that they face the:

> unsightly truth at the heart of the racial divide in Australia: that young Aboriginal people do *not* have the same opportunities as other young Australians.
>
> (Woodhead 2011, 40)

Such representations allow audience access to, and potentially give insight into, the intricate spaces surrounding discursive formations of the 'racial divide' as it intersects with Indigenous childhoods in Australia.

Like the coming-of-age trope, much has been made of the 'lost child' trope as a 'peculiar Australian anxiety' where these stories serve as warnings of the real dangers of the Australian bush and outback (Collins and Davis 2004, 141; Tilley 2012). Back in 1980, Sue Dermody observed that the lost child story was often a romantic quest mode that put the child in a physical challenge in unfamiliar territory and envisioned them as the hero/ine. The protagonist searches or struggles to fulfil an ideal against a backdrop of real anxieties. This trope also has a deeper cultural significance as a hangover of past Anglo-Celtic/settler generations – that is, of never fitting in a place that's not 'home' and possibly will never truly be home (Collins and Davis 2004, 141). For the Indigenous child 'lost' in the lost child trope, like Samson and Delilah in the film of the same name, they are lost in the 'alien and hostile environment of white urban Australia'. This common theme is arguably reworked to 'signify Aboriginal anxiety about not belonging in contemporary Australian mainstream society' (Ryan-Fazileau 2012, 33). The films of Sen and Thornton do perhaps suggest this sense of the Indigenous child not belonging in a Western society, and if not an 'anxiety' per se, certainly an ambiguous position around identity, belonging and survival:

> The fears of the colonial period may be a thing of the past for settler Australians, but, even if today's Aboriginal children no longer face the dangers of the Stolen Generations, they are still suffering very real after-effects of this trauma.
>
> (Ryan-Fazileau 2011, 5)

It seems then, that Indigenous trauma, and the loss of culture, country and kin that might go with it, could be felt through this broader theme of being at a loss and being a 'lost child' in a kind of 'hostile wilderness'. For Indigenous Australian scholar, Aileen Moreton-Robinson (2003), this sense of home and belonging is felt even more profoundly by Indigenous people given the illegal dispossession of their land. The question raised here is how one can be at home when you can never return home, when your country has been taken from you. But Moreton-Robinson also argues that Indigenous Australian's 'omnipresent' and deep spiritual connection to country 'continues to unsettle non-Indigenous belonging' on a land that was never theirs (2003, 24). Samson and Delilah, like Lena and Vaughn in *Beneath Clouds* and Daniel in *Toomelah*, can be seen as 'a new generation of lost ones, lost by their own people as well as white culture, making their final struggle and the final image of their possible survival doubly poignant' (Gallasch 2009, 25).

What the next section will demonstrate through an analysis of *Beneath Clouds*, *Toomelah* and *Samson and Delilah* is how the Indigenous child protagonists are seen as at risk, vulnerable and sick due to contexts of poverty, racism, neglect, marginalisation, drug abuse and violence. However, the films also show how these young people are capable and strong, and they become agents of social cohesion and symbols of 'reconciliation'. In this sense, these films take up and reaffirm normative childhood discourses, while at other times challenging them. It is this ambiguous and complex space of 'racial difference' that this analysis shifts to now. In particular I show how this 'racial difference' is inscribed within the textual features and key visual, aural and verbal discursive metaphors of these films. I also discuss the ways in which audiences are potentially positioned in relation to this racial difference via these filmic features.

Representations of Indigenous childhoods in film

In the film Toomelah, a 10-year-old Aboriginal boy, Daniel, wakes up on a mattress on the floor of an isolated Aboriginal community in far north-west New South Wales (NSW) called Toomelah. Dogs bark outside. A smaller child is still sleeping on the couch. Daniel goes to the fridge and finds there is nothing to eat. He looks under the lid of the frying pan and finds there is nothing to eat. He goes into his mum's room as she sleeps and looks in her purse and finds there is no money.

Daniel spends his days playing up at school, or not going to school and hanging out with the local drug dealer and his mates. There only seem to be two paths for Aboriginal men in this community and Daniel needs to decide what kind of man he is going to be: a drunk like his father in the gutter, or a 'bad cunt' like his criminal mates.

In the film Samson and Delilah, scruffy-haired Aboriginal teenager Samson wakes up on a mattress on the floor at an isolated and remote NT Aboriginal community outside Alice Springs. He sits up and puts on a shirt and grabs a container with petrol in it and sniffs. A cheesy country song by Charlie Pride plays, 'Everyday is goin' to be a sun shiny day'.

Samson spends his days getting high to break the tedium and bleakness of his life. There is very little to do, very little purpose. He takes a shine to Delilah down the road.

A teenage Aboriginal girl named Delilah wakes up on a mattress in the dirt under the veranda of a rundown house. There are wrecked cars and rubbish surrounding the yard. She collects wood for the fire to make breakfast, wakes her headstrong but infirm Nana and, in language, tells her to take her tablets and forces them into her hand.

Later, after the death of Delilah's grandmother and a beating by her aunties, Samson takes Delilah to Alice Springs, the closest regional city. There the two youngsters – *homeless, starving and alone – suffer neglect, racism, injury and abuse; forgotten by their community and rejected by the predominantly white city. But against all the odds, they survive.*

Somewhere in rural NSW an Aboriginal teenager called Vaughn (in Beneath Clouds*) wakes up early in his cot at the juvenile detention centre and thinks about escaping to see his dying mother. At the dusty rural NSW town of Moree, an Aboriginal teenager, Lena, dreams of escaping her 'shit hole' of a town and the problems of her family and friends (and maybe even her Aboriginal identity) for the city to find her father and the romantic ideal his Irish identity symbolises for her.*

Meeting up on the road, angry Vaughn and judgemental Lena become unlikely allies, suffering racism, injury and abuse along the way. Learning painful lessons about their selves and the racial divide between Indigenous and non-Indigenous Australians, they head toward the metropolis of Sydney in the hope of finding 'home'.

'What you going to do with yourself?': Making meaning with/through Daniel, Lena and Vaughn, and Samson and Delilah

On one level, the child protagonists in these films are suffering the effects of living in 'rural' and 'remote' places positioned as poor and isolated places forgotten by mainstream Australia. The 'rural' is discursively, semiotically and affectively envisaged as a deficit; a 'shit hole' with images of run-down houses, garbage in the streets and dogs running everywhere. Audiences arguably feel the desolation and poverty of such a place. Then again, even though Vaughn and Lena in *Beneath Clouds* have hopes for the city, the feeling rapidly vanishes once there, and as Samson and Delilah show, cities can be harsh places for Indigenous kids too. The child protagonists are members of communities that have lost many of their cultural knowledges, connections and relationships as a direct result of colonisation, dispossession and the Stolen Generations. These young people are angry (Daniel, Vaughn, Lena, Samson), sick (Samson), sad, lonely, neglected, vulnerable and 'at risk' of being further marginalised and of remaining in cycles of poverty, unemployment, criminality, drug and alcohol addiction, violence, ill-health, teenage pregnancy and maybe even early death. Almost every 'white' person that comes into contact with them examines them, exploits them, dismisses them, threatens or abuses them. In these films we get to see what marginalisation looks like, but from the eyes of the marginalised 'black child' subject.

Ten-year-old Daniel in *Toomelah* seems on his way down the particular path of marginalisation, disadvantage and destruction. The following scene works discursively, semiotically and affectively to incite spectators towards making meanings with regard to childhood (and adulthood), masculinity and Indigeneity as they converge to form Daniel's subjectivity in this particular place. After a day of 'wagging', or deliberately skipping school, he goes home and gets into trouble from his mum who says a teacher came over to say he was absent. She exclaims 'How many times I gotta tell you!' and says she is going to tell his estranged father. She then gives him $20 and sends him to get some drugs for her from the local drug dealer, Linden and his mates:

Linden: Looks boys, here comes little bad boy Dan!

Daniel: What you cunts doing? . . .

Linden: Someone said you were fucking up at school, man? Said you stabbed Tupac with a pencil or something?

Daniel: Yeah, I don't fuck around, me, bro.

(Linden and his mates laugh)

Linden: Trying to be a bad-arse boxer like his old father, boys! That's right, until the metho knocked him, boys.

(Linden and his mates laugh)

Linden: Hey Dan, who you mad on?

Daniel: No one.

Scammer: Tanitia, ain't it?

Linden: Tanitia, ay?

Daniel: Neh!

Linden: Tanitia! You scooping her yet or what?

(Linden and his mates laugh. Daniel, straight-faced, leaves)

How Daniel talks rough and talks himself up to impress the local gangsters, and how Linden and his mates tease and laugh at him about his alcoholic father and little 'girlfriend' Tanitia, are key ways of discursively and performatively reiterating this kind of hyper black 'gangster' masculinity that is a desirable subjectivity here. Later we see how much time Daniel spends with Linden and his mates and even though they joke about him wanting to be a 'little gangster', Daniel more than proves himself capable as a member of the 'manly' gang.

Spectators might feel shocked by the 'profane language' and content of the conversations, like Julie Rigg on ABC Radio National (25 November, 2011), particularly given that Daniel is a young *child*. Certainly, when Daniel walks away, we can see that his little skinny legs have not yet grown into his big feet, and his over-sized floppy shoelaces arguably make us see his smallness, and feel he is vulnerable and in need of protection. He also doesn't seem to understand the full content of the conversation and looks blankly when the boys talk about 'scooping', as a misogynist reference to females and sex. Sen shows us this scene but doesn't give much away in terms what we're meant to make of it. Perhaps audiences might feel anxious about what the young men might do to impressionable Daniel at his expense, or how they will negatively influence him as 'bad' role models. Perhaps they may feel angered that Linden and the boys don't look after him as adults are meant to do, particularly in light of Daniel's seemingly neglectful and damaged parents.

But is it possible not to see Daniel as 'poor' or 'little', stuck in a harsh, unloving, unforgiving, violent, horrible world and/or as the victim of his surroundings including poverty, boredom, drug and alcohol abuse, and neglect? Is it possible to think of Daniel as a 'player', equal to the big boys and not in a completely negative way? Daniel knows things and has had experience beyond his years. He has learned much along the way from all the people in his world, and has learned essential things about his culture and his peoples, including from Linden and his mates. And certainly Daniel is actively figuring out things as he goes along too, trying to figure out who he can be in this world and to what ends. In this sense, the film opens up a space for readings around Indigenous childhood that might mobilise normative childhood (and racial and gendered) discourses, while at other times, might be working to challenge them. Instead of the black child being doubly at risk due to their 'childhood' status and their 'race', and further compounded by the 'rural/remote' place, the child protagonists in these films are shown to '*do* things instead of having things *done to* and *for them* by adults. The child is conceptualised as an active, independent person with rights, interests' (Meyer 2007, 88; original emphasis).

Sen has said that the divisions between 'childhood', 'adolescence' and 'adulthood' aren't that clear cut in places like Toomelah and that men and boys often speak on the same 'level' (Sen in interview with Daniel Browning, ABC Radio National *Awaye!*, 3 December 2011). Perhaps, then, white/Western spectators who bring their own moral values, judgements and expectations into a film like *Toomelah*, might miss something significant and unique. Sen has argued that:

> the film also displays a lot of humour through the characters, and I guess it depends on your perception and your background and your cultural experience . . . For me I think, there are many funny moments in *Toomelah* and I think the audience, when they go and see the film, should be open to that.
> (Sen in DVD extras of *Toomelah*)

Can white/Western audiences see the humour in *Toomelah*, in a scene like the one above? Can they overcome their own moral judgements and Western worldviews to see this scene differently, and to what effect? Would Western concepts of 'childhood' as incompleteness or a 'becoming' personhood, as a time of vulnerability and innocence need to be turned on their heads?

I argue that it is possible to see Daniel and the rest of the young protagonists as being far from vulnerable or easily led, and they are far from helpless 'victims'. The deficit model of Indigenous childhoods is potentially shifted towards a more agentic one in this light. The child subjects are savvy and smart, with undeniable strength, endurance and spirit or 'fight'. Vaughn opens up Lena's eyes to black politics even though she is supposedly more educated. Virtually illiterate, deaf in one ear, with a crippling stutter and damaged due to petrol sniffing, Samson makes the stubborn and 'hard' Delilah laugh and love. The girls in particular are far from 'victims', and in fact, as noted previously, are arguably positioned as the nurturers and saviours of not only themselves and those around them, but their culture and people too. Lena is constantly criticising the way her family and community live their lives, and is initially scathing of Vaughn's angry black politics. To her, Aboriginal identity means poverty, criminality, unemployment, single (teenage) motherhood, drug addiction and suffering. She wants to escape all this and with her light skin colour can 'pass' as white. But by hitching the backroads of NSW with the darker skinned Vaughn, Lena experiences direct prejudice, racism and violence from almost all the white people and white authority figures along the way. It is then she learns that some of the reasons behind the quality of life of many of her people are more complex than being simply about their 'bad choices'. By the end of *Beneath Clouds*, audiences arguably get the sense that with a whole new appreciation of black identity, Lena will fight on, more determined than ever. She has left her impression on her fellow-traveller, Vaughn, too. Audiences might feel he is doomed to being shot down by the police like so many filmic young (black, Australian) males before him. The police have been hunting him for escaping from the juvenile detention centre and have now, finally, caught up with him. But, the ambiguous finale perhaps suggests that another kind of ending *is* possible for black adolescent males like Vaughn. Perhaps audiences might sense Lena's influence on him and the profound change that has occurred in him so that his future will not be about further devastation and death.

Delilah, even more than Lena, illustrates the Indigenous girl subject as strong, capable, a nurturer and healer. It is Delilah who is beaten, kidnapped, raped, run over by a car and broken physically and spiritually in the course of the film. Yet it is Delilah who cares for the drugged-out and despondent Samson. She rescues him from under the bridge in Alice Springs and takes him back to her country for them to heal. Healing herself and healing Samson is a metaphor for healing her people. In the absence of any adults, Delilah takes it on her young, 'good' shoulders as an agent of social cohesion, a symbol of 'reconciliation', and with all the wisdom and experience of a 'mature' subject, an elder 'beyond her years'. Whether the extra burden of this weighty responsibility placed on the (female) child subject, actually excuses the (colonial, white, black, masculine) adult world/s, needs further thought. However, what is clear is that there is more going on here than simply the deficit model of Indigenous childhoods that usually dominates.

Concluding thoughts

This chapter has argued for the usefulness of a cultural analysis of popular films, as an engagement with such films opens spaces to think about the complexities around issues such as poverty, development, childhood, gender and Indigeneity. The discursive frames used to bring the Indigenous child to the screen, and the means by which audiences make meaning from them, are a part of wider public realms that enact influence upon social policy and practice regarding Indigenous peoples and poverty in the Australian context.

Close analytical readings of *Beneath Clouds*, *Toomelah* and *Samson and Delilah* offer some insights into formations of filmic Indigenous Australian childhoods and the Indigenous Australian child subject. This chapter has highlighted discursive, semiotic and affective textual features, and has explored the ways in which audiences might be positioned in relation to these. Ultimately, it brought into focus how meaning might be made from the screen, framing ways of understanding formations of 'black'/'white', 'child'/'adult', 'masculinity', 'girlhood', 'rurality' and 'poverty' in the making of Indigenous childhood.

There are advantages and disadvantages to being subjects of Indigenous childhood seen as at risk, vulnerable and sick – *and/or* as capable, good, cohesive subjects. The Indigenous filmmakers of the films under analysis in this chapter are challenging viewers (and society more broadly) to rethink the discursive assumptions around childhood, race and poverty that inform so much of our social policy. As developmental theorists, sociologists, educationalists and cultural scholars, we must reflect on how our thinking is potentially enabled and constrained by such discourses. We need to consider how the realities of Indigenous children are made and remade, and to what effects. This kind of thinking is, after all, the basis for change.

Notes

1 The data source here is the Australian Bureau of Statistics Income and Expenditure surveys for 2009–10 and previous years. The poverty line is calculated as a proportion of the disposable income of a 'middle income' (median) household. The report uses the austere 50 per cent measure, but also makes a comparison at the higher 60 per cent measure used in the UK and the European Union.
2 See for instance the landmark case Mabo v Queensland (1992) where the High Court of Australia recognised Indigenous or native title to ancestral lands due to the claim of Torres Strait Islander man Eddie Koiki Mabo.
3 The position of Abbott's current conservative coalition government on the Intervention/Stronger Futures is still unclear. Lovell (2012) has recently shown, that while both the Howard and Rudd/Gillard governments have been committed to the Intervention, the major political discourses used by the Coalition and Labor governments have been very different. In contrast to the Coalition's discourses noted above, the Labor government has shown a focus on human rights on one hand, and on the other, a single Western pathway to development (Altman, 2009; Altman and Russell 2012).
4 *Where the Wild Things Are* by Maurice Sendak (1963).
5 Films about Indigenous childhood or youth include: *Jedda* (1955), *Walkabout* (1971), *The Chant of Jimmie Blacksmith* (1978), *Manganinnie* (1980), *Initiation* (1987), *The Fringe Dwellers* (1986), *Blackfellas* (1993), *Radiance* (1998), *Yolngu Boy* (2001), *Serenades* (2001), *Australian Rules* (2002), *Beneath Clouds* (2002), *Rabbit Proof Fence* (2002), *Jindabyne* (2006), *September* (2007), *Australia* (2008), *Stone Bros* (2009), *Bran Nue Dae* (2009), *Samson and Delilah* (2009), *Mad Bastards* (2010), *Here I Am* (2011), *Toomelah* (2011), *The Sapphires* (2012) and *Mystery Road* (2013).

6 Like *The Year My Voice Broke* (1987).
7 See for instance *Looking for Alibrandi* (2000), *Head On* (1998) and *Beneath Clouds* (2004).
8 See for instance *September* (2007) where the reconciliation of the main black and white male children acts as a metaphor for the nation.

References

Altman, Jon. 2007. 'Alleviating Poverty in Remote Indigenous Australia: The Role of the Hybrid Economy.' *Centre for Aboriginal Economic Policy Research* 10: 1–9.

Altman, Jon. 2009. *Beyond Closing the Gap: Valuing Diversity in Indigenous Australia*. CAEPR Working Paper 54. http://caepr.anu.edu.au/Publications/WP/2009WP54.php.

Altman, Jon, and Susie Russell. 2012. 'Too Much 'Dreaming': Evaluations of the Northern Territory National Emergency Response Intervention 2007–2012.' *Evidence Base: A Journal of Evidence Reviews in Key Policy Areas* 3: 1–28.

Australian Council of Social Service and Social Policy Research Centre at the University of NSW. 2013. *Poverty in Australia 2012*. 3rd edn. Strawberry Hills, NSW: Australian Council of Social Service.

Beresford, Bruce, dir. 1986. *The Fringe Dwellers*. Australia: Fringe Dwellers Productions.

Bhabha, Homi. 1992. 'The Other Question: The Stereotype and Colonial Discourse.' In *The Sexual Subject: A Screen Reader in Sexuality*, edited by Mandy Merck, 312–331. London: Routledge.

Blair, Wayne, dir. 2012. *The Sapphires*. Australia: Goalpost Pictures.

Blatterer, Harry. 2007. 'Contemporary Adulthood: Reconceptualizing an Uncontested Category.' *Current Sociology* 55: 771–792.

Blatterer, Harry. 2010. 'The Changing Semantics of Youth and Adulthood.' *Cultural Sociology* 4(1): 63–79.

Cain, Deborah. 2004. 'A Fence too Far?: Postcolonial Guilt and the Myth of Distance in *Rabbit Proof Fence*.' *Third Text* 18(4): 297–303.

Caputo, Raffaele. 1993. 'Coming of Age: Notes towards Reappraisal.' *Cinema Papers* 94: 12–16.

Carstairs, Peter, dir. 2007. *September*. Australia: Tropfest Feature Program.

Chauvel, Charles, dir. 1955. *Jedda*. Australia: Charles Chauvel Productions.

Chouinard, Vera. 2009. 'Placing the 'Mad Woman': Troubling Cultural Representations of Being a Woman with Mental Illness in *Girl, Interrupted*.' *Social & Cultural Geography* 10(7): 791–804.

Cole, Beck, dir. 2011. *Here I Am*. Australia: Scarlett Pictures.

Collins, Felicity, and Therese Davis. 2004. *Australian Cinema After Mabo*. Cambridge, UK: Cambridge University Press.

Crilly, Shane. 2001. 'Reading Aboriginalities in Australian Cinema: From Jedda to Dead Heart (and a few in between).' *Australian Screen Education* 26–27: 36–44.

Dermody, Susan. 1980. 'Action and Adventure.' In *The New Australian Cinema*, edited by Scott Murray, 81–93. Melbourne: Nelson.

Dermody, Susan, and Elizabeth Jacka. 1988. *The Screening of Australia: An Anatomy of a National Cinema*. Vol. 2. Sydney: Currency Press.

Duigan, Jon, dir. 1987. *The Year My Voice Broke*. Australia: Kennedy Miller.

Ellsworth, Elizabeth. 1997. *Teaching Positions: Difference, Pedagogy and the Power of Address.* New York: Teachers' College, Columbia University.
Ellsworth, Elizabeth. 2005. *Places of Learning: Media, Architecture, Pedagogy.* New York: RoutledgeFalmer.
Fletcher, Brendan, dir. 2010. *Mad Bastards.* Broome, Western Australia: Bush Turkey Films.
Frankland, Richard, dir. 2009. *Stone Bros.* Australia: ScreenWest.
Gallasch, Keith. 2009. 'The Seeing Ear, The Hearing Eye.' *Real Time* 90(April–May): 23–25.
Giroux, Henry. 1994. *Disturbing Pleasures: Learning Popular Culture.* New York: Routledge.
Giroux, Henry. 2000. 'Public Pedagogy as Cultural Politics: Stuart Hall and the 'Crisis' of Culture.' *Cultural Studies* 14(2): 341–360.
Goldman, Paul, dir. 2002. *Australian Rules.* Australia: Adelaide Festival of Arts.
Gonick, Marnina. 2006. 'Between 'Girl Power' and 'Reviving Ophelia': Constituting the Neoliberal Girl Subject.' *NSWA Journal* 18(2): 1–23.
Gonick, Marnina. 2010. 'Indigenizing Girl Power: *The Whale Rider*, Decolonization, and the Project of Remembering.' *Feminist Media Studies* 10(3): 305–319.
Gottschall, Kristina. 2010. 'Coming-Of-Age.' In *Directory of World Cinema: Australia and New Zealand*, edited by Ben Goldsmith and Geoff Lealand, Vol. 3, 176–187. Bristol: Intellect Publishers.
Gottschall, Kristina. 2011. '"Jesus! A Geriatric – That's All I Need!": Learning to Come of Age with/in Australian film.' *Global Studies of Childhood* 1(4): 332–342.
Hamilton, Emma. 2012. 'Introduction: Stories of Adolescence.' In *Making Film and Television Histories: Australian and New Zealand*, edited by James Bennett and Rebecca Beirne, 151–152. London: I.B.Tauris.
Honey, John, dir. 1980. *Manganinnie.* Australia: Tasmanian Film Corporation.
Huijser, Henk, and Brooke Collins-Gearing. 2007. 'Representing Indigenous Stories in the Cinema: between Collaboration and Appropriation.' *The International Journal of Diversity in Organisations, Communities and Nations* 7(3): 1–9.
Jenks, Chris. 1996. *Childhood.* London: Sage.
Jennings, Karen. 1993. *Sites of Difference: Cinematic Representations of Aboriginality and Gender.* Melbourne: Australian Film Institute.
Johnson, Stephen, dir. 2001. *Yolngu Boy.* Australia: Australian Children's Television Foundation.
Kelada, Odette. 2008. 'White Nation Fantasy and the Northern Territory 'Intervention'.' *ACRAWSA e-journal* 4(1): 1–11.
Kenway, Jane, and Elizabeth Bullen. 2001. *Consuming Children: Education-Entertainment-Advertising.* Buckingham and Philadelphia: Open University Press.
Khadem, Mojgan, dir. 2001. *Serenades.* Australia: Australian Film Finance Corporation.
Knopf, Kerstin. 2013. 'Kangaroos, Petrol, Joints and Sacred Rocks: Australian Cinema Decolonized.' *Studies in Australasian Cinema* 7(2/3): 189–200.
Kokkinos, Ana, dir. 1998. *Head On.* Australia: Head On Productions.
Langton, Marcia. 1993. *'Well, I Heard It on the Radio and I Saw It on the Television': An Essay for the Australian Film Commission on the Politics and Aesthetics of Filmmaking by and about Aboriginal People and Things.* Sydney: Australian Film Commission.
Lather, Patti. 1991. *Getting Smart: Feminist Research and Pedagogy with/in The Postmodern.* New York: Routledge.

Lawrence, Ray. 2006. *Jindabyne*. Australia: April Films.
Lesko, Nancy. 2001. *Act Your Age! A Cultural Construction of Adolescence*. New York: Routledge.
Lovell, Melissa. 2012. 'A Settler Colonial Consensus on the Northern Territory Intervention.' *Arena Journal* 37(38): 199–219.
Luhrmann, Baz, dir. 2008. *Australia*. Australia: Twentieth Century Fox Film Corporation.
Lusted, David. 1986. 'Why Pedagogy?' *Screen* 27(5): 2–14.
Marsh, Pauline. 2013. 'Picturing a Golden Age: *September* and *Australian Rules*.' *Alphaville: Journal of Film and Screen Media* 5: 1–15.
May, Josephine. 2012. 'The Devil's Playground: Coming-of-Age as National Cinema.' In *Making Film and Television Histories: Australian and New Zealand*, edited by James Bennett and Rebecca Beirne, 158–63. London: I.B.Tauris.
McKee, Alan. 1997a. ' Films Vs Real Life: Communicating Aboriginality in Cinema and Television.' *UTS Review* 3(1): 160–182.
McKee, Alan. 1997b. 'The Generic Limitations of Aboriginality: Horror Movies as Case Study.' *Australian Studies* 12(1): 115–138.
Meyer, Anneke. 2007. 'The Moral Rhetoric of Childhood.' *Childhood* 14: 85–104.
Moran, Albert. 2006. 'The Teenpic.' In *Film in Australian: An Introduction*, edited by Albert Moran and Errol Vieth, 172–187. Cambridge: Cambridge University Press.
Moreton-Robinson, Aileen. 2003. 'I Still Call Australia Home: Indigenous Belonging and Place in White Postcolonizing Society.' In *Uprootings/Regroundings: Questions of Home and Migration*, edited by Sara Ahmed, 23–40. Oxford: Berg Publishers.
Noyce, Phillip, dir. 2002. *Rabbit Proof Fence*. Australia: Rumbalara Films.
O'Regan, Tom. 1996. *Australian National Cinema*. London: Routledge.
Palmer, Dave, and Garry Gillard. 2002. 'Aborigines, Ambivalence and Australian Film.' *Metro Magazine: Media and Education Magazine* 134: 128–134.
Palmer, Dave, and Garry Gillard. 2004. 'Indigenous Youth and Ambivalence in Some Australian Films.' *Journal of Australian Studies* 82: 75–84.
Pazzano, Chiara. 2012. 'Factbox: The 'Stronger Futures' legislation.' *SBS World News Australia*, 20 June. http://www.sbs.com.au/news/article/2012/06/20/factbox-stronger-futures-legislation.
Pearce, Michael, dir. 1987. *Initiation*. Australia: FGH.
Perkins, Rachel, dir. 1998. *Radiance*. Australia: AndyInc.
Perkins, Rachel, dir. 2009. *Bran Nue Dae*. Australia: Robyn Kershaw Productions.
Ricketson, James, dir. 1993. *Blackfellas*. Australia: Barron Entertainment.
Roeg, Nicholas, dir. 1971. *Walkabout*. Australia: Max L. Raab Productions.
Ryan-Fazileau, Susan. 2011. '*Samson and Delilah*: Herstory, Trauma and Survival.' *Journal of the Association for the Study of Australian Literature (JASAL)* 11(2): 1–11.
Ryan-Fazileau, Susan. 2012. 'Hybridity, Power Discourse and Evolving Representations of Aboriginality (1970s-today).' *Antipodes* 26(1): 29–34
Said, Edward. 1985. 'Orientalism Reconsidered.' *Race and Class* 27(2): 5–7.
Schepisi, Fred, dir. 1978. *The Chant of Jimmie Blacksmith*. Australia: The Film House.
Sen, Ivan, dir. 2002. *Beneath Clouds*. Australia: Autumn Films.
Sen, Ivan, dir. 2011. *Toomelah*. Sydney: Bunya Productions.
Sen, Ivan, dir. 2013. *Mystery Road*, Australia: Mystery Road Films.
Simon, Roger. 1992. *Teaching Against the Grain: Texts for a Pedagogy of Possibility*. New York: Bergin & Garvey.

Speed, Lesley. 2006. 'When the Sun Sets over Suburbia: Class and Subculture in Bruce Beresford's *Puberty Blues.*' *Continuum: Journal of Media & Cultural Studies* 20(3): 407–418.

Spivak, Gayatri. 1988. 'Can the Subaltern Speak?' In *Marxism and the Interpretation of Culture*, edited by Cary Nelson and Lawrence Grossberg. Illinois: University of Illinois Press.

Thornton, Warwick, dir. 2009. *Samson and Delilah*. Australia: CAAMA Productions.

Threadgold, Terry. 2000. 'Poststructuralism and Discourse Analysis.' In *Culture and Text: Discourse and Methodology in Social Research and Cultural Studies*, edited by Cate Poynton and Alison Lee, 40–58. Sydney: Allen & Unwin.

Tilley, Elspeth. 2012. *White Vanishing: Rethinking Australia's Lost-in-the-Bush Myth*. New York: Editions Rodopi BV.

Walkerdine, Valerie. 1997. *Daddy's Girl: Young Girls and Popular Culture*. Basingstoke, England: Macmillan.

Woodhead, Jacinda. 2011. 'A Remote Possibility?: The Uncomfortable Realities of Toomelah.' *Metro Magazine: Media and Education Magazine* 170: 38–40.

Woods, Kate, dir. 2000. *Looking for Alibrandi*. Australia: Belle Ragazze.

Young, Elspeth. 2002. *Third World in the First: Development and Indigenous Peoples*. E-Library: Taylor & Francis.

Part II
Contextualising the 'poor child'
Children's voices as modes of resistance

4 Child labour, schooling and the reconstruction of childhood
A case study from Kenya

Angela Githitho Muriithi

Introduction

The complex relationship between child labour, schooling and poverty in developing countries continues to capture the imagination of international organisations, non-governmental organisations (NGOs) and researchers alike. Child labour is seen to pose a significant challenge for the achievement of basic formal education for children in poor communities. Canals-Cerdá and Ridao-Cano (2004) and Heady (2003) argue, for instance, that work has a negative and sizeable effect on school progress because the need for children to work often precludes school attendance. Yet many children and young people do attend school *and* work. The preoccupation with the impact of work on children's educational attendance and performance often invokes concerns about the 'rights and wrongs' of child labour that draw on universalised assumptions of childhood, work and education. Debates revolving around 'child labour' or 'child work' vis-à-vis schooling raise fundamental issues about how childhood itself is understood: what childhood is, and what activities are deemed suitable or unsuitable for children. These discussions about childhood, mainly taking place in the global North, have come to shape international discourses on child labour, as well as educational and child labour policies (Fyfe 1989; Boyden *et al.* 1998). For example, the idea of childhood as rigidly separate from adulthood has now been codified into international social policy, the most significant document being the 1989 UN Convention on the Rights of the Child (Fyfe 1989). Declarations like this express a protective view of childhood in which work, particularly hazardous or exploitative work, is seen as detrimental, while schooling is understood to be crucial for 'normal' child development. Extreme versions of this viewpoint even suggest that work and schooling are mutually exclusive.

This chapter seeks to challenge universal assumptions of childhood by demonstrating the need for socio-economically and historically located approaches to understanding the child labour debate. It argues that the concepts of childhood which shape discussions about the ethics of child labour vis-à-vis schooling must be understood within different and ever changing contexts. Policies that rely on dominant Northern theories of childhood fail to take into account contextual variations and are thus not always workable or ethical in developing contexts.

This chapter examines these issues through a case study of Kiratu,[1] a poor community in Kenya with a long history of child labour. It draws on historical and archival research conducted as part of a doctoral study examining the relationship between child labour and schooling in Kenya. The chapter highlights the ways that childhood – and subsequently the relationship between child labour and schooling – has been reconstructed in response to cultural, socio-economic and political changes. It demonstrates that at different points in the last century, the 'child' in the community of Kiratu has been thought of as: a *'socialised child'* – a child preparing and being prepared to be part of the community; a *'labouring child'* – a child who performs work and is part of the economic structure; and a *'schooled child'* – a child who is part of the modern educational project of formal schooling. Empirical data are used to show the continual reconstruction of childhood in this community.

The child in Kiratu currently straddles both the world of work and the world of school within the context of a severely deprived social and economic environment, which results in the child being pulled in both directions. It is important to understand the implications of this pull in the context of Kenya, a nation confronted with the challenges of implementing education reforms in the face of deepening economic constraints. Free Primary Education (FPE) is one such reform. Instituted in 1974 and then again in 2003, it attempts to address a number of challenges, the most important being to bring out-of-school children into formal education and to improve the quality of primary education being offered. The overall goal of FPE has been to build human capital capacity in the country in order to develop the economy and reduce poverty.

Despite these efforts, the UNESCO *EFA Global Monitoring Report Fact Sheet for Kenya* (2012) states that 1 million children are still out of school in the country. While this is almost half the number of 1999, it is still the ninth highest of any country in the world (UNESCO 2012). Additionally, the *Kenyan Integrated Household Budget Survey 2005/2006, Child Labour Analytical Report* (CBS 2008), which is the most recent survey of this kind, states that about 1.01 million children aged 5–17 years are working for pay, profit or family gain. Of these, 773,696 are child labourers.[2] Provision of free and compulsory primary education has long been considered the 'medicine' for the problem of child labour (Weiner 1991). The fact that it seems to be failing in this role in Kenya points to deeper issues than those simply related to access to education (Manda *et al.* 2003, 13). What emerges from this study is evidence that there is a disjuncture between social policy and the socio-historical and economic realities on the ground and the case is made that social policy needs to be sensitive to such realities in order to be meaningful.

The social construction of childhood

Philippe Ariès (1962) in his classic *Centuries of Childhood*, was the first to put forward the theory that 'childhood' was a modern Western invention. According to Ariès, there was no such thing as childhood in medieval Europe. The child was fully integrated from the earliest age into all aspects of daily life including education, work and play. Ariès' assertion that childhood did not exist prior to the fifteenth century was directly opposed to the 'universal' idea of childhood advocated by dominant developmental approaches to childhood in the field of psychology. In these approaches, rationality is the universal mark of adulthood and childhood is the period in which children are trained to become rational. Childhood is seen as a 'biologically determined stage on the path to full human status' (Prout and James 1997, 10). In contrast, Ariès (1962) argued that changing attitudes towards children which stressed their special nature and needs, as well as the introduction of formal education and long periods of schooling for children (particularly in the nineteenth century), had signalled their gradual removal from the everyday life of adult society. In other words, far from being a universal and static notion, childhood had changed over the last five centuries.[3]

Despite interpretivist critiques such as Ariès' and later the new sociologies of childhood suggested by scholars such as Prout and James (1997), the psychological developmental approach to childhood in which the child is considered irrational, vulnerable, innocent, ignorant, dependant and requiring protection still holds sway. Formal schooling is considered key in this developmental approach. Conceptual problems tend to arise, therefore, when this essentially Western developmental idea of childhood is exported to countries where children's work is not necessarily seen as an anathema; where child development is a fluid and unsegmented process in which work is seen to play an important role in the socialisation of children, and, where children's work may be essential for family survival. Boyden et al. (1998) argue, for example, that taking Western childhood as a normative basis for remedial action for working children in developing contexts could potentially have damaging effects on poor families and their children.

While welfare practitioners may believe that working children, or children who are out of school, are aberrations that need to be rectified, parents may consider work as an essential part of socialisation and children might see work as part of their family responsibility or right to survive. Relatedly, the highly individualistic view of children common in industrialised societies is not found in the majority of the world's cultures. White (1999, 134) also contends that 'official policies [on child labour] are often based on static and universalising models of childhood', while Myers (1999, 21) adds that the popular notion that all children develop through the same universal set of biologically determined stages to some end point called 'maturity' is outmoded, and conceptual frameworks based on this idea run the risk of being counterproductive. Their argument is that culture and the social environment exert a powerful influence on childhood, and failure to understand this results in policies that cannot or do not work. These two schools of thought about childhood – childhood as universal, and childhood as relative or particular – have come to form the foundation of 'abolitionist' and 'child centred' discourses of child labour, respectively (Lieten and White 2001).

However Frones (2005) argues that there is a distinction between childhood as an analytical category (e.g. the principles underlying the position of a child in society), and childhood as living social practice:

> Being a child is defined as belonging within the framework of childhood. [On the other hand] The lives of children as social practice are represented by the processes of moving through childhood.
>
> (2005, 281)

This idea is supported by James and James (2008) who argue that there is a distinction between childhood as the early part of the life course, and childhood as the structural space occupied by children and created by institutional arrangements that separate children from adults (for example, schooling or African traditional initiation rites). What this means is that the institution of 'childhood' is a constant feature of the structure of all societies. Although children grow up and develop into adults, in terms of the institutional arrangements of any society, the space of 'childhood' remains and is occupied by the next generation (Qvortrup 1994). However, the *ways* that children go through this space vary in time and space. This is what Frones refers to as 'social practice', the processes of moving through childhood. So in a sense, childhood is both universal *and* relative.

However, Lieten (2008) cautions against dichotomous views of childhood, arguing that while it is important to remain aware of Western ethnocentric views, we should also beware of the pitfalls of cultural relativism. What is missing in the discussion about childhood, he asserts, is the concrete analysis of how poor and/or ethnically marginalised children are made to remain in a state of childhood that puts them at a disadvantage compared to the children from wealthier backgrounds, even though institutions such as education systems have become available to all:

> Defending the separate and specific childhood of deprived children [as the relativists do] would amount to defending, or at least condoning their economic marginalisation. Children may remain bereft of a 'Western' type of childhood not because of a different cultural perspective of childhood but because of the unfortunate impact of globally lopsided economic development.
>
> (Lieten 2008, 6)

Lieten believes that in a modernising and globalising world, it is less important what specific culture children live in or how children used to live traditionally, and more important that they acquire the enabling skills and knowledge that will help them keep up with the challenges and requirements of the new world rather than the traditional world. He therefore leans towards a more universalistic notion of childhood, arguing that not all universal ideals of childhood should be abandoned for being alien or inappropriate.

The challenge of defining and understanding what the terms 'childhood', 'child labour', 'child work' and 'working children' actually mean in hugely diverse socio-economic, political and cultural contexts remains. Hobbs *et al.* (1999, 57) wisely argue that there is no watertight concept of child labour, and that the onus is on all those who use the phrase to attempt to make clear how they are employing it. Similarly, those who read about child labour should be critical in their approach and question whether any given writer is using the phrase in a coherent and consistent manner. In what follows I examine Frones' (2005) and James and James' (2008) idea of childhood as the universal structural space occupied by children, while at the same time being a living and changing social space that is specific to different times and contexts. This is done through a case study of child labourers in Kenya.

From the socialised child to the labouring child to the schooled child: a case study of a reconstructed childhood in Kenya

A reconstruction of childhood, as described by Ariès (1962) and later Frones (2005) and James and James (2008), has taken place in what was formally known as Kiambu District, Kenya, over the last century. As I discuss, this social process of reconstruction had a profound influence on the way child labour and later formal schooling was – and continues to be – understood.

This account draws on historical and archival data on child labour in Kiambu from the Kenya National Archives (KNA) in Nairobi in an effort to relate understandings of child labour and schooling to wider historical and socio-economic structures in Kiratu. Numerous historical documents relating to the district from the early 1900s until the 1950s were analysed. In addition, the research considered historical literature about land use and tenure, child labour and schooling in Kiambu. To explore the contemporary reconstruction of childhood in Kiratu, I also draw on findings from the wider ethnographic study I conducted in the community. Over the course of 9 months between 2008 and 2009, 75 individuals from different sections of the community were involved in this ethnographic study, including 20 child labourers aged between 12 and 17, both in and out of school, and involved mainly in wage labour on coffee farms. Also included were parents of child labourers, teachers, the chief and sub-chiefs, government officials, social workers and religious leaders in the community. Ethnographic methods such as participant observation, focus group discussions, shadowing and in-depth interviews were employed.

In what follows, I detail how the conceptualisation of the child in Kiratu as variously a *socialised child*, a *labouring child* and a *schooled child* have been influenced by the changing social, political and economic contexts in which they exist. The case study demonstrates how these different understandings of childhood have influenced the relationship between child labour and education in this community and have not always been taken into account in blanket policies such as Free Primary Education. Further, I outline how contemporary patterns of existence in Kiratu, characterised by poverty, landlessness, low wages and family breakdown, have continued to shape childhoods.

The socialised child

In the traditional set up of the Kikuyu, who lived in Kiratu before the coming of the British in 1895, children were highly valued. According to Kenyatta (1938), it was the duty of every couple to produce children. They were a means of building and extending family groups and clans, which strengthened the tribe as a whole. Children were not only important culturally, but also important economically to the survival of the community. Childhood, therefore, consisted of a time of socialisation for their various future roles as men and women in the family and society as a whole. Socialising children provided them with a sense of identity with their ethnic group, based on a thorough understanding of the traditions, expectations, customs, economy and history of the community (Ocholla-Ayayo 1976). Children's work was considered an important part of the socialisation process for two main reasons. First, through work children learned specific skills that they would need when they became adults and these skills were usually defined by specific sex roles within that community. According to Erny (1981, 95), the relationship between work and education was close and the two formed a 'unitary whole', with the adults teaching the children skills, encouraging them to imitate and offering help when the child did not succeed, but without doing it for them. Second, participation in work taught the child responsibility for others, perseverance, discipline and other moral values. Kenyatta explains this second function succinctly as 'the idea of education as participating in the life of the community' (1938, 124). During this process of socialisation, children were not expected to be simply passive recipients of parent's knowledge. They were not considered to be vulnerable or incompetent, but resilient and active agents of their own development. Furthermore, practical work integrated children closely with their households by allowing them to see and experience their own contributions (Kenyatta 1938).

According to Kayongo-Male and Walji (1984), land was an important factor in the socialisation process in precolonial times. Because the Kikuyu in Kiratu were an agricultural people, plenty of learning actually took place on the land. Parents and their clan members had considerable power over their children because they controlled the distribution of the land. Children were dependent on their parents until they were given their own piece of land or obtained it through marriage. This helped parents maintain high levels of discipline over their children and empowered them to supervise their education through work, to its ultimate conclusion. However, socialisation processes in Kiratu were soon to be radically changed by colonialism. According to Njeru (1981), land alienation, the hut tax and forced labour caused the traditional mechanisms for the control of children's activities and behaviour to be destroyed in the communities that came into contact with colonialism. In Kiratu, the child was transformed from being a *socialised child* whose education was tied to work within the family division of labour, to a *labouring child* within capitalistic modes of production. Children were now used as a reserve labour force.

The labouring child

Kenya came under the British sphere of influence in 1888 under the administration of the Imperial British East Africa Company (Kitching 1980).[4] When Kenya came under the direct control of the British government in 1895, the impact of colonialism began to be felt throughout the territory, mainly through sweeping changes in land use and the introduction of capitalism (Overton 1988). From the outset, colonial administrators considered Kenya a territory that was to be developed into a white man's country and Europeans were encouraged to migrate to the protectorate through incentives such as land alienation for settlement and settler friendly labour and taxation policies. According to Overton (1988), the earliest land alienation in Kenya began in Kiambu district, where Kiratu is located. Its natural beauty and fertile soils attracted white settlers. From 1905 onwards, the numbers of British colonial settlers moving to Kenya increased, with most of them arriving first in Kiambu, which was then inhabited by the Kikuyu tribe. A vast amount of land was alienated for colonial use. The 1915 Crown Land Ordinance completely nullified the African's legal rights to the land such that every inch of Kenya was under the legal authority of the Crown. This land included 'all lands occupied by native tribes and all lands reserved for the use of any native tribe' (Dilley, as cited in Kilson 1955, 114).

The result of wide-scale land alienation was the creation of a large population of poor squatters with no access to the main means of production: the land. For the settlers, this had the advantage of creating a potential and stable pool of labour (Overton 1988). This was the first step in the proletarianisation of the native population of Kiambu and it caused major changes in the status and position of parents and thus their role in the socialisation of children.[5] The clan no longer solely determined land rights and so parents lost much of their traditional authority over their children and in other areas of life (Kayongo-Male and Walji 1984). The introduction of the hut tax further disrupted traditional socialisation practices and modes of production. Families had to pay taxes on their huts, which helped the colonial government acquire cheap labour on hundreds of farms in the white highlands – men, women and children were drawn into migrant labour in order to obtain cash for the tax. Children were drawn inexorably into the new colonial modes of production and their traditional education was largely compromised.

Most of the alienated land in Kiambu was put to commercial agricultural use, and labour was needed to work the farms. The labour motivated by the hut tax was insufficient to meet the demand, so in 1919 the British government established a compulsory labour policy in Kenya by issuing the *Northey circular*, which declared that the Kikuyu had to leave their native reserves (where they had been forced to live when their land was alienated) and take up work on European farms. Female and child labour was now used, regarded as a reserve force of labour and utilised when casual labour was scarce.

Children were in great demand as the labour shortage had served to highlight the enormous potential of children in the labour force. The *Native Labour Commission (NLC) of 1912–1913*, or the *Barth Commission* as it was commonly known, was the first official body to look into labour practices in Kenya.[6] Much of its report consisted of arguments in favour of forced labour, and better ways to use 'native labour, including that of children' (Kayongo-Male and Walji 1984, 40).

For instance, a Mr. Scott, a British settler from Kiambu, argued in the report that he favoured the use of children, since he found that 'in his experience with boys and girls of about 14 years old, work was done at about half the expense of adult labour'. A Mr. Bowker even suggested that 'young natives should be indentured to farmers' (NLC, as cited in Kayongo-Male and Walji 1984, 40).

These events – land alienation, hut tax, forced labour and ensuing poverty – had profound effects on the children and families in Kiratu. Children were drawn into non-family-based capitalist labour and exploitation began to take place. Whereas work and education had previously been considered part of a unitary whole, there was now a radical break between the two. Work was no longer for purposes of socialisation and participating in the life of the community but for the material survival of the family. The educative aspects of work were lost and the *socialised child* was transformed into the *labouring child*. Labouring on settler farms also had the negative effects of breaking up family and community cohesion. Boys 'did not submit to the elders or their parents on their return to their homes and were very troublesome' (NLC, as cited in Kayongo-Male and Walji 1984, 40). Anti-social behaviour increased. The children in effect became individualised proletarians performing alienated labour. Control over their labour and the pace of their work activity was largely no longer in their or their families' hands. Rather, it was controlled by the overseer and the owner or manager of the farms.

Quijano (2000) argues that such transformations have to be understood in the context of a modern/colonial world system built on a power pattern sustained by ideas of 'race' and Eurocentricism. Two main ideas took centre stage: 'race' as a means of ordering the world, and capitalism as the means for economic growth. This meant that the exploitation of labour, using Indians and Africans as slaves for example, was possible because of the proclaimed superiority of the white race. There was a racial division of work lasting the length of the colonial period and this was a fundamental feature of colonial/modern capitalism (Quijano 2000). As a way to dominate or exploit the population, children were part of the power relations and subject to exploitation. Therefore, while children in Europe gradually became the object of growing pedagogical and medical attention through family and school care, children in European colonies entered into 'productive circuits of servitude and slavery' (Pedraza-Gomez 2007, 25). While European children were gradually liberated from work, their education made compulsory and basic healthcare more available to them, children under colonial regimes continued to work and be part of a racially segregated population. This was the case in Kiratu during the colonial period (1895–1963). The introduction and growth of capitalism in the context of colonial domination, land alienation and forced labour meant that children were drawn into exploitative labour. The child was transformed from a learner into an economic being and this, I suggest, was driven by a 'racialisation' of childhood. Work in the coffee farms was not deemed suitable for European or Indian children. Almost all the child labourers were African, predominantly boys, involved in coffee and tea production.

By the end of the colonial period, records showed that the number of child labourers had decreased from around 60,000 countrywide between 1939 and 1944, to about 11,000 at independence in 1963 (Kayongo-Male and Walji 1984). According to the Ministry of Labour statistics, this figure had fallen to 8,780 by 1966 (Kayongo-Male and Walji 1984).[7] The rapid educational expansion that took place immediately after independence could have had a role to play in the decline of child labour postindependence. However, although the practice diminished in some areas of the economy, it continued in the agricultural sector, albeit illegally. In fact, in Kiambu child labour continued to thrive, driven by deepening poverty in parts of the district. Children's wages were needed to supplement family income as the majority of people in Kiratu remained poor and landless.[8]

While labour was a major preoccupation of children in Kiratu for a large part of the colonial period, the advent of formal education brought with it new demands on children. More importantly, the break in the relationship between work and socialisation/education that had occurred due to the proletarianisation of the population in Kiratu was now further strengthened, at least for those who were able to attend school. With independence in 1963, the government emphasised the urgent need for a well-educated workforce (Chege and Sifuna 2006). In this postcolonial context, the child was now required to attend school instead of working.

The schooled child

The foundations of formal education in Africa were laid principally by nineteenth century missionaries from Britain and France who saw formal education as a tool of conversion to Christianity (Watson 1982). Anglican, Catholic and Presbyterian missionaries raced to convert as many Africans as possible to their individual denominations, and schools were the vehicle for this task. There were some opportunities for Kenyan children to attend school during the colonial period, although these were limited to areas with missionary activity. Throughout the colonial period, the content of African education remained subject to contest between Africans who saw formal education as a tool for economic and political liberation, the missionaries who saw it a tool for missionary expansion, and the colonial government who felt that an academic education was unsuitable for the needs of Africans and even 'dangerous' (Wamagatta 2008).

Formal education came to Kiratu mainly through the establishment of primary schools by missionaries in the 1950s. The development of a schooling culture in Kiratu after independence in 1963 was driven largely by events taking place in the education sector nationally. There was an unprecedented rush to expand educational opportunities and facilities at all levels in Kenya. The new government felt it necessary to change the educational structures urgently to eliminate the racial and ethnic prejudices that had been nurtured over the years and to promote a cohesive multiracial society (Eshiwani 1993). In addition, a more appropriate education was necessary to prepare Africans for the roles they were to play in the new nation. Children were therefore considered by the government to be potential human capital that would contribute to national development and poverty eradication (Eshiwani 1993). This idea of the potentiality of the child was in contrast to the 'presentness' of the *socialised child* who was a learning worker, one who was making his/her contribution to the community in that moment in time, and indeed in contrast to the *labouring child* whose wages were crucial for family survival.

According to the District Education Officer working in Kiratu during the research period, enrolment patterns followed national trends for the time. National primary school net enrolment rates (NER)[9] rose in the period after independence and throughout the 1970s and 1980s, especially when free primary education was declared in 1974 (Hazelwood *et al.* 1989). It was during this postindependence era that the idea of the *schooled child* became firmly established. The break in the relationship between work and socialisation/education was re-enforced, at least in principle, by this institutionalisation of children in schools. At the same time, the new Kenyan government appeared committed to stamping out the practice of child labour. Laws banning some forms of child labour were enacted and enforced more strictly than previously, with employment premises being frequently raided (Kayongo-Male and Walji 1984).[10] The schools in Kiratu were therefore very well attended in the decades after independence because of the coffee boom that characterised these decades, increasing family earnings, as well as the free primary programme of 1974–75. The pull to attend school rather than work on the coffee plantations caused the gradual decline of child labour in Kiambu district and in Kiratu in the last decades before and after independence. However, the practice did not disappear completely, as poverty levels were still quite high and children still needed to work to supplement family incomes. In fact, in the 1980s and 1990s, their numbers began to rise again and school enrolment fell as poverty levels increased. Enrolment levels only picked up again in 2003 when free primary education was declared a second time. Enrolment levels have continued to rise in the years since, but are sporadically affected by natural disasters such as droughts.

The changing path of childhood in Kiratu traced so far shows the strong historical influences of culture and political economy. As I discuss below, childhood in Kiratu continues to be shaped by present-day socio-economic factors such as poverty, landlessness, poor housing and family breakdown.

Contemporary childhood in Kiratu

One of the strongest influences on community understandings of childhood in Kiratu postindependence is poverty. Government documents on Kiambu district state that there are various forms of poverty in the district, including rural poverty, urban poverty, absolute poverty and food poverty (MOPND 2005). They further state that 25.08 per cent of Kiambu's population is living below the poverty line. This implies that 102,506 people in the district are living on less than US$1.25 a day. Paradoxically, the district's contribution to national poverty is only 1.48 per cent and it is considered to be one of the richest districts in the country, its wealth derived from large-scale commercial farming.

Farming is still the main economic activity in Kiratu, and land is the main means of production. However, it is scarce and at a premium as a result of wide-scale land alienation and the disruption of traditional land tenure systems discussed earlier. Landless families are forced to supplement their food needs by buying food with their meagre salaries. According to Wambui, a social worker, 80 per cent of the Kiratu population live below the poverty line, and hunger and malnutrition are major difficulties. Teachers see first-hand the effects of hunger in the community when children fail to come to school or attend sporadically. Mrs. Murage, head teacher of a primary school in Kiratu, explained that:

> things are really bad . . . [pause] especially now with the absence of the feeding programme in most schools. Because even if the child could only feed once in a day, it is far much better than when you come to school hungry and go back home hungry, and sleep hungry . . . [pause] you don't expect that child to go to school the following day. The school feeding programme is one of the most important ways of getting children to come to school every day in this community.

The majority of people in Kiratu community are engaged in wage or casual labour to survive and there is a large, fluid migrant and local casual labour force. The majority engage in jobs such as coffee berry and tea picking, with the former employing most of the wage labourers. However, conversations with community members revealed that casual labour is sporadic and the income from it cannot be depended on. Wages fluctuate depending on the seasons, but are generally low, too low for parents to provide for their own needs and those of their children.

For poor families in Kiratu, child labour is a kind of coping mechanism. Children have no choice but to work or face starvation. However, conversations with parents also revealed that work prepared children well for an uncertain future. This idea of working as a means to build resilience was remarked on by teachers in Kiratu who felt strongly that children's labour on the coffee farms is not only considered 'normal' because of poverty but is also a kind of 'orientation' for the future. In one teacher's words:

> Parents will say that they have to prepare their children for the reality of a harsh future and they do this through work. They say 'let the child learn how to pick coffee. It will help them'.

This view is normally held by parents who cannot afford secondary-school fees and whose children's future in the education system is uncertain. In the minds of parents, children need to be prepared for the reality *now* rather than a potential life that education promises in the future. This outlook has echoes of the *socialised child* discussed above in an earlier section. In the case of Kiratu, children need to be prepared for the harsh economic realities on the ground. Unwittingly, this facilitates a kind of social reproduction, and the cycle of poverty is repeated. Hence, parents with this view are often in conflict with teachers and child labour officers, who subscribe to the idea of the 'potentiality' of children.

Many children in Kiratu live in very poor social conditions. Families live in cramped one-room houses with poor sanitation. There is theft, violence, drug abuse, alcoholism and prostitution. Family breakdowns are commonplace. The family unit is in crisis. Teachers in Kiratu see first-hand the effects of family disintegration because of their close contact with children. Many children miss school because their often single parent cannot not afford the related costs. Writing about the psycho-social environment of childhood poverty, Evans contends that poor children (such as those in Kiratu) are disproportionately exposed to more adverse social and physical environmental conditions:

> They suffer greater family turmoil, violence, and separation from their parents. Their parents are more nonresponsive and harsh, and they live in more chaotic households, with fewer routines, less structure, and greater instability.
>
> (2004, 88)

Deprived economic and social environments offer neither the stability nor the flexibility needed for families to overcome the difficulties they face every day (Bonnet 1993). Therefore, children are often put to work, or make the decision themselves to work, as a means to breakout: 'To send a child to work is, for a family, an attempt to escape from a situation deteriorating day by day' (375).

Poverty and family breakdown in Kiratu mean that parents often lack the economic means to support school engagement in ways expected of them by social institutions. Although the main impetus for child labour in Kiratu seems to be poverty, some children run away from their homes and schools and work to support themselves. The District Development Officer for Kiambu also claimed that boys were 'an endangered species' because they had no role models as their fathers were mostly alcoholics. Boys in their final years of primary school were being lured away by other boys who were working and 'earning big money' and were susceptible to the problems of drug abuse and crime. According to the chief of Kiratu, these young men are the bane of the community, terrorising people at night:

> Many boys in this community have no one to look up to. Their fathers are absent or unknown and their mothers have a hard time disciplining them [...] they are an authority unto themselves and are influenced by their older friends who did not go to secondary school to quit school and engage in antisocial behaviour.

Therefore, while working to be resilient may have some 'benefits' at least in the eyes of the parents in terms of socialising children to survive in a harsh world, working does not always have the capacity to instil moral values in children, so the intentions of parents are sometimes unfulfilled. Currently childhood in

Kiratu is a time characterised by daily struggle and precluding, for the most part, the playfulness and security that typifies it in wealthier families.

Working and schooling: a balancing act

In Kenya, any work that violates the rights of children, including the right to attend school, is defined as child labour. It was not clear exactly how many child labourers there were in Kiratu and the wider Kiambu district during the research period. Current government documents estimate the number of child labourers in the district at about 29,000 and these were working mainly in the commercial agricultural sector (MOPND 2005). Mr. Wambugu, the head teacher of Kiratu primary school, also remarked that it is a matter of the extent to which children are working, rather than whether they are working or not:

> Child labour is rampant in this area. Most if not all the children at my school have [been] or are involved in it. Most of the children in this school are the children of casual labourers from the nearby farms. They are very poor; therefore, work for the children is a must.

Children are involved in various forms of work, mainly coffee berry picking, but also farm cultivation, domestic work, and the worst forms of child labour according to the International Labour Organization: drug trafficking and prostitution. Working on coffee farms is not allowed, but this rule is generally flouted. Children as young as 3 years of age can be found working on the farms. The *labouring child*, involved in non-family capitalist labour where work is, for the most part, not for purposes of socialisation and participating in the life of the community but for the material survival of the family, is alive and well.

While working for wages is a big part of children's lives, going to school is also seen as being important. Schooling means a great deal to the child labourers because it is a source of hope for a brighter future for them. One girl, Waruguru, with whom I talked during my many visits to the primary school, remarked:

> School is good. Because if you study hard, you can remove yourself and your parents from poverty. If you study hard, get a chance to go to secondary school or even college, you will get a good job and money and food . . . and clothes.

Positive views about schooling were manifested in enrolment rates in Kiratu. The majority of children join between 6 and 7 years of age and spend an average of 8–10 years in primary school, depending on whether they repeat classes or not. The dropout rate is quite low, ranging from less than 1 per cent to 2 per cent. Most of these children drop out of school because of requirements that parents have to purchase school uniforms, shoes, exercise books and, as there are frequent teacher shortages, raise money to pay new teachers. Work is the next viable alternative for these children, highlighting that access to 'free' education is still not a reality.

Transition rates to secondary school are low.[11] About 40 per cent of all examination candidates in Kiratu proceed to secondary school, a lower percentage than at district level (50 per cent) and still lower than the national average (60 per cent).[12] The main reason for this situation is the high cost of secondary school education. Moreover, the overall performance of the four primary schools in Kiratu in national examinations has been poor, which has also contributed to poor transition rates.[13] For the 60 per cent of the exam cohort in Kiratu who did not proceed to secondary school, joining the labour force permanently becomes a viable option, often the only one left. Many girls marry young and start families.

Work and schooling exist in tandem in Kiratu, as many children attend school and engage in wage labour to survive. The child is pulled between two worlds: the world of work, which is necessary for survival, often encouraged by parents and sometimes children but frowned upon by teachers; and the world of school, which holds the promise of a better future. The children themselves are receiving mixed messages: that child labour is wrong and an abuse of their rights; and that it is normal and necessary. The picture that emerges is of a community struggling to embrace and sponsor the idea of the *schooled child* in the context of oppressive and intergenerational structural poverty and family breakdown.

Implications for social policy

By tracing the historical development of the notion of childhood in Kiratu this research vindicates Ariès' (1962) and James and James' (2008) argument that although childhood is a constant feature of all societies, the *ways* that children go through that childhood vary in time and space. The role of children in Kiratu has changed over time, responding to cultural, socio-economic and political winds of change. The child has been understood as a *socialised child*, whose job was to gain knowledge of their future roles as men and women in the community through work; as a *labouring child*, whose paid work provided for the material needs of the family; and as a *schooled child*, whose main preoccupation, at least in principle, should be the attendance of school. Table 4.1 summarises this.

This account of childhood also urges us to interrogate two main assumptions related to the implementation of Education for All (EFA) policies in developing countries like Kenya. First, EFA, with its attendant demands for free and compulsory primary education, assumes a certain 'universality' of childhood; the idea that children are individuals with unique (but universally applicable) characteristics, that they are vulnerable and subject to protection, and that their main occupation should be school and play. This is the ideal of childhood put forward in the UN Convention on the Rights of the Child and reinforced in declarations such as EFA.[14] However, discussions in this chapter shed light on the limitations of such assumptions. While the idea of childhood as the structural space occupied by children may be universal, the experiences they may have while occupying this space vary in time and space. Indeed, the experience of many of the children in Kiratu over the last century has shown this. Penn (2005) strongly argues that childhood is a diverse and often unequal time for children across the globe, one

Table 4.1 Reconstructed understandings of childhood in Kiratu

Period	Notion of childhood	Characteristics of childhood	Relationship between child labour and education	Main role of children
Pre-colonial	The socialised child	Children are resilient and active agents of their own development	Very close positive relationship	*Learning* – the child is a social being
Colonial	The labouring child	Akin to slavery. Children must work to survive	Relationship severed. Education/socialisation removed from the equation	*Working* – the child is an economic being
Postcolonial	The schooled child	Children are vulnerable and in need of protection and guidance	Break in relationship set. Working and schooling perceived to have a negative relationship	*Schooling* – the child is still an economic being, understood to be potential human capital

that is influenced by powerful cultural, historical and socio-economic factors. The harsh reality of children's lives in Kiratu, in which they navigate an existence of poverty, hunger, family breakdown and dangerous and deprived living environments while incongruously being expected to attend school regularly and avoid engaging in paid labour on the coffee farms, is one that policies such as EFA fail to take into account.

This unacknowledged tension has the effect of undermining not only the relevance of EFA, but its implementation. As of 2012, there were still over 1 million children out of school in Kenya, many of whom are engaged in work for survival despite policies such as *Free Primary Education* (UNESCO 2012). The way that EFA constitutes or considers childhood as a time that should be free from work or labour is not always relevant or practical in the context of many developing countries. Ethnographic data from this research have shown that while primary education is 'free', as we see through the accounts presented in this study, many children remain out of school or only sporadically attend school for various reasons including poverty and hunger. And yet the new Kenyan constitution, promulgated in 2010, dictates that primary education shall be both free and compulsory. How this law will be enforced in poor communities like Kiratu remains to be seen.

What this case study has therefore demonstrated is the disjuncture between Kenyan (and international) social policy and the socio-historical and economic realities on the ground; a problem common to many countries in Africa. This research has shown that it is possible for the *labouring child* to co-exist with the *schooled child* and social policies need to take this into account by being more flexible to their needs. There should be provision in these policies for schooling *and* work under certain conditions, in which hazardous and exploitative aspects are addressed. The child labourers in this study clearly expressed the opinion that although being educated was an important agency goal, working was equally important for their survival. Flexibility like this would require some level of decentralisation of the education system to allow, for example, school calendars to be synchronised with peak demands for family labour, such as harvesting seasons, and to enable curricula that are socially, culturally and economically relevant to particular contexts.[15] For global agendas for education and international development to be meaningful, the disjuncture between policies and socio-historical and economic realities has to be addressed, first, through an understanding of the changing nature of childhood in different contexts over time and second, through the adoption of educational policies and practices that take into account these shifts.

Notes

1. Not the real name of the community.
2. This chapter differentiates between *working children* and *child labourers*. Working children are children working for pay, profit or family gain. Child labourers on the other hand are considered to be children whose work prevents them from going to school, and which may be hazardous or exploitative.
3. Not everyone agreed with Ariès of course. For example, Lloyd De Mause (1976) refuted Ariès's claims, arguing that childhood was the same; it was the parents who had changed. Child rearing methods had changed from the more brutal and exploitative forms to what they are today in modern Western societies.
4. Being under the British 'sphere of influence' meant that the British companies had a monopoly of commercial and other interests in Kenya.
5. Stichter (1975) refers to proletarianisation as the separation of peasant producers from all means of production. In the African context, this is the land upon which they could realise their material and social reproduction. Dispossessed, they are compelled to exchange their labour power for wages. Through the sale of labour power, capital gains ownership and control of labour for the purpose of extracting surplus value in the form of profit.
6. See the *East Africa Protectorate Native Labour Commission 1912–1913, Evidence and Report*.
7. From 1936 until independence, the Labour Department, through its annual reports, kept records of the number of working children in the country and types of contracts under which they worked.
8. The coming of independence in 1963 did not bring with it the hoped-for land reforms. The vast majority of land in Kiratu passed from the hands of the colonial settlers to wealthy African individuals who continued to use the land for large-scale commercial farming.
9. NER is the total number of school-age children who are enrolled in school. National primary school enrolments increased from 890,000 in 1963 to 4.3 million in 1983 (Hazelwood *et al.* 1989).

10 For example, the Employment Act of 1976 (Cap 226) placed restrictions on the employment of women and juveniles and established penalties for their unlawful employment in order to prevent children's exploitation and abuse. This law was repealed and replaced by the Employment Act Number 1 of 2007 (see the Kenya Law Reports at http://kenyalaw.org/kl/).
11 The Kenyan education system consists of 8 years of primary school, 4 years of secondary school and 4 years of university education.
12 Education facts and figures obtained from the Ministry of Education on 1 October 2009
13 Entry into secondary school is based on academic performance.
14 Kenya is a signatory to both these global campaigns.
15 A good example of this kind of flexible education would be the *earn and learn* schools in Zimbabwe. Bourdillon (2000) conducted a study of selected secondary schools run by tea estates in Chipinge district in Zimbabwe, in a scheme known as *earn and learn*. Pupils were provided with education, meals and boarding facilities on condition that they spent substantial amounts of time plucking tea. The curriculum was specially structured to take this into account.

References

Ariès, Philippe. 1962. *Centuries of Childhood: A Social History of Family Life*. New York: Vintage Publishers.

Bonnet, Michel. 1993. 'Child Labour in Africa.' *International Labour Review* 132 (3): 371–389. http://search.proquest.com.ezproxy.uws.edu.au/docview/224006330?accountid=36155.

Bourdillon, M., ed. 2000. *Earning a Life. Working Children in Zimbabwe*. Harare: Weaver Press.

Boyden, Jo, Birgitta Ling, and William E. Myers. 1998. *What Works for Working Children*. Stockholm: Radda Barnen/UNICEF.

Canals-Cerdá, José, and Cristóbal Ridao-Cano. 2004. 'The Dynamics of School and Work in Rural Bangladesh.' World Bank Policy Research Working Paper No. 3330. Washington, DC: World Bank.

CBS (Central Bureau of Statistics) 2008. *Kenyan Integrated Household Budget Survey 2005/2006, Child Labour Analytical Report (KIHBS)*. Nairobi: Ministry of State for Planning, National Development and Vision 2030.

Chege, Fatuma, and Daniel N. Sifuna. 2006. *Girls' and Women's Education in Kenya: Gender Perspectives and Trends*. Nairobi: UNESCO.

De Mause, Lloyd, ed. 1976. *The History of Childhood*. London: Souvenir Press.

Erny, Pierre. 1981. *The Child and His Environment in Black Africa*. Nairobi: University of Nairobi Press.

Eshiwani, George S. 1993. *Education in Kenya since Independence*. Nairobi: East African Publishers.

Evans, Gary W. 2004. 'The Environment of Childhood Poverty.' *American Psychologist* 59 (2): 77–92. doi: 10.1037/0003-066X.59.2.77.

Frones, Ivar. 2005. 'Structuration and Childhood: An Essay of the Structuring of Childhood and Anticipatory Socialization.' In *Studies in Modern Childhood: Society, Agency, Culture*, edited by Jens Qvortrup, 267–282. Basingstoke: Palgrave Macmillan.

Fyfe, Alec. 1989. *Child Labour*. Cambridge: Polity Press.

Hazelwood, Arthur, in collaboration with Jane Armitage, Albert Berry, John Knight and Richard Sabot. 1989. *Education, Work and Pay in East Africa*. Oxford: Clarendon Press.

Heady, Christopher. 2003. 'The Effect of Child Labour on Learning Achievement.' *World Development* 31 (2): 385–398. http://dx.doi.org/10.1016/S0305-750X(02)00186-9.

Hobbs, Sandy, Jim McKechnie, and Michael Lavalette. 1999. *Child Labour: A World History Companion*. Oxford: ABC-CLIO Ltd.

James, Allison, and Adrian James. 2008. *Key Concepts in Childhood Studies*. London: Sage.

Kayongo-Male, Diane, and Parveen Walji. 1984. *Children at Work in Kenya*. Nairobi: Oxford University Press.

Kenyatta, Jomo. 1938. *Facing Mount Kenya*. London: Secker and Warburg.

Kilson, M.L. 1955. 'Land and the Kikuyu: A Study of the Relationship between Land and Kikuyu Political Movements.' *The Journal of Negro History* 40 (2): 103–153.

Kitching, Gavin. 1980. *Class and Economic Change in Kenya: The Making of an African Petite-Bourgeoisie*. New Haven: Yale University Press.

Lieten, Georges Kristoffel. 2008. *Children, Structure and Agency*. New York: Routledge.

Lieten, Kristoffel, and Benjamin White. 2001. 'Children, Work and Education: Perspectives on Policy.' In *Child Labour, Policy Options*, edited by Kristoffel Lieten and Benjamin White, 1. Amsterdam: Askant Academic Publishers.

Manda, Damiano Kulundu, P.K. Kimalu, N. Nafula, D.N. Kimani, R.K. Nyaga, J. Mutua, G. Mwabu, and M.K. Kimenyi. 2003. *Costs and Benefits of Eliminating Child Labour in Kenya*. Nairobi: Kenya Institute for Policy Research and Analysis.

MOPND (Ministry of Planning and National Development). 2005. *Kiambu District Development Plan 2005–2010*. Nairobi: Government Printers.

Myers, William E. 1999. 'Considering Child Labour: Changing Terms, Issues and Actors at the International Level.' *Childhood* 6 (1): 13–26. doi: 10.1177/0907568299006001002.

Njeru, Enos Hudson. 1981. 'Land Adjudication and Its Implications for the Social Organization of the Mbere.' *African Journal of Sociology* 1: 101–125. http://www.getcited.org/pub/102121283.

Ocholla-Ayayo, Andrev B.C. 1976. *Traditional Ideology and Ethics among the Southern Luo*. Uppsala: Scandinavian Institute for African Studies.

Overton, John. 1988. 'The Origins of the Kikuyu Land Problem: Land Alienation and Land Use in Kiambu, Kenya, 1895–1920.' *African Studies Review* 31 (2): 109–126. doi: 10.2307/524421.

Pedraza-Gomez, Zandra. 2007. 'Working Children and the Cultural Perception of Childhood.' In *Working to Be Someone: Child Focused Research and Practice with Working Children*, edited by Beatrice Hungerland, Manfred Liebel, Brian Milne and Anne Wihstutz, 23–30. London: Jessica Kingsley Publishers.

Penn, Helen. 2005. *Unequal Childhoods: Young Children's Lives in Poor Countries*. Abingdon: Routledge.

Prout, Alan, and Allison James. 1997. 'A New Paradigm of the Sociology of Childhood? Provenance, Promise and Problems.' In *Constructing and Reconstructing Childhood*, edited by Allison James and Alan Prout, 7–32. London: Falmer Press.

Quijano, A. 2000. 'Colonialidad del poder, eurocentrismo y América Latina.' ['Coloniality of Power, Eurocentrism and Latin America.'] In *Colonialidad del saber: eurocentrismo y ciencias sociales. Perspectivas latinoamericanas* [*The Coloniality of Knowledge: Eurocentrism and Social Sciences. Latin American Perspectives*], edited by E. Lander, 201–246. Buenos Aires: CLACSO, UNESCO.

Qvortrup, Jens, ed. 1994. *Childhood Matters: Social Theory, Practice and Politics.* Aldershot: Avebury.

Stichter, Sharon B. 1975. 'The Formation of a Working Class in Kenya.' In *The Development of an African Working Class*, edited by Richard Sandbrook and Robin Cohen, 21–48. London: Longman.

UNESCO (United Nations Educational, Scientific and Cultural Organization). 2012. *EFA Global Monitoring Report Fact Sheet for Kenya.* http://www.unesco.org/new/fileadmin/MULTIMEDIA/HQ/ED/pdf/EDUCATION_IN_KENYA_A_FACT_SHEET.pdf (accessed 15 September 2014).

Wamagatta, Evanson N. 2008. 'African Quest and Struggle for High Schools in Colonial Kenya: The Case of the Abortive Kiambu Local Native Council Central High School at Githunguri, 1926–34.' *Journal of African and Asian Studies* 43 (3): 345–362. doi: 10.1177/0021909608089258.

Watson, Keith. ed. 1982. *Education in the Third World.* London: Croom Helm.

Weiner, Myron. 1991. *The Child and the State in India: Child Labour and Education Policy in Comparative Perspective.* Princeton: Princeton University Press.

White, Ben. 1999. 'Defining the Intolerable: Child Work, Global Standards and Cultural Relativism.' *Childhood* 6 (1): 133–144. doi: 10.1177/0907568299006001010.

5 Victims of what? Misunderstandings of anti-trafficking child protection policies in Benin

Simona Morganti

Introduction

During the last 15 years, child trafficking has emerged as a major international child protection issue and there has been a particular focus on West Africa, where the problem has often been represented as tragically endemic. This chapter aims to demonstrate the evident discrepancies between the dominant discursive representations of child trafficking in international policy and the manifold and overlapping realities of child work and child mobility practices in Benin.

The dominant trafficking discourse constructs departures from the family home as the result of corrupted tradition (particularly in the form of 'child placement'), economic crisis or criminality (Morganti 2008, 2011; Howard 2011, 2012). In focusing on the inadequacies and the rigidity of these assumptions, I demonstrate that high levels of movement are an integral part of Beninese children's lives and are rarely perceived by these children in terms of trauma or rupture. On the contrary, youth labour mobility is often an important step in their social and economic development, which implies both maintaining pre-existing social ties (to parental lineages, and to the village of origin) and the creation of new ones (with fostering parents, employers, companions).

The chapter draws on an ethnographic study conducted in Benin (Abomey, Cotonou and villages of southern districts) from 2003 to 2009, over a 16-month period. Participant observation and interviews were conducted with both adults (parents, authorities, ex-domestics) and children. One hundred and fourteen girls aged between 5 and 15 years who were identified by non-government organisations (NGOs) and authorities as 'trafficked', participated in the study. Ninety-eight of these girls had rural origins and had been employed in domestic service, while 16 girls were currently working as itinerant sellers in Dantokpa market in Cotonou. As I discuss, the study revealed that most of these girls did not perceive themselves as victims of 'trafficking'. Whether it is they or their families who decide that they should migrate, they do so in the pursuit of personal and familial advancement.

This chapter's focus on children's voices is underpinned by the understanding that listening to presumed victims' stories may help us to better understand mobility practices in contemporary Benin. With Mannion (2007), I argue that listening to children is always important in order to recognise and address their disempowered positioning within society, despite the methodological and ethical problems that it entails (Razy and Rodet 2011, 32–33). This research sees as crucial the privileging of children's voices, even in societies – such as in Benin – where giving voice to children is uncommon, as it provides a way to discover how children perceive themselves and how they perceive the adults questioning them (such as authority figures, people from NGOs and even me as a researcher and an NGO consultant). These are adults who all too often decide their future. Seeing as they are the 'beneficiaries' of protection policies against child trafficking, consulting children and their families is vital in order to assess these policies' pertinence and effectiveness (Hashim and Thorsen 2011).

In the first section of this chapter, I outline the local conceptions of childhood, the socialisation process and migration, in order to show that in Benin child mobility and child work are an integral part of juvenile education. I draw on a critical theoretical framework that challenges the assumptions in dominant Western understandings of the child and the nuclear family. In the section that follows, I examine anti-trafficking actions elaborated in Benin, arguing that these are both limiting and restrictive. I then present a case study of *vidomègons*, young domestic workers who child protection actors consider as trafficked children, in order to illustrate the tensions between the ways in which these girls conceptualise themselves and their work and the ways in which they are conceptualised by authoritative bodies. The conclusion is drawn that child migration in Benin is an ever-changing but deeply embedded social reality and that standard international civil society characterisations of it are often simplistic and ill-informed.

Western discourses and Beninese conceptualisations of the child

This chapter examines the tensions between the dominant discourse on child trafficking emerging from international (Western) child protection organisations and the local conceptualisation of the child in the Beninese context. In doing so, it highlights the importance of a contextual analysis by suggesting that the omission of context risks reproducing a form of neo-colonial violence hidden beneath a 'mask of protection' (Morganti 2011).

In the dominant Western discourse, much influenced by child psychology, any movement of unaccompanied minors is described as a negative process, something which is in itself 'pathological' (Hashim 2003; Howard 2008). The bare fact of moving away is seen to interfere with the 'normal', 'natural', 'healthy' development of children by prematurely removing them from the care of parents (Ouensavi and Kielland 2001; UNICEF 2002, 2004, 2006; ASI 2003). In the dominant discursive representations of child mobility that underpin international child protection policies, any departure from home is inexorably connected with a high-risk situation by exposing children to exploitation; this risk is double for migrant girls who are also described as inevitably exposed to sexual abuse

(Moujoud and Pourette 2005). This conceptualising of independent migrant children as vulnerable rests on stereotypes of child and family that are far from being universal, although they are often assumed within dominant discourses to be so. At the same time, it insists on the concept of risk and exploitation in a non-reflexive manner. Without denying that independent child migration can potentially expose children to dangerous circumstances, it is important to consider local understandings of the presumed 'risks' of moving away as well as the risks that can occur when children do not leave (Razy and Rodet 2011, 29–30).

The elision of mobility with exploitation significantly impacts the ways in which anti-trafficking policy is conceptualised. The executive reports of international agencies and NGOs acting in Benin assert that there is a direct link between fostering, migration and trafficking: according to these reports, the latter has its roots in the corrupt fostering system and in child migration, and thus it is implied that the fight against trafficking is a fight against all forms of mobility. Therefore the fundamental actions carried out during the last 10 years aimed at combating child trafficking in Benin were: prevention of any child mobility through the adoption of a strict law on child displacement and by awareness-raising activities about the risk of fostering practices and migration; detection, care and support of presumed victims; and repatriation of presumed victims to their villages (Howard 2012). The strict adherence of child protection actors to these actions is a clear indication that, despite the differences in language and method, all organisations and agencies agree that the best interest of the children[1] lies in staying at home (Howard 2013).

Unlike some Western notions of the need for children to grow up in a child's world specifically created for them, children in West Africa are very soon considered to be an integral part of the adult world. They have responsibility for domestic chores and the duty of contributing to the family income by a paid activity outside the home is very common. In Southern Benin this form of child work is known as *djoko* and it is based on the idea of socialising children through economic activities. Rural families are financially relieved when their children leave home and open the possibility for future monetary returns. As there is no local term to translate the concept of trafficking, child protection actors continue to use the term *djoko* in the 'sensitisation campaign' to alert the population about the (perceived) danger of *all* children's departures. But trafficking and other forms of child mobility (fostering, work migration, etc.) are not synonymous and to set off the alarm about the former does not mean that people will stop encouraging the latter (Howard and Morganti 2015). Within this context, there is a thin line between child work – acceptable and encouraged by tradition – and child labour – unacceptable because it entails economic exploitation – which blurs the boundaries between youth labour mobility and trafficking, and makes it difficult to recognise trafficking as a problem and even more so as illegal.

Furthermore, in Southern Beninese tradition an experience of hardship is socially accepted as a way to strengthen the character of the child. Biological parents are not considered good educators because they are seen to be too soft and, in contrast, the rough reality that children experience away from home is seen as a fundamental part of the educational process (Morganti 2006, 2007). Children mainly occupy a low rank in the family hierarchy and a certain amount of violence against them is a given. There is no clear line separating socially acceptable punishment from socially non-acceptable violence.

The cultural acceptability of searching for employment away from the home is demonstrated by the readiness of underage people to migrate: this movement itself is seen as an act of emancipation, rather than exploitation. According to the dominant Western discourse, children are absolutely dependent upon adults: it is not acceptable to let children work and even more, it is not acceptable to let them go away to do work. In direct contrast, from Beninese children's point of view, migration represents both a taking of responsibility for themselves and for others (Morganti 2011), as well as an initiation (Imorou 2008). Northern Beninese girls, for instance, usually migrate to collect dowry money to equip *themselves* for marriage.

A well-consolidated migratory tradition is a main factor in explaining the high level of consent given by family heads to children's departure in search of work or training. The involvement of community members in child transfers is far more frequent than that of external organised crime (MFE 2007). Migration is perceived positively because it is considered to be a way of increasing the economic capital and the social status of the migrant and of her community. The mobility of the child population in fact enables a family to widen their network of relations and to prevent the risk of isolation. Notwithstanding any strong economic motivations, it is reductive to imagine that every departure is simply a crisis strategy that is inevitably adopted to combat poverty, as a reaction to the lack of land or a dwindling food supply; one could instead make the hypothesis that sending a child away is a strategy to prevent such crises since it acts as the creation of a possible emergency plan for the future (Howard 2008).

The analysis of the migratory experiences of children is now central to a number of disciplines and institutional and professional spheres, even if they still do not talk to each other nearly enough (Razy and Rodet 2011, 6). A chorus of criticism has begun to question the dominant representation of the child-victim who is in danger of falling into the hands of traffickers as soon as s/he leaves the parental home (Hashim 2003; Howard 2008, 2011; Morganti 2008, 2011; Imorou 2009; Hashim and Thorsen 2011; Baker and Huijsmans 2012; Howard and Morganti 2015). From 2008 to 2010, a regional study supported by a broad platform of child protection agencies documented and analysed the many forms of mobility practiced by children and young people on the move in West and Central Africa.[2] This process has enabled the project stakeholders to get closer to empirical realities, to listen better to the children and to develop a comprehensive approach to the issue, with common positions and recommendations.

The ethnographic study of childhoods on which this chapter is based allows me to engage empirically with tensions of child mobility. I question persistent Euro-American assumptions such as the 'nuclear family' as a privileged habitat for an ideal childhood, and that of the 'home' as a space which is delimited geographically and genetically (Whitehead *et al.* 2007). Further, it allows me to examine how various figures carry out parental duties in ways that contradict the parental roles naturalised in the West (Goody 1999). Focusing on family structure, the place of the child within the family, the nature of social bonds and the socialisation process, this ethnography begins to 'rethink childhood' (Bonnet *et al.* 2006), considering who should be a child, not just in terms of biological age, but also taking into account the social status held within society. In addition, examining the historical and anthropological nature of migration allows me to elucidate the place that it occupies in the construction of local identities, and to discover whether child departures are taking place over customary routes or flowing against routes traditionally taken by their families. This works to identify the individual and collective pressures to move away from home and to understand children's aspirations and expectations.

To contrast the blind protectionism of the dominant Western discourse on migrant children's vulnerability, one would be tempted to insist on the need for child agency. But child agency and child vulnerability are the two opposite faces of the Western child as a historical and geographical product (Lancy 2012). Thus, this analysis takes a more nuanced approach, exploring the ways in which children – and their families – are both caught up in and negotiate migration and work experiences, acknowledging the role that (adult and institutional) power plays in these negotiations. Furthermore, in focusing on girls' mobility, this study deals with a Western gendered presumption of a 'double' lack of agency: migrant girls are twice different from the standard adult male migrant that research on migration has long considered as the normal, tolerable model (Razy and Rodet 2011).

Western intervention: a restrictive law as response to two scandals

The different conceptualisations of the child outlined above inevitably lead to tensions between local context and international laws on trafficking. Here I explore how the imposition of international trafficking laws on the Beninese contexts played out in relation to two major trafficking events in the region.

Child trafficking emerged as the central child protection issue across most of the world at the start of the last decade (Castle and Diarra 2003; Hashim 2003; Thorsen 2007; O'Connell Davidson 2011; Baker and Huijsmans 2012). This was nowhere more apparent than in Benin, where two high-profile events saw trafficking catapulted to the top of Benin's social policy agenda. The first was the interception in April 2001 of a Nigerian trawler, the *Etinero*, smuggling Beninese adolescents to work in Gabon. The second was the high-profile 'rescue' of Beninese adolescent labour migrants from the region of Zakpota working in the artisanal quarries of Abeokuta, Nigeria.[3] During the Abeokuta crisis, old quarrels flared up again between the relevant Beninese government ministries and the NGOs working in Benin, who had already been accused of creating excessive publicity about the *Etinero*. Terms such as 'child slaves', 'slave trade' and 'trafficking' were used as labels that the Beninese would find very difficult to live down. Both episodes led to Benin being marred as the new 'epicentre' of the international traffic in children (TDH 2005; Morganti 2008, 2011; Alber 2011; Howard 2011, 2012).

In the West African context, the demonstration of commitment to preventing child trafficking on behalf of governments seemed sincere and the breathless rush to legal regulation was stimulated by civic society. The representatives of local governments involved took part in numerous regional meetings which in their turn led to the stipulation of multilateral agreements between the states of origin, of transit and the destinations of trafficked children (UNICEF 2004, 10–25). Constantly put under pressure by international agencies, they worked out local community initiatives aimed at intercepting and denouncing cases of trafficking. The 'anti-trafficking committees' set up in various villages in Benin, Togo and Burkina Faso by the United Nations Children's Fund (UNICEF) are an example of such initiatives (CEFORP-UNICEF 2004; UNICEF-MFPSS 2004) even though for some they represent a substantial failure (Botte 2004). Despite a massive deployment of resources, it was rare for anyone to concern themselves with trying to adapt standards established elsewhere to local conditions (Dottridge and Feneyrol 2007, 2). The laws against trafficking were arguably an emergency response to silence the criticisms of the international community and above all to avoid cuts in economic aid (Morganti 2008).

Sometimes bills were written to combat child trafficking; on other occasions laws focused on the worst forms of child labour[4] (Dottridge and Feneyrol 2007, 1). However, the efforts made over the last 15 years for the most part consisted in the setting out of specific norms to conform to the *Protocol to Prevent, Suppress and Punish Trafficking in Persons, especially Women and Children*, adopted by the United Nations in Palermo in 2000. This is the first of three documents supplementing the UN *Convention against Transnational Organized Crime*. The second one is aimed at people-smuggling or the trade in migrants. Whilst people-smuggling goes against migration policies and is a problem of law and order, people trafficking is a human rights violation. While people-smuggling presupposes a wish to migrate by those involved and implies the crossing of frontiers, trafficking can take place within a state, is always the result of some act of constriction and has as its aim the exploitation of the victim (Esclavage moderne et trafic d'êtres humains 2000; Botte 2003; La Rocca 2003; Dottridge 2004; Vaz Cabral 2006). Children (under 18 years old) who are involved in migration, both in national and international contexts, are in any case considered to be victims of trafficking. The presumption is that they have always been subjected to being led or coerced and so unable to give free and willing consent to their departure.[5]

In Benin the *Loi N° 2006–04 Portant conditions de déplacement des mineurs et répression de la traite d'enfants en République du Bénin*[6] was elaborated between 2005 and early 2006. It automatically abrogated previous regulations and in the name of their rights banned children from moving around at all. In particular article 7, page 2, states:

> No child between 0 and 18 may be transferred within the state without his or her biological parents or a person with authority over him or without a special authorisation given by the administrative authorities of the place of residence, except with judicial permission or in special cases on recommendation of the social services or medical services.
>
> (my translation)

If one overlooks the fact that 'a person with authority over a child' would be interpreted locally as anyone who is older than the child, even another minor, we can imagine the paradoxes of applying such a law in a context where the majority of the population is illiterate and without documents given the very low rate of registering births. Most tried to get around the law rather than resort to the legal procedure which might remedy any unjust arrest (Wibrin and Chaumont 2010). This is what happened in Benin. The new directives rained down on people from above in the form of prescriptions and prohibitions seemingly irreconcilable with century-old practices and the efforts to seize children on the part of the police officers and the local communities frequently produced results which oscillated between the tragic and the grotesque. For example, when one young boy was repatriated from Abeokuta, the tragicomic reaction of his father reveals the gap in perceptions. On the return of his son, he remarked it was a pity he had not got back 2 days earlier so as to have been able to leave for the plantations in the Ivory Coast with his brother.

The gap between norms and reality is probably one of the worst effects of an over-extension and consequent emptying of meaning of terms such as 'exploitation' and 'trafficking'.[7] In turn, the gap between imposed prescriptions and pre-existing customs caused, as a specific corollary, an immense confusion between the various kinds of traditional child mobility and the unjust outcomes that some migratory experiences can lead to. While the very young could be at risk of exploitation in labour migration, the efforts made at the state level are too often an impediment to any kind of mobility whatsoever, independent of the age, motives and aspirations of the young people and their families.

Are *vidomègons* trafficking victims?

A crucial sub-element of the trafficking discourse revolves around the *vidomègon* ('child who is with someone') who is the subject of the widespread tradition of child fostering in Southern Benin. In this section I make use of a case study on *vidomègons* in order to illustrate the tensions between the ways in which these girls conceptualise themselves and their work, and the ways in which they are conceptualised by authoritative bodies. In doing so, I highlight the potentially damaging impact of the uptake of internationally dominant discourses of childhood and child protection, which frequently work to disempower the children they seek to protect. Yet, as the case study demonstrates, this is not a straightforward opposition: changes in how this foster care system plays out work to complicate potential readings of this work as either agentic or exploitative.

By far the best example of the discursive construction of the *vidomègon* system as a corrupt tradition that leads to trafficking is the nationwide 'sensitisation campaign' centring on the film and cartoon strip *Anna, Bazil et le Trafiquant*. Created as part of UNICEF's anti-trafficking work in the early 2000s, *Ana, Bazil and the Trafficker* alerts adults and children to the risks run by *vidomègons*. Even the singer Angelique Kidjo wrote the song *Ces Petits Riens*[8] to raise the alarm about the dangers hidden behind the very young leaving home. The implied reasoning is that if they were suitably informed of the dangers that every child is exposed to when away from home, parents would never choose to let them go. So how can we explain the evident persistence of such practices if they lead so inexorably to trafficking? Should one surrender to the facile idea that the naivety and ignorance of parents are so deeply rooted that another 10 years of campaigns and repression are necessary?

According to oral testimonies collected in Southern Benin, the socio-cultural phenomenon of *vidomègon* is predicated on the idea of collective education to foster social solidarity within the extended family. Children are temporally entrusted to someone in town, especially in the economic capital of Cotonou, who can ensure alternatives which are absent in remote areas. This system works because villagers who have moved to town are expected to offer assistance to children from the same village who are searching for support. They are also responsible for children's informal education. On their part, *vidomègons* have to demonstrate obedience and respect for the adults who host them and exactly as they would with their own parents they have to collaborate in carrying out the domestic chores and help with the family business. The chores carried out by fostered children are seen as a duty linked to rights to lodging and protection (Stella 1996) and as being an integral part of their domestic apprenticeship (Morganti 2007).

However, over the last three decades traditional fostering has changed. If in the past *vidomègons* were usually boys of school age who left rural villages to get an education or to attend an apprenticeship in town, most of today's *vidomègons* are girls aged 5–15. They have never attended school or leave school very early and are 'placed' (Adihou 1998) in city households to carry out domestic tasks (baby care, housekeeping) and duties outside the home (such as selling goods).

According to data collected in care centres for underage people in difficult situations, most of the girls that arrive there and considered victims of trafficking are aged 10–15 years. They have been through more than one 'placement' as domestic servants, and have decided to leave their previous employer's house. They have usually left the village to follow an 'auntie' – generally a relative or acquaintance – who is looking for a young helper in town. Traditional fostering may be invoked but it is evident that parents and girls themselves expect a monetary gain from the departure. Some parents may receive a symbolic figure or some gifts (alcohol, fabrics) before the child leaves. After only a few months of domestic and commercial training within the foster family, the 'auntie', inexorably considered a trafficker by child protection authorities, often places her *vidomègon* with another employer who offers payment to the 'auntie' for the girl's service. Generally, the 'auntie' sends some money to the girl's parents every 2 or 3 months or even more rarely, whilst keeping extra gains for herself with the pretence that the girl will receive a 'marriage case' (money, clothes, household tools) on returning to the village.

Usually, the girls in these centres affirmed that host families had no consideration for their young domestics, be they relatives or not, and often had found themselves exposed to food and rest deprivation, excessive chores, injuries and physical violence. They considered their working conditions quite hard (working 12–16 hours a day, 6 days a week), but they believed that by leaving their employers they could avoid especially excessive circumstantial injustice. Normally, they were not ready to give up on their urban experience: they did not want to return to their village and instead hoped to get a 'better employer' who would give them remuneration, or help them start a small business, or place them into training (such as hairdressing, dressmaking).

In contrast, the girls who I met in Dantokpa, the central market of Cotonou, were still living with their host families or with their employers. They too are considered victims of economic exploitation and trafficking by child protection actors, simply because they are children working away from their parents. This is the case even if their working conditions are exactly the same as those experienced by children still living with their family. Indeed, within the family, Beninese girls learn business skills very quickly and are expected to contribute to their mothers' activities.

From a focus group with 16 girls in Dantokpa who did not attend school and dedicated themselves full-time to commerce spending about 12–14 hours a day in the streets, it emerged that 15 participants out of the 16 did not regret not going to school. Furthermore, they disliked the competition of schoolgirls who spend their holidays in the market. Some of the participants were free to work for themselves on their day off. Others already had their own business and the women they live with acted as 'economic godmothers' who supported and trained them. All of the participants showed with enthusiasm small tricks they had learned and claimed to want to dedicate themselves to trade. According these girls, these abilities are their most useful skills. They all avoided saying that relations with their employers and with customers were often pressured; however, from their narratives the context of the market seems to be a scenario where even the youngest vendors soon learn to move with cunning, alertness and resourcefulness.

Listening to presumed victims' voices

The narratives constructed by child protection agencies and those told by children themselves in *vidomègon* situations are clearly vastly different. In this section I demonstrate that the major implication of the disjuncture so far highlighted (between the trafficking discourse and the children's realities) is that the policies designed to 'protect' young Beninese from trafficking remain largely ineffective, if not completely counterproductive. In particular I use the voices of two presumed victims to highlight that the perception they have of themselves as workers is in stark contrast to the assumption that they needed to be repatriated to their village to protect them from work.

A collaboration with the Salesian Sisters' NGO provided the most important access to the stories of presumed victims of trafficking. The main activities of the missionaries take place in the *Foyer Laura Vicuña* in Cotonou, which in 2001 was set up as a transit centre and shelter for female victims of trafficking and economic exploitation. In 2005, 362 girls aged 4–18 came through the centre, while in the first 7 months of 2006, 211 had already been registered. The girls are 12 years old on average and come from all the regions of the country. According to the data over these 2 years, 55 per cent were *vidomègons*, 1.4 per cent were victims of internal trafficking, 14.8 per cent were victims of international trafficking, 8 per cent were housemaids (*bonnes*), 6.6 per cent young girls with family problems, 11 per cent were 'lost' children, and 2 per cent were victims of sexual violence or forced marriage.

After many discussions with the social workers in the centre about how they chose to classify children, I came to understand that they had been using the terms trafficked, *vidomègons*, lost, housemaids and so on, for a long time in good faith, and at their own discretion. Then with the signing of Law N° 2006-04 all displacements of children became automatically classified as trafficking. In 2008 the Families Ministry, with the support of UNICEF, distributed to all such organisations the 'Identification form for children in need of special protection measures' and an instruction manual of about 40 pages on how to fill in the form. Since then the workers confessed that, frequently, on having to put the reason for the child being in the centre, they would tick 'trafficking' so as not to make mistakes. A heading such as 'child work' would seem more appropriate, especially for young girls employed in domestic service. But the instructions are clear, if there is a combination of work and transfer from their original home then there can be no hesitation. However, the social workers very rarely use the term when talking amongst themselves.

Most of the girls arrive in *Laura Vicuña* and in similar centres after passing briefly through what used to be known as the *Brigade de Protection des Mineurs*, today called the Central Office for the Protection of Minors, or OCPM.[9] Usually the staff of the OCPM simply register the transit and sometimes question the children before handing them over to the centre where it is decided who to entrust with their care. Only in very complex cases does the official follow the so-called 'social inquiry' carried out by NGOs to learn more about the presumed victim's situation. After some weeks in care centres, children are accompanied back to their village and their parents are encouraged to put them in an apprenticeship or send them to school. By returning children home, organisations try to get parents to face up to their responsibilities. However, in this context, these responsibilities are Western constructs that regard proximity to the nuclear family as a primary priority and a form of protection for the child. To be sure that children live in what they consider to be a 'safe' context and are not at risk of new 'placements', social workers organise periodic visits to villages. Yet it is evident that the large number of presumed victims does not allow social workers efficient control of children's movements.

Following activities in the *Laura Vicuña* centre, I attended the hearings that open the 'social inquiry'. The interviews usually took place in the centre's courtyard, under the shade of a tree or in the social workers' small office alongside. On average they lasted around half an hour and were held in *Fongbé*, the most widespread local language. The girls rarely spoke French and even if they did, I didn't want social workers' habits to change because of my presence. I did not audio-record interviews but took notes of social workers' simultaneous translations. At the end of the interviews I was free to ask questions. On several occasions, participants came to see me some days after the initial interview to tell me their stories again. When this opportunity presented itself, I sought the assistance of other girls for translation. My age, my gender and my status seemed to make me more approachable and the girls spoke to me openly; my being 'white' and my proximity to the project chiefs were an advantage because they hoped I could participate in the decision about their future.

The experiences of the two girls illustrated here reveal the limitations of repatriating presumed trafficking victims to their village. The interviews showed that it is simplistic to assume that the biological family is the safest environment for underage people. The girls' narratives illustrate how the dominant presumptions of child protection actions of children's vulnerability and incapacity to decide what is better for themselves risks hindering their personal plans and those of their families.

Sabine, interviewed by me on 02/12/2005

> *Sabine is about 12 or 13. She speaks French quite well even though she never attended school because she didn't want to. She learned some French during her stay with her employer in Cotonou. Her parents are separated: she lived in Abomey with her mother and her father lives in a village nearby with his second wife. Sabine and her younger sister were entrusted to two different women in town.*

> *Before leaving she worked sporadically in Abomey market. "You can offer your help to a stallholder and she will give you some money." She explains she was not obliged to leave the village. Her mother said that she could refuse but Sabine didn't. "When I've had enough, I will leave", she thought. "Now is enough", she says.*

> *She knows that her parents got some money from the transaction but she doesn't know how much. She stayed several months with a couple that also employs another housemaid. She is a bad woman who injured Sabine more than her employer did. "It is also for that reason that I left." The employer is a very bad woman too: "I'm the only one she hurt in the house!" Sabine shows me the scars from bites on her arms.*

Every morning Sabine would get up at 05:30 am and start her domestic chores. During the day Sabine would also sell sandwiches for her employer in Dantokpa. Every evening the employer would count the amount of money: if she was not satisfied, she accused Sabine of being a thief and would beat her with a wooden stick. On the last occasion of being accused of thieving, Sabine decided to run away and tried to reach her father's village in vain. Then, wandering in the street, she met someone who suggested that she go to the police station.

Sabine asserts that she doesn't want to go back to Abomey. "I want to stay in Cotonou, I want to work for someone as a maid to earn some money and start a business. If it's not someone bad, I will stay with her." She is convinced that in town, if you do not meet a bad person, life is better. "There's no job for me in Abomey and my mother she is bad too. She hurts me frequently. She did this to me with a knife", and she shows me a scar on her head. I ask Sabine if her mother hurts her sister too and she replies immediately, "Yes, really hard! That is why my father sent us to town. If this here is your situation, he said, you must leave, and I agreed".

Sabine feels that employment gives her the opportunity to choose her living conditions in a manner that family life did not. To avoid unjust treatments and accusations, she breaks the relationship and she leaves the house of her employer. In contrast, she wouldn't be able to react against her mother in that way: leaving her own family is not so simple. Sabine tried to reach her father's village herself and she's aware that she must talk to him about leaving her employer. Returning to her mother's house would however mean exposing herself again to physical violence. She also reacts against economic exploitation: she wants to work for someone as a maid to earn some money and start her own small business. She is fully aware of the town's economic potential. Like most of the girls I met, she likes the town's amenities and is convinced that even with a few coins you can always get by. Sabine's sister's experience represents an important example of 'good' fostering: her sister does carry out some domestic duties, as traditional education recommends, but she goes to school and her foster mother takes care of her. *Vidomègons*' destiny depends on their foster parents' behaviour and Sabine knows this: she wants to find 'someone who isn't mean'. This approach to employment and family life highlights how important the migratory experience is for children as it can lead to economic emancipation and at the same time loosen particularly constrictive family ties.

Mama, interviewed on 06/12/2005 by a social worker

Mama doesn't know how old she is. She's probably 13 or 14. She doesn't speak very much and her French isn't good. Finally, the social worker managed to communicate in Mina, *the most widespread language in Southern Togo, where her family come from.*

Mama went to primary school for 1 or 2 years. "Then", she says, "they told me to stop; my father said that". Before moving to Cotonou she made and sold palm oil

> in Parakou, where her family live at present. She used to buy nuts and transform them herself into oil. She left because a woman was looking for a maid in town. The agreement between Mama or Mama's family and her employer is not completely clear: she was to carry out domestic chores without getting paid, for about 3 months or maybe more. Instead of money, she would receive a stock of clothes that her mother could sell in Parakou. Only after having accomplished her mission would she return home. While working for her mother's creditor, Mama produced and sold palm oil keeping some earnings for herself. She has to collect her dowry money and the palm oil market in Cotonou is much better.
>
> Mama describes her host family as well off. They also had another maid. One day Mama decided to leave: her employer hurt her very badly because she broke a vase falling over in the market. Then, wandering in the street, someone escorted her to the police station.
>
> I requested the social worker to ask her what she wants to do now and Mama replied she doesn't want to go back to Parakou yet. "If I find someone to work for, I will work as a maid before leaving." She explains to us that she will work for free, until her employer agrees to buy a stock of clothes for her mother as compensation. "I want to finish before (leaving). I have not finished yet."

Mama's story reveals how common migration is. Mama's family migrated from Togo to Benin, while her brother migrated from Benin to Nigeria, and Mama herself moved from Northern to Southern Benin. She considers her stay and work in town to be an opportunity for herself – collecting dowry money – and a mission she has to accomplish for her family – procuring clothes for her mother. In leaving her employer Mama reacts against circumstantial excessive violence but she is satisfied with her job. To return her to the village would affect her personal plans for her social and economic emancipation and destroy her family's survival strategies.

Most of the girls I met who had escaped from their employer preferred to delay their return to the village, especially teenagers. In general, these domestics lamented excessive job instability because their employers frequently threatened to replace them with younger and more docile helpers. In such cases, the girls attempted to fully use their social network in the city in order to follow a 'career' as salaried housemaids or as stall keepers' assistants (Jacquemin 2012).

For these migrants, returning home before having accomplished their mission means failure: migrants, including young ones, were often unwilling to consider themselves as victims but rather position themselves as workers. During an interview, the social worker of the St Joseph centre of Parakou[10] complained that the main problem was keeping in the centre the adolescent males who had been stopped by the police when trying to reach cotton plantations in Banikoara (Northern Benin) or fields in Nigeria. Often they are farm workers or even high school students used to working as seasonal farm labourers during the school holidays in order to pay the school fees or buy a bike to travel to school. They are often arrested as a group and do not consider themselves to be victims of trafficking but rather of overzealous police officers. In their eyes, the protection offered by NGOs is a deprivation of their freedom and an impediment to their wish to migrate. Aid programmes offer no equivalent compensation for the sums they could hope to earn in a season's work and no alternative to the frustration of having to come home empty handed. Although the plantation work is badly paid and even if their departures are imposed by their parents, these young people take charge of themselves and their families. Returning home with money needed for education or to cover the costs of metal sheets for roofing the family home, increases their status and their sense of social responsibility.

Conclusion

To enter into the life of these children and young people is to reveal the multiple connections they are a part of and allows us to better understand their 'migrant worlds' (Razy and Rodet 2011, 7). When we consider their stories, we understand how difficult it is to categorise the different cases and to decide which label fits: fostering, voluntary or forced migration; reaction or submission to authority; or something else. There is a fluid *continuum* of possible situations and circumstances of displacement, somewhere between the extremes of a spontaneous search for freedom on the one hand and a forced migration to find work on the other. Whilst one extreme implies freewill, decision-making power and a desire for emancipation, the other implies constriction and being unable to determine one's own future.

Without wishing to deny any of the problems which may be posed by one situation or another, it is important to highlight that the official diagnosis proposed by the protectors of childhood is often simplistic, flawed and can even be deliberately misleading. As Boyden (1997, 207–208) rightly points out, to consider minors on the move as a problem – and more so a problem that has to be resolved – is to legitimise state intervention in family life in ways that do not attend to the wider social, economic and cultural contexts shaping a family's life. The presence and interference of international agencies and organisations which work for the protection of the child in many African states have their whole *raison d'être* in just such a construction of a problem. Law N° 2006–04 has managed to criminalise any movement whatsoever: if there was some reasonable doubt beforehand, the problem has now become a real one.

This chapter demonstrates that what is officially considered as trafficking in Benin is very often something else. Although some of the child 'victims' that I met were actually subjected to economic exploitation and hard living conditions, very few would class themselves as anything other than young labour migrants. I do not wish to deny the harsh realities of these children's lives; on the contrary, it is only by understanding the socio-economic context that perceives positively their move and work that we can actually evaluate both their labour and their mobility. The failure of current anti-trafficking social policies can be largely explained by a flawed conception of the realities of child work and mobility practices in Benin. When the official discourse is able to understand and reflect on such dynamics, the actions to which it is related will be better placed to address the real problems of young workers.

Notes

1 Article 3 of the *Convention on the Rights of the Child* (CRC). Approved by the UN General Assembly on 20 November 1989 in New York, is the most important legal instrument in child protection. States that have ratified the CRC are legally bound to make their national laws conform to the articles contained within it.
2 *Project of Joint Regional Study on the Mobility of Children and Youths in West Africa. Which Protection for children Involved in Mobility in West Africa. Our Positions and Recommendations* by AMWCY-ENDA Jeunesse Action (African Movement of Working Children and Youths-Environment and Development in the Third World), ILO (International Labour Organization), IOM (International Organization for Migration), PLAN WARO (West African Regional Office of Plan International), Save the Children, Terre des hommes and UNICEF WCARO (Regional Office of the United Nations Fund for Children for West and Central Africa).
3 The regions of Zakpota and Abeokuta have in fact been used to a continuous exchange of goods and population since the mid-eighteenth century, and the economy of a number of villages in the area of Zakpota has been linked to the quarries and Nigerian plantations at least since the 1970s. Continuous contact has encouraged the setting up of organised groups specialised in the recruitment of a workforce, both seasonal and otherwise (TDH 2005, 13).
4 The concept of the worst forms of child labour developed at the end of the 1990s and was defined in *Convention N° 182* of the International Labour Organization (ILO) in 1999. This document identifies four forms of unacceptable child labour: a) all forms of slavery and practices similar to slavery, such as sale, trafficking, bondage and forced labour; b) sexual exploitation for commercial purposes; c) involvement in illegal activities such as drug trafficking; and d) employment in activities which put at risk the health, safety or morality of the child. The convention asked all signatory states to prohibit the first three forms unconditionally while the fourth category was to be discussed and established at national level (Dottridge 2004, 2005; Botte 2005).
5 Sections c) and d), article 3, *Protocol on Trafficking*.
6 *Law No. 2006–04 of 05 April 2006 on the Conditions of Displaced Minors and the Suppression of Child Trafficking*.
7 The definition of exploitation adopted in the *Trafficking Protocol*, for example, is not particularly helpful. The text uses broad definitions of exploitation practices rather than referring to specific actions.
8 *These little nothings*, in a direct translation.
9 The office was created in June 1983. It answers to the Director of the Judicial Police, it has jurisdiction over the whole national territory and has a branch in every department of the country.
10 In 2007 the collaboration with this home allowed the Salesian Sisters to operate more efficiently in Northern Benin and to provide shelter also for male minors.

References

Adihou, A. 1998. *Les Enfants Placés au Bénin*. London: ASI (Anti-Slavery International) and Cotonou: ESAM (Enfants Solidaires d'Afrique et du Monde).
Alber, E. 2011. 'Child Trafficking in West Africa.' In *Frontiers of Globalization: Kinship and Family Structure in Africa*, edited by A.M. Gonzalez, 71–93. London: Africa World Press.
ASI (Anti-Slavery International). 2003. *Sub Regional Project on Eradicating Child Domestic Work and Child Trafficking in West and Central Africa*. London: ASI.

Baker, S., and R. Huijsmans. 2012. 'Child Trafficking: 'Worst Form' of Child Labour, or Worst Approach to Young Migrants?' *Development and Change* 43 (4): 919–946.

Bonnet, M., K. Hanson, M.F. Lange, G. Paillet, O. Nieuwenhuys, and B. Schlemmer, eds. 2006. *Enfants travailleurs, repenser l'enfance*. Lausanne: Page deux.

Botte, R. 2003. 'Traite des êtres humaines et esclavage. Du congres de Vienne (1815) au protocole de Palerme (2000): les réponses du droit.' *La Pensée* 336 (oct.–déc.): 7–21.

Botte, R. 2005. *Documentation des stratégies et activités de prévention et de réinsertion mise en place par les comites de village dans le cadre de la lutte contre la traite des enfants (Bénin, Mali, Burkina Faso)*. Dakar: UNICEF-BRAOC.

Botte, R. 2005. 'Les habits neufs de l'esclavage. Métamorphoses de l'oppression au travail.' *Cahiers d'Etudes Africaines* 179–180: 651–666.

Boyden, J. 1997. 'Childhood and the Policy Makers: A Comparative Perspective on the Globalisation of Childhood.' In *Constructing and Reconstructing Childhood: Contemporary Issues in the Sociological Study of Childhood*, edited by A. James and A. Prout, 190–216. London: Falmer Press.

Castle, S., and A. Diarra. 2003. *The International Migration of Young Malians: Tradition, Necessity, or Rite of Passage?* Research Report. London: London School of Hygiene & Tropical Medicine.

Ceforp-Unicef. 2004. *Evaluation de l'action des comités villageois et des CPS dans la lutte contre le trafic des enfants. Rapport final*. Ceforp-Unicef.

Convention N° 182 – Worst Forms of Child Labour Convention. 1999. Geneva: ILO.

Convention on the Rights of the Child. 1989. New York: UN Assembly.

Dottridge, M. 2004. *Kids as Commodities? Child Trafficking and What to Do about It*. Lausanne: Terre des Hommes Foundation.

Dottridge, M. 2005. 'Types of Forced Labour and Slavery-like Abuse Occurring in Africa Today. A Preliminary Classification.' *Cahiers d'Etudes Africaines* 179–180: 689–712.

Dottridge, M., and O. Feneyrol. 2007. *Action to Strengthen Indigenous Child Protection Mechanisms in West Africa to Prevent Migrant Children from Being Subjected to Abuse*. Lausanne: Terre des Hommes Foundation.

Esclavage moderne et trafic d'êtres humains quelles approches européennes. 2000. Actes du colloque du 17 novembre 2000. Paris: Centre de Conférences Internationales.

Goody, E. 1999. 'Sharing and Transferring Components of Parenthood: The West African Case.' In *Adoption et fosterage*, edited by M. Corbier, 369–388. Paris: De Boccard.

Hashim, I.M. 2003. 'Child Migration: Pathological or Positive?' Paper presented at the International Workshop on Migration and Poverty in West Africa, University of Sussex.

Hashim, I., and D. Thorsen. 2011. *Child Migration in Africa*. Uppsala: The Nordic Africa Institute and London: Zed Books.

Howard, N.P. 2008. 'Independent Child Migration in Southern Benin: An Ethnographic Challenge to the 'Pathological' Paradigm.' Paper given at the Research Workshop on Independent Child and Youth Migrants, Migration DRC, 6–8 May 2008, University of Sussex.

Howard, N.P. 2011. 'Is 'Child Placement' Trafficking? Questioning the Validity of an Accepted Discourse.' *Anthropology Today* 27 (6): 3–8.

Howard, N.P. 2012. 'An Overview of Anti-Child Trafficking Discourse and Policy in Southern Benin.' *Childhood* 20 (2): 554–558.

Howard, N.P. 2013. 'Promoting 'Healthy Childhoods' and Keeping Children 'At Home': Beninese Anti-Trafficking Policy in Times of Neoliberalism.' *International Migration* 51 (4): 87–102.

Howard, N.P., and S. Morganti. 2015. '(Not!) Child Trafficking in Benin.' In *Global Human Trafficking. Critical Issues and Contexts*, edited by M. Dragiewicz, 91–104. London: Routledge.

Imorou, A.-B. 2008. *Le coton et la mobilité: les implications d'une culture de rente sur les trajectoires sociales des jeunes et enfants au Nord-Bénin.* Dakar: Plan WARO, Plan UK, TDH, LASDEL.

Imorou, A.-B. 2009. 'Children's and Young People's Mobility: A Study of Tactics and Strategies and Involvement in Managing Their Social Trajectories.' Paper presented at the Workshop on Child and Youth Migration in West Africa: Research Progress and Implications for Policy, University of Sussex and Centre for Migration Studies, University of Ghana, Accra, 9–10 June 2009.

Jacquemin, M. 2012. *'Petites bonnes' d'Abidjan. Sociologie des filles en service domestique.* Paris: L'Harmattan.

Lancy, D. 2012. 'Unmasking Children's Agency.' *AnthropoChildren* Issue 2, October 2012. http://popups.ulg.ac.be/2034-8517/index.php?id=1253.

La Rocca, S. 2003. 'La schiavitù nel diritto internazionale e nazionale.' In *Il lavoro servile e le nuove schiavitù*, edited by F. Carchedi, G. Mottura and E. Pugliese, 168–196. Milan: Franco Angeli.

Loi N° 2006–04 Portant conditions de déplacement des mineurs et répression de la traite d'enfants en République du Bénin. Benin: Assemblée Nationale. http://www.protectionproject.org/wp-content/uploads/2010/09/BENIN-FRENCH.pdf.

Mannion, G. 2007. 'Going Spatial, Going Relational: Why 'Listening to Children' and Children's Participation Needs Reframing.' *Discourse* 28 (3): 405–420.

MFE (Ministère de la famille et de l'enfant). 2007. *Etude nationale sur la traite des enfants, rapport d'analyse.* Cotonou: MFE.

Morganti, S. 2006. 'Il bambino comunitario. Pratiche di socializzazione infantile nel Sud Bénin.' In *Antropologia dei rapporti di dipendenza personale*, edited by F. Viti, 105–130. Modena: Il Fiorino.

Morganti, S. 2007. 'Il lavoro dei bambini in Bénin.' In *La vita in prestito: debito, lavoro, dipendenza*, edited by P.G. Solinas, 75–104. Lecce: Argo.

Morganti, S. 2008. 'Bambini dell'altro mondo. Rituali, mobilità e lavoro nell'infanzia del Benin meridionale.' PhD dissertation, University of Modena.

Morganti, S. 2011. 'La mobilità dei minori in Benin. Migrazione o tratta?' In *Migrazioni. Dal lato dell'Africa*, edited by A. Bellagamba, 127–156. Padua: Edizioni Altravista.

Moujoud, N., and D. Pourette. 2005. 'Traite des femmes migrantes, domesticité et prostitution. A propos de migrations internes et externes.' *Cahiers d'Etudes Africaines* 179–180: 1093–1121.

O'Connell Davidson, J. 2011. 'Moving Children? Child Trafficking, Child Migration and Child Rights.' *Critical Social Policy* 31 (3): 454–477.

Ouensavi, R., and A. Kielland. 2001. *Le Phénomène des Enfants Travailleurs Migrants Du Bénin: Ampleur et Déterminants.* The World Bank/CEO.

Project of Joint Regional Study on the Mobility of Children and Youths in West Africa. Which Protection for Children Involved in Mobility in West Africa? Our Positions and Recommendations. AMWCY-ENDA Jeunesse Action, ILO, IOM, PLAN WARO, Save the Children, Terre des hommes, UNICEF WCARO.

Protocol to Prevent, Suppress and Punish Trafficking in Persons, especially Women and Children. 2000. Palermo: United Nations.

Razy, E., and M. Rodet. 2011. 'Introduction. Les migrations africaines dans l'enfance, des parcours individuels entre institutions locales et institutions globales.' *Journal des Africanistes* 81 (2): 5–48.

Stella, A. 1996. 'Pour une histoire de l'enfant exploité.' In *L'enfant exploité. Oppression, mise au travail, prolétarisation*, edited by B. Schlemmer, 31–48. Paris: Karthala.

TDH (Terre des hommes). 2005. *Les petites mains des carrières de pierre. Enquête sur un trafic d'enfants entre le Bénin et le Nigeria.* Benin: TDH.

Thorsen, D. 2007. "If Only I Get Enough Money for a Bicycle!' A Study of Child Migration against a Backdrop of Exploitation and Trafficking in Burkina Faso.' Occasional paper, Centre for African Studies, University of Copenhagen.

UNICEF. 2002. *La traite des enfants en Afrique de l'Ouest: reponses politiques.* Florence: Centro di Ricerca Innocenti.

UNICEF. 2004. *La traite des êtres humains en Afrique, en particulaire des femmes et des enfants.* Firenze: Centro di Ricerca Innocenti.

UNICEF. 2006. *Principes directeurs pour la protection des droits des enfants victimes de la traite.* Cotonou : UNICEF.

UNICEF-MFPSS. 2004. *Étude relative à l'évaluation de l'action des comités locaux et des centres de promotion sociales dans la lutte contre le trafic d'enfants.* Cotonou : UNICEF-MFPSS.

Vaz Cabral, G. 2006. *La Traite des êtres humains. Réalités de l'esclavage contemporain.* Paris: La Découverte.

Whitehead, A., I. Hashim, and V. Iversen. 2007. 'Child Migration, Child Agency and Inter-generational Relations in Africa and South Asia.' Working paper T24, Working Paper Series, Migration DRC. Brighton: University of Sussex.

Wibrin A.-L., and J.M. Chaumont. 2010. 'La lutte contre le trafic d'enfants au Bénin: le point de vue des mineurs.' In *Mouvements*, 18 Novembre 2010. http://mouvements.info/la-lutte-contre-le-trafic-denfants-au-benin-le-point-de-vue-des-mineurs/.

6 The construction of resilience
Voices of poor children in Mexico

Luz María Stella Moreno Medrano

Introduction

The lives of poor children in the 'developing world' are often characterised as being deficient or simplistically as 'lacking opportunity'. However, the ways in which children understand their own worlds often challenge this reductionist perspective (Viruru and Cannella 2005). The purpose of this chapter is to analyse the voices of Mexican children in contexts of poverty to highlight children's perspectives on and understandings of the complexities of their socio-economic conditions. The data used are part of a larger ethnographic study on the schooling experiences of children who were observed and interviewed within their school contexts over a period of 14 months from 2006 to 2007. The results of the study show that not only do the politics of schooling and families' messages have an important influence on the experience of childhood, but also that children develop mechanisms of resilience that allow them to build aspirations for a better future, in spite of their current socio-economic adversities. Analysing resilience in children's lives enables me to expand discussions on the factors that promote human capacities beyond reductive understandings of the conditions faced by poor children. It also demonstrates the power of narrative approaches for educational and social policy making (Roe 1992; Hajer 1995; Fischer 2002; Stone 2002; Jones and McBeth 2010). Boswell *et al.* argue that:

> policy problems do not simply flow from the objective 'facts' of the situation, nor can policy preferences simply be inferred from objective, rational interests. Instead, both problems and preferred solutions are constructed by different actors (politicians, the media, academics), drawing on available ideational resources of patterns of thought.
>
> (2011, 2)

The narrative approach in this chapter allows us to open up spaces for seeing children as policy actors with specific social interests and ideational resources; a view that urges social and education policy makers to respond to the lives, concerns and concepts of the children they seek to govern.

Trying to understand the different worlds of children is a difficult task. This chapter seeks to explore the ways in which 'resilience' is negotiated in the lives of poor immigrant indigenous children in Jalisco, Mexico. It highlights the importance of analysing childhoods from a socio-historical perspective to avoid essentialisms or impositions from middle-class standpoints. It is my intention to open up spaces to hear children's voices and consider their multiple constructions and negotiations of resiliency rather than make claims about their socio-economic 'realities' from a unilateral position.

The socio-historical context of migration and urbanisation in Mexico is central to this study. Mexico has a strong and painful colonial history, and there are vast social and cultural differences between the north, centre and south of the country. The struggles of poverty are acutely felt in rural parts of the country, leading to significant economic migration to urban areas. Nowadays, the big cities in Mexico have a myriad of cultures, creating spaces for renewed cultural identities and possibilities of social organisation. Rural families who migrate to the cities are faced with new dynamics of social organisation and labour demands, and they often encounter difficult conditions of urban poverty. How do migrant children of these families experience the challenges of urban poverty? How do many of them develop forms of resilience through their experiences of social and economic adversity? These are the central questions guiding the discussions in this chapter.

The chapter begins with a discussion about the dominant notions of childhood shaping the understanding of Mexican children's lives. I highlight the contradictions between these essentialising discourses and the multiple experiences of many children in developing countries. I then introduce the context of the research project, including the methodologies and data analysis used for this chapter. The chapter then critically examines the concept of resiliency focusing on the notions of risk, protection and developmental assets. I then present four case studies of Mexican immigrant indigenous children living in urban poverty to show how their negotiations of resiliency interact in different moments in their lives, sometimes in even contradictory ways. Finally, some concluding ideas and implications are discussed with the objective of opening up the debate around the importance of recognising resiliency as a continuous but highly contingent process in children's lives that is shaped by multiple aspects of their social realities.

Challenging the concept of childhood

Childhood is a complex period in life: it is a stage of discoveries and contradictions; it is a period where many of the workings of the world are not only learned, but also questioned. It is a time where family and culture have a primary role in the construction of identities, but also where dominant practices and discourses are imposed on those identities through schooling, social policies and everyday practices. Being poor and being a child is considered in much of the development literature as disadvantage and vulnerability (Kellett *et al.* 2004). The image of the child in the modern world is one that invokes ideas of protection and in the face of social struggles, this image is sometimes utilised to promote conceptions of suffering and deficit. Dominant discourses about childhood in Western societies are sometimes static and monolithic, as Leonard argues:

> While children often experience multiple realities, the dominant notion of childhood in contemporary western societies is one in which children are considered immature, naïve, innocent and incompetent and thus in need of protection by and from mature, worldly, experienced and competent adults.
> (2006, 441)

Within these Western discourses, children living in contexts of poverty are usually seen only as vulnerable and therefore they are positioned as targets of social interventions. However, little has been said about the capacities that children develop from social struggles, and the possibility that they may negotiate from their experiences constructs and practices of resiliency (González Arratia 2009). In this sense, poor children are positioned as passive rather than active subjects.

In Mexico, as a multicultural country with more than 69 indigenous languages and with more than 45 per cent of the population living in poverty, it is almost impossible to think about childhood as a homogenous category. Childhood is constructed through the interaction of cultural, historical and socio-economic realities; it is necessary to understand the daily struggles of poor families that promote practices which children learn to navigate. It is within this process that children develop, sometimes even without the help of adults, the tools to navigate the struggles of poverty. Therefore it is crucial for analyses to focus on the strengths and capacities that children can and do have within contexts of poverty, instead of assuming an inherently deficit and passive notion of the 'poor child'.

I argue that the colonial history of Mexico has an important role to play in elucidating the nature of children's resilience. It could be said that Mexico itself is resilient; the syncretism of the Spanish and indigenous cultures and religions is only one example of this characteristic. Almost half the children in Mexico struggle in poverty, and current economic conditions need to be understood with respect to the unequal and exploitative system left behind by colonialism. As Balagopalan explains, colonial legacies have had a profound impact on the ways in which childhoods are experienced in postcolonial settings:

> Although the move to recognize multiple childhoods is an attempt to move away from the functioning of the western bourgeois childhood as the hegemonic ideal, how does the fixity we assign childhoods of the poor in the Third World ignore the disjunctions that the history of colonialism has produced in these lives?
> (2002, 20)

The history of colonialism in Mexico and in most Latin American countries still has a strong impact on people's lives. The wounds of the past including abuse, religious and cultural impositions, and Western social practices, still profoundly influence the present. Little has been said about the consequences of colonialism in children's lives: how do we relate their voices to a history of cultural impositions? What are the new postcolonial impositions that children face in their daily lives? There is a lot of racism in Mexican society not only against indigenous peoples, but also against different social groups in the population. Colonisation of the mind (see Nandy 2009) does not allow us to value our internal cultural and social diversity as an asset, so there is a tendency to regard Western societies as more 'civilised' and 'desirable'.

Researching childhoods in Mexico: an ethnographic approach

The research project on which this chapter is based took place in the municipality of Zapopan in the state of Jalisco, Mexico, in 2006–2007. The initial aim of the project was to understand, using an ethnographic approach, the schooling experiences of immigrant indigenous children attending urban schools in this municipality. Semi-structured interviews and participant observations were used to gather information. Forty-four children between the ages of 8 and 12 years were interviewed, along with several teachers, parents and the principals of two primary schools (one public and one private).

Ethnography is a research methodology that allows us 'to see' and indeed the results of the research project exceeded my initial objectives (Wade 1997). The children's data are tremendously rich regardless of my sometimes short-sighted questions and limited research approaches. I followed, as much as possible, a child-friendly approach in the interviews (Kellett *et al.* 2004; Punch 2004; Greene and Hill 2005; Thomson 2008). I used drawings and photographs as catalysts for discussion during the interviews, but the core of the information came from the interviews themselves. The voices of the children were strong enough to be heard through the traditional methods of semi-structured interviews. As a *mestizo* researcher (mixed Spanish and indigenous ancestry, like the majority of the population in Mexico), coming from a privileged, educated, middle-class background, my voice is also embedded in the colonial history of my country. Through the process of the ethnographic research, I myself was also able expand my field of vision by becoming more attentive to a postcolonial view (Viruru and Cannella 2005; Smith 2006).

Understanding resilience

There are insufficient data on the construction of resilient practices in children's lives, especially in contexts of poverty. Studying resilience among children opens up possibilities for understanding children's lives from a diversity of angles, considering culture, history and socio-economic conditions. Indeed, I argue that the study of resilience must be a situated analysis that takes these contexts into account. If not, there is a danger that 'resilience' (or its lack) will be seen as a personal or individual attribute that is disconnected from socio-economic conditions of possibility. Such a reading risks perpetuating a 'deficit' view of the child who does not enact 'resilient' behaviours; this 'failure' is attributed to individual deficiencies rather than being a product of the socio-material conditions, contexts and resources available to her. For the 'poor child', the notion of 'resilience' must not provide a way for society to side-step our obligations to address the inequalities that differentially distribute resources. As the discussions in this chapter show, children's practices of 'resilience' are situated, contingent, negotiated and sometimes contradictory.

Gordon defines resilience as 'the ability to thrive, mature, and increase competence in the face of adverse circumstances' (1998, 47). Resilience is a concept originally used in 1976 in the psychological and mental health fields by Murphy and Moriarty (Gordon 1998). It was not until the mid-eighties that the concept gained more importance in the field of sociology (Werner and Smith 1982; Goldstein and Brooks 2013). Most research studies on children's resilience are conducted using standardised instruments of cognitive and behavioural competences (e.g. Stanford Binet, Achenbach Child Behaviour Checklist, Salgado 2005, among others). However, very few studies focus on the voices and experiences of the children themselves from a narrative perspective. It is difficult to study children's resilience when they are very young; most of the research studies on resilience follow a longitudinal approach in order to show the decisions and life trajectories of the children in young adulthood or middle age. In this study, however, I was able to see the capacity of young children to show signs of resilience. This suggests that resilience is a dynamic process that changes along one's life trajectory depending on factors that might promote or limit an ability to successfully adapt to current adversities.

The formation of children's resilience must be viewed from a perspective that takes into account complex, often contradictory and multi-layered experience resulting from specific socio-historical contexts (Seccombe 2002). Indeed, I argue that it is necessary to study children's resilience in interaction with the socio-economic structures in children's lives. Resilience cannot be viewed as a fixed attribute that children might or might not possess (Zimmerman and Arunkumar 1994), and resiliency changes at different points in children's lives. One of the purposes of this chapter is to determine the factors in children's lives that suggest resilient practices. For the purpose of this analysis, I seek to ascertain in the children's narratives factors contributing to resilience that have been identified in the field of psychology. Following Burley *et al.* (2010), these factors are:

1 **Risk factors:** such as low socio-economic status, dropping out of school, participation in violence, recent divorce, neglect, teenage pregnancy, and teenage parenthood.
2 **Protective factors:** support from family, friends, teachers and the community. Supportive relationships comprise caring with high expectations, a presence that produces a sense of belonging, and guidance focused on increasing self-esteem.
3 **Developmental assets:** behaviours and opportunities in students' lives that help them adapt to new contexts.

Risk factors

Although the schools in which this research study took place are located in a neighbourhood of high marginality, children did not use the term 'poor' to define their living situation. Rather, the children provided much more complex and nuanced analyses of their contexts. They were able to describe a number of factors to explain their family conditions, mostly around three main themes: income, housing and neighbourhood (including the dynamics within them), and finally, the lack of educational opportunities for their parents during their childhoods, as shown in Figure 6.1. In doing so, these children challenged the dominant perspective of risk factors and resilience which, as Seccombe (2002) argues:

> still places the primary responsibility upon individual versus structural level-conditions. Poverty (and other risk factors) are not fully contextualized as a byproduct of broader social forces. I suggest that people are poor not simply because they are lacking in human or social capital or because they lack social support. They are poor or may experience deleterious consequences because of structural factors such as an inadequate job, unequal pay structure, sexism, or racism.
>
> (Seccombe 2002, 389)

I was able to find the structural factors that Seccombe (2002) identifies in the children's data, as summarised in Figure 6.1. The children themselves seem to be aware of the effects that these risk factors have on the lives of their families. The lack of a proper job and appropriate housing with basic services, the discrimination that many of them face or see in their neighbourhoods, and the lack of

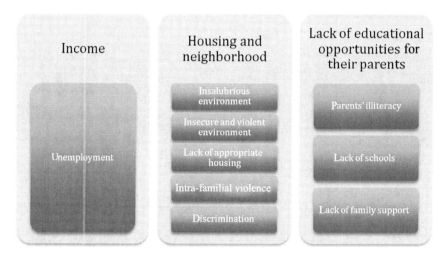

Figure 6.1 Risk factors among participants associated with income, housing and parents' lack of educational opportunities in Jalisco, Mexico

educational opportunities for their parents are associated with the current social conditions that the children are facing.

Protective factors

In the children's narratives, as described in Figure 6.2, I was able to identify protective factors in four social spheres: family, community, friends and schools. In the family sphere, all case studies revealed experiences of migration in the different generations, leading to the development of strong connections between family members in their communities of origin and their current city. Work and collaboration is also related to the experiences of migration, with family members tending to create networks of support. The community, as another social field, is also a protective factor that promotes a sense of belonging and strengthens identity. Friends are seen by the children as providing strong relationships of support, within dynamics of acceptance and rejection at different moments, but as important influences on children's sense of security. Schools are an important social field in which children also feel protected. The children's motivations and aspirations are reinforced by the messages they receive at school and by the role models they encounter through their experiences with children and their friends.

Developmental assets

I was able to identify two types of developmental assets in the data: personal characteristics and adaptation skills. These factors directly relate to the construction of resilient identities in the ways that children develop mechanisms to navigate their current living situations. Within the personal characteristics, I was able to identify a sense of autonomy, responsibility, empathy, creativity and reflexivity. Within the adaptation skills, I identified problem solving, ways to respond to adverse situations, strategies to avoid conflict at home and at

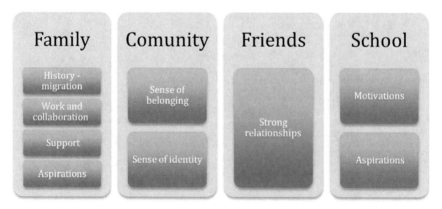

Figure 6.2 Protective factors among participants associated with family, community, friends and school in Jalisco, Mexico

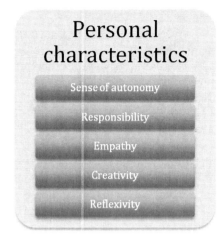 

Figure 6.3 Developmental assets among participants associated with personal characteristics and adaptation skills in Jalisco, Mexico

school, paid work that seems to also contribute to the children's sense of autonomy, and the recognition of what they have instead of what they lack (see Figure 6.3).

These factors (risk factors, protective factors and adaptation skills) were present through different dynamics in the children's narratives. As will be discussed in the following section, Natalia, for instance, has more risk and fewer protective factors in her experience of intra-familial violence, lack of proper housing and lack of parental employment, but has developed a lot of adaptation skill. On the other hand, another child, Pantera Negra, also has risk factors in terms of socio-economic conditions, but he has a strong family support system and has developed a great capacity to creatively respond to his current conditions. Differently again, Mirian seems to have developed resiliency to adapt to the new conditions that immigration brings; however, it seems that there is little space at this point in her life to make a different choice from the one her parents are planning. Marcos, as the fourth and last case of this analysis, is a very powerful example of children's and families' resilience. His indigenous culture and strong family bonding in both his parents' community of origin and his family in the city have created a protection for Marcos that allows him to thrive effectively within a context of racial discrimination in his school and neighbourhood.

Interactions of resilience: the lived realities of four children

The following discussion attempts to show how the resilience factors of protection, risk and developmental assets interact in children's lives in rather complex and sometimes contradictory ways. The four cases were selected because they highlight different aspects in children's resiliency processes. Table 6.1 summarises the demographic data of the children. All the children go to the same public school in a poor neighbourhood in Zapopan, Jalisco, Mexico. They are between 10 and 12 years old and all have experiences of immigration within their families (see community of origin). The children's mothers' occupations are related to housekeeping in middle-class houses in the city, and their fathers' jobs are related to the informal market, although Natalia's father is a gardener. All parents have no or just a few years of schooling, and some of them do not know how to read or write.

To different degrees, the four children demonstrate a range of ways of constructing resilient identities in the face of different types of adversities: economic struggles, intra-familial violence, cultural discrimination, lack of family support, and so on. It was almost impossible to describe these analytical themes separately, since they are inter-related in the children's lives.

I found that in order to be loyal to the children's own voices and experiences, it was important to maintain a holistic analysis of the data, without fragmenting it or taking it out of context. Therefore, my discussion of each case constructs a story that shows the inter-relationship of the elements of resilience mentioned above to illustrate the complexity of the children's experiences intertwined with their aspirations and personal desires.

Table 6.1 Demographic information about the participants

	Natalia	Pantera Negra	Mirian	Marcos
Age	12	11	12	10
Grade	4th	6th	6th	5th
Community of origin	Zapopan	Michoacan	Puebla	Guadalajara
Mother's schooling	Illiterate	4th grade in elementary school	Elementary school	Incomplete Secondary school
Mother's occupation	Not employed	Housekeeper	Housekeeper	Housekeeper
Mother's community of origin	Tapalpa	Michoacan	Puebla	Oaxaca
Father's schooling	Few years in elementary school	Secondary school	Elementary school	Incomplete Secondary school
Father's occupation	Gardener	Informal seller	Informal seller	Informal seller
Father's community of origin	Zacatecas	Michoacan	Puebla	Oaxaca

Natalia: risk, protection and a sense of responsibility

Natalia's case opens up the possibility of reflecting on children's resilience and poverty. Even though she lives in a difficult economic situation with family dynamics that are sometimes violent, she has developed a number of ways to navigate the adversities in successful ways to protect herself, outside of the norm of the 'middle-class' child of the Western model. Natalia's family is one of the poorest families in the school. The teachers and the principal identified both Natalia and her brother as the students from the most underprivileged environments. I had a very special emotional connection with Natalia, I found her to be a very sensitive girl and she seemed to enjoy our interviews. Natalia's father is originally from the state of Zacatecas and her mother is from Tapalpa, Jalisco. Natalia was born in Zapopan and she has five siblings. They live in a neighbourhood of irregular housing. From her descriptions of her home, I noticed that her family spends much time and many resources to maintain the structure of their house:

> *Natalia:* [out of the scholarship[1]], my mom buys the material for the house, since we only have one room but it gets wet, and we are already building [another room], but my dad doesn't have the [money] for the pieces, he uses . . . what's its name? He's putting, what's its name? . . . tables above and now we have aluminium, but it gets wet . . .
>
> *Interviewer:* And do you have electricity?
>
> *Natalia:* Yes, and we are stealing it, when there is nobody, they could shut it down, and the water too, and it goes away [. . .] right where the street is, there is a pole and all of us [take electricity] from it.

In Natalia's account, the risk factor of vulnerable housing appears in interaction with the ability to problem solve. Although Natalia recognises her father's lack of resources to build a proper roof, she focuses on what they are currently doing – although as yet insufficient – to protect them with tables and aluminium. The structural poverty in which Natalia lives, without regular water and electricity, is a reality that she recognises, but at the same time, she identifies the alternative mechanisms that allow her family to have access to these services. Creativity has been identified as one of the personal factors that promote children's resilience (Rodríguez *et al.* 2012), and this account shows how creativity might be taking place in children's lives even in the middle of difficult economic conditions.

Natalia seems to have the ability to recognise what she and her family have, rather than what they lack. Her description of her house is full of examples of her capacity to find the alternatives of adaptation to her current living conditions:

Natalia: In my house, I only have radio, beds, stove, not refrigerator or telly because it isn't working, and a couch, and, what's its name? ... and only a wood table, and the [house] is built with layers, but it doesn't have pillars, the [room] in the front [. . .] because my dad hasn't have money for the beams.

Interviewer: And what is the floor made of?

Natalia: The floor is of soil.

Interviewer: And how do you get water?

Natalia: We don't have a faucet; we have a hose.

Interviewer: And toilet?

Natalia: We have a toilet bowl, and once it's full, we go and take it out to the other side, behind the room I mean . . .

The need to find economic resources in Natalia's family seems to be a task of shared responsibility, where she and her siblings try to find ways to help her father get some money. Natalia, for instance, works as a domestic assistant for a neighbour; she says she likes working and she gets paid sometimes; and this social network gives Natalia the possibility of finding money when her father needs a loan:

Natalia: I work with a woman, I like to help her and I got paid sometimes [. . .] [I help] her to wash the dishes, to sweep, to make the beds, but not everything, only that . . . and my dad sometimes doesn't have money, and we help him to get some, and then my dad pays it back to the people we asked, that's why . . .

There is a strong sense of solidarity and collaboration in Natalia's account. Regardless of the economic adversities, Natalia shows great loyalty and a strong sense of responsibility for her family's needs, looking for money in different ways when required.

The stress of lack of money in Natalia's family is also a source of conflict. The same neighbour that Natalia works for as a domestic assistant is not only a source of help but also a source of conflict. The protective factors in Natalia's life are complex and sometimes contradictory: they take the form of protection and at other times, the form of risk:

Natalia: [. . .] I sometimes got beaten, because I say [bad] things to my mum or I beat my siblings.

Interviewer: Do you get beaten hard?

Natalia: Well, but dad does, when he's mad, he beats me real hard . . . mmm . . . sometimes I cry and my dad . . . a woman near my house who is my mum, my dad says, because I'm always with her, because she, she [is very nice] and my dad says 'tell your mum to give you money' . . .

Natalia experiences severe physical abuse from her mother and father, and the protection of the mother comes and goes; when it is absent, Natalia leaves the house:

Natalia: My mum [beats me more than my dad], sometimes my mum defends me from my dad and sometimes I go out to the street so they don't beat me

[. . .]

Natalia: Sometimes I got beaten with cables, well not with cables, I got beaten with the belt or with a hose, and my sister too, because she is very rude, my sister, that's why she gets beaten . . .

Grade repetition, intra-familial violence and the danger of sexual abuse in her neighbourhood are some of the risks that Natalia faces on a regular basis. Her 10-year-old sister was sexually abused and Natalia does not go out to play in the street when it is dark to avoid the danger.

The protective factors in Natalia's life, viewed from an 'academic' perspective, are quite controversial. Her mother is illiterate and, according to Natalia, she has some issues with her mental health because she was severely beaten by her father when she was a child:

Natalia: [I repeated first grade] because I didn't know anything, and I don't know what happened to me, I couldn't, I couldn't read, and since my mum didn't know how to read, and my dad does [read], but since my dad works, he can't help me

[. . .]

Natalia: . . . my mum doesn't know how to read [. . .] because [her family] gave her a hard time in the ranch, my mum used to carry heavy things, they took x rays of her head, because her father beaten her real bad, that's why my mum never learned to read, they gave her a hard time, and if she didn't do what they said, she got beaten real hard, she had bruises in her feet and everything, and one day, her dad tried to kill her with a knife, her dad is drunk . . .

The factors of protection that Natalia has access to are limited; in school she is 2 years behind; in her social relationships with her peers, she experiences social discrimination because other children call her 'dirty', and Natalia also experiences a violent family environment. However, Natalia's accounts are full of explanations of the reasons behind each of the situations she lives in. She does not complain about her life, nor does she present it from a deficit perspective.

Natalia's case opens up the possibilities of thinking about children's poverty differently and highlights the importance of listening to children's voices and their own perspectives before imposing middle-class/white/academic prejudices on others' realities. I am not suggesting taking a highly relativist perspective when looking at poverty and inequality, but I highlight the fact that there are children with a great capacity to face adverse situations with their own resources despite the lack of protection by social institutions. This situation calls for the positioning of academics, practitioners and policy makers in a very different standpoint, one that considers the possibilities and capacities of children to identify their own needs and desires, listening to their own interpretations of their worlds, affections and experiences.

Pantera Negra: risk, protection and creativity

While Natalia's story demonstrates ways of reading poverty outside a deficit model of a middle-class child, the narrative of Pantera Negra (Black Panther) foregrounds how resilience can reframe traditional ideas of child work and child labour. Pantera Negra, as he decided to call himself for the purpose of this research, is a 12-year-old boy full of interests and positive perspectives about his life. He lives in an impoverished neighbourhood, and his parents work long hours to provide for him and his siblings. Although poverty might be seen as a risk factor in Pantera Negra's childhood, he shows a strong sense of autonomy and determination in the decisions that he is able to make on daily basis:

Pantera Negra: I don't like onions. I'm a vegetarian, I don't like meat [...] since I was little I didn't like either meat or onions.

Interviewer: Then what do you eat?

Pantera Negra: Well on Mondays I like to buy vegetables, because on Sunday I get [some vegetables] in case my mom runs out of money and she needs some, but they make their food and I tell my mom to cook my vegetables, since they sell little bags of chopped vegetables, I buy and my mom makes me some, or beans or lentils.

The possibility of having paid work empowers Pantera Negra to get some money to make choices such as deciding the type of food he prefers to eat. He is very secure and determined in defining what he likes and dislikes, and he is able to make some adaptations, such as buying his food on Sunday, in the face of possible scarcity of resources in his family during the week.

As part of the research study, I gave some of the children cameras so they could take pictures of their daily activities, as well as of the things they liked and disliked. In relation to one of his photographs, Pantera Negra said that he likes to play guitar:

Pantera Negra:	[In this picture] it's me where I play [guitar] when I don't have anything else to do.
Interviewer:	You have had a lot of lessons, right?
Pantera Negra:	Baking, swimming, football, basketball, circus, jelly and all that . . .
Interviewer:	And who tells you to go to your lessons?
Pantera Negra:	Well, myself [. . .] since they're monthly, my dad entered a raffle for ten pesos a week and I get some out of it and he pays and my mom sometimes helps me too . . .

In our interviews, he made reference on different occasions to several extra-curricular activities that he has been involved in. He has taken baking and jelly-making, swimming, football, basketball, and circus classes – all activities in different institutions around his home. He has the capacity to pay for his class fees by conducting raffles or saving a little amount each week from the work he is able to do in the local market at weekends.

Pantera Negra's accounts challenge the traditional view of child labour. In some contexts, child labour is considered exploitative and a way to 'limit' childhood; however, the Latin American reality shows the children continue working to help their families (Post 2002). For some children, like Pantera Negra, who is immersed in a structurally unequal economic system, gaining some money not only empowers him to make choices about his life, but also gives him a different set of skills such as negotiation, planning and problem solving in a concrete way that schools are not able to replicate. This set of skills allows Pantera Negra to build a resilient identity, one that is creative and autonomous.

Mirian: between the city and the countryside

Mirian's narrative demonstrates the tensions between life in the city and in the countryside. Her story also shows how resilience works in the middle of contradictions between family bonds and individual aspirations. For some children, whose parents migrated to a bigger city, their current economic conditions seem to be better than those back in their communities of origin. For instance, Mirian migrated with her parents from the countryside in the state of Puebla:

Interviewer:	Why did your parents come here [Jalisco]?
Mirian:	Since over there [in Puebla] they almost didn't have a good job, hum, they didn't make all that money and it wasn't enough so they came here to find something better over here . . .

She explains that when her parents were in the countryside, they had significantly less money than when they are in the city. She knows that in the countryside, people are poorly paid and social and educational opportunities are more limited. She said:

Mirian: We live further from Puebla and almost every year we go there to Puebla, or my parents sometimes they almost don't have money, and this year only my brothers and I went and my parents stayed here and when over there, they almost don't buy anything for us, and here they do. Over there my parents worked like from 6 until 3 or 6 in the afternoon and from those hours they made very little . . .

Mirian's father wants to go back to Puebla to work his land again; however, this decision represents a sacrifice for the family since they will be making less money and the economic opportunities for Mirian will be more limited. She is in 6th grade, and she is expecting to finish secondary school 'here', before going back to Puebla again.

Interviewer: What are your plans now when you finish elementary school?

Mirian: I am going to middle school and I don't know if my mom, I don't know if I will keep on studying, my dad wants to go to Puebla, he wants to go back, he wants to go back this year, because over there he works the land, he won't have [money] for books and school uniforms so we better return when I finish middle school, when I get myself out of middle school I don't know if we're going back or I will keep on studying.

[. . .]

Interviewer: If you go back, you cannot keep on studying over there?

Mirian: I don't know if there's a high school over there, but my mom says that . . . my dad works the land, and what he makes out of it is not much, that's why I finish studying here.

Mirian knows that she may soon go back to Puebla, but she is expecting she will be able to at least finish secondary school.

It is interesting to see how her familial situation contrasts with Mirian's aspirations for her own future. When I asked her whether she wanted to stay 'here' (in the city) when she grows up, she said:

Mirian (laughing): . . . not my whole life. Over there, there are like different traditions, and more family members, I almost wouldn't like to stay here.

Mirian's family decision to return to Puebla is, in a way, aligned with her wish to go back to her larger family and cultural traditions; however, when I asked what she wanted to do when she grows up, she said:

Mirian: To finish my studies and to finish a career to get a better job.

Later on, when I was substituting for her teacher one day, I asked the group to write down on a piece of paper, their goals within school, Mirian wrote:

> *Mirian:* To finish work and homeworks, study hard to pass my subjects, and to pass to the next grade, to become someone important in life.

Mirian's aspirations seem to be related to finding a professional career in order to get a better job and become an 'important person' in life; at the same time, she wants to go back to Puebla to be with her family, although she knows that the job opportunities and economic conditions are not as good. Mirian experiences a contradiction between what she knows might open economic opportunities for her on the one hand, and on the other, her family's wish, that might seem difficult for her at this point in her life, to take a different path from her own. It is possible in her accounts to discern some doubt and not much determination or autonomy. Family, in this case, might seem to be an important protective factor in Mirian's life, but might also leave little space at this point in her life to think about different possibilities regarding her future choices. Resiliency here seems contradictory; however, Mirian's aspirations and reflections on her own future are clear and she is able to consider the advantages and limitations of living in the city and in the countryside.

Marcos: culture and family as protectors

Marcos's narrative highlights the importance of culture in the formation of children's resilience. His strong bonds with his family's traditions back in his parents' community of origin has developed in Marcos a great capacity to evaluate racism in the city and learn to navigate it in successful ways. Marcos is a boy in 6th grade, whose parents migrated from the state of Veracruz. They are originally from an indigenous community and speak Totonaca, although Marcos is not as fluent as his parents. They visit Zimatlan most years and his relationship with his grandparents is very strong. Marcos can navigate successfully in different social contexts – in his parents' community of origin as well as in the city. In his account Marcos is very critical of the difficulties his parents faced back in their communities, as he explains:

> *Interviewer:* And when you go to [Veracruz], how do you like it? Do you think life is difficult over there?
>
> *Marcos:* I've seen it there, over there, the people who help to cultivate are called servants [*mozos*] and when they cultivate they get paid 25 pesos and a plate of food, and that's it. That's why [my parents] said no, we don't want you to be like us that we didn't learn much and I want you to be more than us.

Marcos has a clear picture of the social struggles his parents faced when they were children. In this account, it is possible to see how Marcos is able to analyse structural socio-economic problems such as the exploitative labour systems and lack of educational opportunities.

The colonial history of indigenous culture is embedded in Marcos's accounts as well: being indigenous is synonymous with lack of opportunities, as he explains in the following quote:

> *Interviewer:* Why your did parents not keep studying?
>
> *Marcos:* When my mum was little, they were like the indigenous and they didn't let her quite study, and she finished primary, she finished primary and she came here, she came with a grandma because over there, you see how they have to prepare *nixtamal*[2] and that . . . and that's why my mum came here with an uncle and then my mum got together with my dad. My dad did study here, he studied in a technical school and he was taught well, but now that he's older I think he forgot a little about secondary school.

For Marcos, being indigenous explained some of the conditions his mother experienced back in her community of origin. It is possible to see how colonial experiences are still embedded in indigenous families and communities through the ongoing consequences of economic and social exclusion and inequality. Blame is still placed on the individual and her culture, not on the oppressive systems that have operated for centuries.

Discrimination as a result of cultural differences is a reality that Marcos has seen at school. Marcos has noticed that children make fun of other children who speak an indigenous language, or their parents:

> *Interviewer:* Have you noticed any difference in how other children see indigenous peoples?
>
> *Marcos:* No because I don't tell my classmates because they make fun, they say I don't know what, and they start saying things like that, I'd better not say anything . . .
>
> *Interviewer:* You haven't told them?
>
> *Marcos:* More or less, I only say that [my parents] come from Veracruz and they speak Totonaco.
>
> *Interviewer:* Did you decide that or did someone recommended it?
>
> *Marcos:* No, I decided it, because I had a classmate who made fun of him and because of that I don't want them to make fun of me, and that's why I haven't told them.
>
> *Interviewer:* What type of mockery?

Marcos: They say that his dad I don't what and they start talking like them, you see how they talk about [indigenous languages] on the telly and all that, and they start talking like that, and they make fun, that's why it is better not to say anything.

Interviewer: Have they made fun of you?

Marcos: No, that's why I don't say anything, because I see how it is and it must feel very bad, how I see they make fun of them and I don't want to feel like that.

Marcos is not necessarily taking steps towards a dignified recognition of his cultural identity, but he is developing the skills to navigate in a racist society. Resilience is a process constructed within contexts of adversities, and for children like Marcos, this adversity takes the form of intolerance and discrimination.

Marcos has a strong protection factor in his family. His mother is very active and is constantly taking a range of classes in the community centre. Marcos's family is very proud of their Totonaca background, and although Marcos downplays his background when he sees discrimination in school and his neighbourhood, he also values and wishes to know more about his culture and traditions:

Interviewer: Your parents consider themselves indigenous?

Marcos: Yes

Interviewer: And you?

Marcos: I'd say yes because my parents are indigenous.

Interviewer: And your children?

Marcos: I wouldn't know very well, because if I marry an indigenous they will be indigenous, but if [my wife] is from here from Guadalajara, they almost won't be. If I'd learnt to speak Totonaco, like my parents, I'd teach my children, that'd be like a heritage that my mum gives me.

Interviewer: And would you like to take care of the land [in Veracruz] when your mother gives it to you?

Marcos: Yes, and be there for some time to know how the traditions are, what they do, what they eat and what they do . . .

I argue that this cultural attachment to his parents' communities of origin gives Marcos a strong sense of belonging even in the middle of the difficulties in city. He has learned to navigate two social systems differently and to be successful in both of them, identifying the knowledge and skills that he needs to learn to respond to future challenges.

As is the case for Pantera Negra, another factor that is important in Marcos's experiences is the importance of a paid job. Marcos works at weekends with his uncle who is a jeweller. He has learned to make silver bracelets and necklaces and with his earnings has been able to buy shoes by himself, and he feels happy that he does not have to ask his mother for money for the week:

> *Interviewer:* If you make more money and start working, would you leave school?
>
> *Marcos:* No, I'll keep on studying, because I want to be a better person not like, I want to be better, like right now I am studying and working on Saturdays, and with the money I make I have for my [expenses] during the week, so I don't have to ask my mum for money, and if I want something at school I buy it, it is less expense for my mum. This Easter I will start saving for our vacations . . .

In contrast to what is expected in a middle-class context, Marcos has a clear idea that a paid job is not necessarily incompatible with studying. The possibility of having a job and getting paid gives children like Marcos a sense of autonomy and the confidence to make small choices in their daily lives.

Conclusions and implications

As I have demonstrated in the four cases, Mirian, Pantera Negra, Marcos and Natalia all face, although to different degrees, a situation of poverty and social difficulty. It is noticeable in all cases that the school is not necessarily the place where they are learning the strength and getting the protection to construct resilient practices. From their experiences, it seems that schools are also spaces of conflict and confrontation, where the children have developed their own resources to survive and learn to navigate in a positive way.

Children's resilience is dynamic, contingent, negotiated and sometimes contradictory. Children are living a number of experiences that might be determining their future skills and they are able to construct their own interpretations of their present situations in creative ways. It is impossible to look at children's experiences without taking into account the historical and socio-economic conditions shaping their lives. Analysing children's histories from a postcolonial point of view (Viruru and Cannella 2005) allows us to question the new ways in which children and youth are considered subjects of a new 'middle-class colonisation'.

These children's narratives challenge the images of childhood as innocent and vulnerable. The four case studies demonstrated that children living in contexts of poverty have developed assets, even if protective factors are not clearly present in their lives, that allow them to successfully navigate their current living conditions. This challenges the dominant ideas that the poor child is passive and lacking; ideas that are assumed in their positioning as silent subjects of social interventions. It also challenges normative discourses of childhood which emerge from the specific economic and political interests of a nation, for example, imposing 'middle class values on working class families, eschewing many of their more flexible, traditional practices in favour of rigid rules' (Kellett *et al.* 2004, 30). Rigid notions of child labour, for instance, are analysed from a political, middle-class and Western perspective in which children's processes of identity formation are not recognised (see Morganti's discussions in this volume). Children's narratives show that in many cases, having a job promotes autonomy and security, and therefore contributes to the formation of 'resilient' identities.

This analysis opens up new lines of research inquiry; more participatory and child-centred approaches are needed to balance the power inequalities between the adult and child worlds (Robinson and Kellett 2004). Such approaches also require a strong sense of reflexivity on the part of academics, researchers and policy makers, to encourage awareness of colonial impositions through discourses and interpretations that might silence the voices of the children themselves (Coffey 1999). As Greene and Hill argue:

> the researcher who values children's perspectives and wishes to understand their lived experiences will be motivated to find out more about how children understand and interpret, negotiate and feel about their daily lives. If we accept a view of children as persons, the nature of children's experiential life becomes of central interest.
>
> (2005, 3)

The voices of the children present a different picture for the social development agendas in Mexico and Latin America. A reflexive look at children's capacities and possibilities for navigating conditions of adversity is a way to start. Mexican children's voices are strong enough to inform local policies, avoiding the reproduction of the colonial practices of importing ideologies and policies from centres of power. The process of policy making informed by a narrative approach is a compelling and challenging task. It implies that the policy process must be founded on multiple sources of knowledge, 'whether these be drawn from personal experience, practitioner knowledge or academic research' (Boswell *et al.* 2011, 2). As this chapter has shown, we can learn a great deal about the complexities of policy 'problems' from children's narratives. How these poor children negotiate their experiences and contexts of adversity, often in unanticipated or boundary-pushing ways, demonstrates too that policy 'solutions' for the poor child cannot be reductive or simplistic.

Notes

1 Natalia receives cash payments from a social assistance programme called Oportunidades that provides economic resources to those in extreme poverty in Mexico.
2 Nixtamal is treated corn used to make *tortillas*, the basis of the Mexican diet.

References

Balagopalan, Sarada. 2002. 'Constructing Indigenous Childhoods: Colonialism, Vocational Education and the Working Child.' *Childhood* 9 (1): 19–34.

Boswell, Christina, Andrew Geddes, and Peter Scholten. 2011. 'The Role of Narratives in Migration Policy-Making: A Research Framework.' *The British Journal of Politics and International Relations* (13): 1–11.

Burley, Hansel, Lucy Banard-Brak, Aretha Faye Marbley, and Christopher Deason. 2010. 'African American Millennials. A Profile of Promise.' *Gifted Child Today* 32 (2): 47–54.

Coffey, Amanda. 1999. *The Ethnographic Self: Fieldwork and the Representation of Identity*. London: Sage.

Fischer, Frank. 2002. *Reframing Public Policy: Discursive Politics and Deliberative Practices*. Oxford: Oxford University Press.

Goldstein, Sam, and Robert B. Brooks. 2013. 'Why Study Resilience?' In *Handbook of Resilience in Children*, edited by Sam Goldsten and Robert B. Brooks, 3–14. New York: Springer.

González Arratia, Norma Ivonne. 2009. 'Resiliencia en niños en situación de pobreza de una comunidad rural.' *Universidad Católica del Maule – Revista Académica* 37: 32–48.

Gordon, Kimberly A. 1998. 'Infant and Toddler Resilience.' *Early Childhood Education Journal* 26 (1): 47–52.

Greene, Sheila, and Malcolm Hill. 2005. 'Researching Children's Experience: Methods and Methodological Issues.' In *Researching Children's Experience. Approaches and Methods*, edited by Sheila Greene and Diane Hogan, 1–21. London: Sage.

Hajer, Maarten A. 1995. *The Politics of Environmental Discourse: Ecological Modernization and the Policy Process*. New York: Oxford University Press.

Jones, Michael D., and McBeth, Mark K. 2010. 'A Narrative Policy Framework: Clear Enough to be Wrong?' *Policy Studies Journal* 38 (2): 329–353.

Kellett, Mary, Chris Robinson, and Rachel Burr. 2004. 'Images of Childhood.' In *Doing Research with Children and Young People*, edited by Sandy Fraser, Vicky Lewis, Sharon Ding, Mary Kellett and Chris Robinson, 27–42. London: Sage.

Leonard, Madeleine. 2006. 'Segregated Schools in Segregated Societies: Issues of Safety and Risk.' *Childhood* 13 (4): 441–458.

Nandy, Ashis. 2009. *The Intimate Enemy: Loss and Recovery of Self under Colonialism*. 2nd edn. Oxford: Oxford University Press.

Post, David. 2002. *Children's Work, Schooling, and Welfare in Latin American*. Boulder: Westview Press.

Punch, Samantha. 2004. 'Negotiating Autonomy: Children's Use of Time and Space in Rural Bolivia.' In *The Reality of Research with Children and Young People*, edited by Vicky Lewis, Mary Kellet, Chris Robinson, Sandy Fraser and Sharon Ding, 94–114. London: Sage.

Robinson, Chris, and Mary Kellett. 2004. 'Power.' In *Doing Research with Children and Young People*, edited by Sandy Fraser, Vicky Lewis, Sharon Ding, Mary Kellett and Chris Robinson, 81–96. London: Sage.

Rodríguez, Hernán, Laura Guzmán, and Nataly Yela. 2012. 'Factores personales que influyen en el desarrollo de la resiliencia en niños y niñas en edades comprendidas entre 7 y 12 años que se desarrollan en extrema pobreza.' *International Journal of Psychological Research* 5 (2): 98–107.

Roe, Emery M. (1992). 'Applied Narrative Analysis: The Tangency of Literary Criticism, Social Science and Policy Analysis.' *New Literary History* 23 (3): 555–581.

Salgado, Ana Cecilia. 2005. 'Métodos e instrumentos para medir la resiliencia: una alternativa peruana.' *Liberabit Revista de Psicología* 1 (11): 41–48.

Seccombe, Karen. 2002. "Beating the Odds' versus 'Changing the Odds': Poverty, Resilience, and Family Policy.' *Journal of Marriage and Family* 64 (2): 384–394.

Smith, Linda Tuhiwai. 2006. *Decolonizing Methodologies*. London: Zed Books.

Stone, Deborah. 2002. *Policy Paradox: The Art of Political Decision Making. Revised Edition*. 3rd edn. New York: W.W. Norton.

Thomson, Pat. 2008. 'Children and Young People: Voices in Visual Research.' In *Doing Visual Research with Children and Young People*, edited by Pat Thomson, 1–20. London: Routledge.

Viruru, Radhika, and Gaile Cannella. 2005. 'La etnografía poscolonial, los niños y la voz.' In *Las identidades en la educación temprana*, edited by Susan Grieshaber and Gaile S. Cannella, 239–256. México: Fondo de Cultura Económica.

Wade, Peter. 1997. *Race and Ethnicity in Latin America*. London: Pluto Press.

Werner, Emmy, and Ruth Smith. 1982. *Vulnerable but Invincible: A Study of Resilient Children and Youth*. New York: McGraw Hill.

Zimmerman, Marc A., and Revathy Arunkumar. 1994. 'Resiliency Research: Implications for Schools and Policy.' *Social Policy Report: Society for Research in Child Development* 8 (4): 13–35.

Part III
Questioning the project of schooling and the politics of development

7 Policy constructions of childhoods

Impacts of multi-level education and development policy processes in Southeast Asia and the South Pacific

Alexandra McCormick

Educational development policy discourses position the 'poor child' in aid-receiving countries, via her formal schooling, as the central hope for national development and growth. In this chapter I demonstrate this with respect to the ways that globally engineered policy discourses have circulated in the postcolonial contexts of Southeast Asia and the South Pacific. These discourses – and the processes that drive their transmission – have shaped two major and current development initiatives: the United Nations' *Education for All* (EFA) initiative established in 1990, and the *Millennium Development Goals* (MDGs) of 2000. Both of these global development campaigns promote the universalisation of primary schooling and gender equality, with the aim of achieving these two goals by 2015. Importantly, EFA proffers four additional education goals, for: early childhood care and education, adult literacy, quality of education and life-long training opportunities. The six policy areas included in EFA promote a holistic approach for education beyond formal primary schooling, and are founded on understanding education as a human right. However, they have been elided with the two MDGs in pursuit of access to formal primary schooling, with a focus on girls. This narrowed emphasis has been translated into aid-receiving, postcolonial contexts by many donors and governments, with civil society organisations (CSOs) advocating the wider programme.

This chapter contributes evidence that, in practice, inequitable policy processes, that is, policy construction, negotiation, promotion and delivery, have determined the ways in which these global agendas have been interpreted and portrayed. These policy processes have led to the neglect of broader EFA dimensions that are significant both in their own right and for achieving relevant education for children in diverse contexts. Paradoxical portrayals of the 'poor child' as vulnerable and as the hope for national development have underpinned these discursive interpretations of education for growth. The close analysis of policy processes presented in this chapter disrupts simplistic and reductive notions of 'education development policy' that position it as a singular, coherent and uncontested entity. I argue that in order to challenge universalising discourses of the 'poor child', we must understand how these discourses take shape through inequitable policy participation and representation that is informed by power relations at multiple levels and in multiple contexts. Policy actors and mechanisms for organisation are historically and politically located through processes of contestation and governance. Within these negotiations particular choices – and voices – are deliberated, proposed and supported over others.

Research into multi-scalar (global, regional, sub-regional and national) policy processes can help us understand why global approaches to development via EFA and MDG frameworks have been viewed as ineffective or of limited relevance in diverse local contexts. This chapter reports on key findings from a critical discourse analysis (CDA) of multi-scalar education development policy to illustrate how policy processes have been exclusionary to differing degrees, and have maintained the neglect of the wider areas of EFA. By tracing the norms and political processes of how multi-scalar policy discourses have been adapted, imposed and/or rejected through sub-regions and national contexts in Southeast Asia and the South Pacific, this chapter illustrates the importance of renewed attention to how policies represent children and education, especially with the construction of 'post-2015 development' agendas underway.

The chapter draws on findings from a research project on education and development policies in the Asia Pacific region, funded by the former Australian Agency for International Development (AusAID). The research involved the CDA of multi-scalar educational development policy construction and transfer, including globally, regionally in Asia and the Pacific, and in six countries and their sub-regions: Cambodia, Laos, Indonesia, the Philippines, Papua New Guinea (PNG) and Vanuatu. In this chapter I present analysis of the ways in which particular purveyors of development discourses at multiple levels of policy activity have constructed, negotiated and promoted EFA and the MDGs to emphasise normative representations of children and their access to primary schooling in situations where the quality, relevance and even safety of schooling have been challenged. The multi-scalar scope of the analysis illustrates the processes and tools by which the global social policies of the MDGs and EFA have been articulated to sustain limiting conceptions of children, education and gender for development in strikingly similar ways across strikingly diverse contexts. In the latter part of the chapter I demonstrate the extensive influence of, and resistance to, these discursive interpretations in national policy processes through layers of contextual analysis of education and development in the sub-regions of the South Pacific/Melanesia, the Mekong Delta and insular Southeast Asia.

Investigating multi-level policies through critical discourse analysis

Critical discourse analysis is derived from critical theory, and here tied to critical development theories, in its emphasis on the roles of politics, power and language in shaping our social worlds (Fairclough 2003). It enables close contextual readings of how conceptions of education are represented in educational development policy mechanisms and documentation. This requires paying attention to the economic and political power of policy actors and the language used in naturalising and cementing particular policy conceptions and activities over others. The ways that discourses – comprising images, language and voice – are related to the construction of policy actors', including children's identities, is an area of increasing interest in education and development policy research (Stromquist 2007; Vavrus and Seghers 2010; McCormick 2012, 2014; Robinson 2013). Using CDA to analyse the legitimation and transfer of educational development discourses through multi-level policy activity enables systematic interrogation of education policy actors, in distinct and overlapping policy contexts, by asking such questions as: Who controls policy representations? Who is being represented in policies and processes? How are representations of education needs and priorities constructed and deployed? (Fairclough 2003; Blommaert 2009).

With the EFA and MDG 'deadline' of 2015, reflection on the significance of these global policies has increased in recent years in an attempt to understand their influence and to construct global 'post-2015 development' approaches (UNDP 2013). Understanding the roles of multi-level policy discourses in defining and framing issues is particularly important in the arena of official development aid. Bilateral funding agencies of richer nations – often former colonial rulers – strategically influence aid-receiving governments' policy options and decisions. They in turn work alongside or with multi-lateral agencies. Applying discourse analysis comparatively to multi-level policy documentation and non-written discursive activities and groups *denaturalises* the composition and direction of policy processes. This process is particularly significant to this book's project of denaturalising the notion of the 'poor child' and her 'development' (see introductory chapter by Hopkins and Sriprakash); it reveals and interrogates the norms and cultural politics driving representations of childhood at the policy level.

This chapter reports on the critical discourse analysis (CDA) of the EFA *National Action Plans* (NAP) and related multi-scalar educational development policy activities and documents, including from civil society actors.[1] The study from which this analysis is drawn used the tools of systemic functional linguistics to compare contexts, discursive content, inter-textuality and to produce an EFA 'genre chain' that instantiates EFA activities across different genres of actors, documents and meetings (Fairclough 2003; McCormick 2011, 2012). A genre chain demonstrates how distinct types of activities and documentation mutually reinforce and naturalise one another through repetition and representation in various types of documents, fora and activities (of different genres). The substance of these activities and documents in turn inter-textually reinforces particular representations and representatives' authority over others, as for example seen in the emphasis on the MDG goals. The EFA genre chain in Table 7.1 depicts the range of EFA activities for the global, Asia Pacific and sub-regional and national contexts within this study. It captures the depth, flows and range of discursive activity involved in these policy processes. Of course, any representation can be only partial in light of the ongoing proscriptive reach of EFA activities, and the dense as well as broad reach of inter-references. The research made use of interviews, focus groups and observation with education policy actors (government, aid agency and civil society employees) from six nations in three sub-regions in Southeast Asia and the South Pacific to supplement the document analysis. These research tools worked to identify, analyse and map policy actors and mechanisms that constitute enacted discourses.

As the information collected in the genre chain in Table 7.1 demonstrates, the EFA initiative has arguably increased the range of social actors who are involved in education and development policy, from politicians and organisation employees to advocates and educators (see examples of activities and actors in columns two and four), as well as the kind of attention given to education policy articulation and integration. The genre chain serves to make taken-for-granted aspects of educational development policy more explicit. These often-obscured aspects of process concern both agents and education-related topics or substance, including the actors involved in policy debates and decision-making, as well as the content and types of education for analytical scrutiny. Moreover, in being analysed discretely according to geographical scale as they are here (see column one of Table 7.1), and in deconstructing these activities, documents and actors by genre, the table demonstrates how polices 'travel' and are reinforced in multiple contexts by these different actors. The descriptions in column two serve to map the activities and documentation that establish and maintain education – and EFA – as a shared social issue. The third column locates the activities and documents generically in order to document and trace what Blommaert (2009) identifies as re-entextualisation (and so reinforcement), and how that occurs within the field of EFA. The fourth column deconstructs the texts by the characteristics of actor, language, location, orientation, purpose and other relevant elements.

The analysis that is reported throughout this chapter was conducted across the multi-scalar inter-textual contexts represented in Table 7.1. It considers historical and political elements that in turn shape the construction of and responses to EFA as a globally orchestrated initiative that is conducted through the range of genres demonstrated. Within this wider scale of discursive activities, the national EFA plans and their creators were proposed as the core tool to implement and transmit EFA and, as such, are the focus of the close document analysis discussed later in the chapter.

EFA and MDG representations of education and childhoods

The EFA goals and MDGs have been promoted by diverse development actors identified in the genre chain, including governments, international agencies, local development organisations and influential donors. While this diversity leads to differing interpretations of development by policy actors, globalised policy statements from powerful 'global' actors such as UNESCO, the World Bank and the OECD, legitimise and sanction constructions of childhood that have, by and

Table 7.1 Partial overview of a genre chain for *Education for All* (EFA)

Scale	Document/Event	Genre(s)	Characteristics
Global	World Conference on EFA (2000); World Education Forum (1990) Ministerial EFA meetings	Multiple: global conferences; associated preparatory documents; meetings	Senior level formal and informal discussions; consensus-building; plan preparation, strategy; presentations; networking; English language; multiple actors, mainly educated elite
	Jomtien Declaration (1990); Dakar Framework for Action (DFA) 2000	Report; action statement; policy guide	Formal text – statement of intent; English; normative strategy; socialisation
	Global Campaign for Education (GCE) campaigns	Campaigns: web-based, flyers, reports	Information sharing; networking; non-state actors; English
	UNESCO EFA National Plan Guidelines	Formal policy document	Normative statement; written guidelines; English
	EFA websites	Multiple: advocacy statements; reports; fundraising	Campaign statements; information-sharing; English, some translations; multiple government and NGO agencies
	EFA research	Academic/agency/organisation interviews, papers, books	Academic/research conventions/norms; information-gathering and sharing; reviewed
	UNESCO Global Monitoring Reports/ (agency) reviews	Comparative assessment report; action statement	Global and national monitoring; English statistical evaluation; renews DFA

(*continued*)

Table 7.1 (continued)

Scale	Document/Event	Genre(s)	Characteristics
Regional Asia Pacific (therefore other world regions also have similar) ⇔	Regional pre-Dakar meeting	Senior and mid-level planning meeting	Mid-level bureaucratic meetings; presentations; predominantly English
	Dakar regional statement	Action strategy	Written text; multiple actors; English
	Multi-stakeholder regional EFA seminars	Planning/assessment/training groups; formal and informal preparatory and outcome documentation	Combinations of actors, various purposes; English, some translation
	Ministerial EFA meetings	Formal and informal preparatory and outcome documentation	Normative strategy; socialisation; English
	EFA mid-decade assessments (MDA) + guidelines	Comparative assessment report	Qualitative and quantitative evaluation; English
	Regional assessment reports		
	Asia South Pacific Association for Basic and Adult Education (ASPBAE, regional NGO) website; research; workshops	Multiple and hybrid; formal and informal preparatory and outcome documentation	Multiple media and locations; information sharing; networking; advocacy; English; socialisation
Sub-regional ⇔	Pacific forum meetings	Senior and mid-level government planning meeting	Mid-level bureaucratic meeting; comparison of national experiences/strategies; English
	UNESCO Bangkok/Apia; Pacific multi-stakeholder EFA seminars (EFAMDA)	UN-led/combined planning; assessment/training	Discussions; strategising; combinations of actors; English
	Training workshops	Planning/assessment/training	Multiple media and locations; English
	Assessment reports/EFA research	Formal documents/reports	Written texts; English

National ⇕	Post-Jomtien EFA activities	Multiple planning/activities	Senior planning, meetings; English and national language
	EFA forum	Plans/consultations/meetings/invitations	Information gathering; sharing; EFA National Action Plan (EFANAP) formation; multiple languages including English
	EFANAP	Policy and strategy document	Medium- to long-term policy structure; English and some national languages
	EFA 2000 reviews; EFAMDA; EFA end of decade assessment	Final report; assessment/monitoring	Education ministries' review process; assessment; English/national language
	EFA research (by academics, coalitions, ASPBAE, etc.)	Academic/agency/organisation interviews, papers, books	Academic/research conventions/norms; information-gathering and sharing; reviewed
	Bilateral strategies and documents; civil society organisations (CSOs) campaigns	Multiple: news, radio; training	Publicity/invitations/meeting; information exchange; updates; socialisation; multiple languages including English
Sub-national ⇐	Provincial/local EFA forums	Meetings; training	Mid-level bureaucrats; local leaders; local, national languages
	Provincial EFA plans	Provincial/local strategies	Localised plans; specific problems/strategies; local/national language (i.e. not English)
	Promotion of EFA	Multi-media information dissemination: news, radio; theatre	Socialisation; information sharing; range of actors, and languages
	Education activities	Formal/non-formal education, multiple types	Multiple learning/'classroom' situations; adults and children; local, national languages, including English (taught)

large, emerged from enlightenment and Victorian discourses (Kendall 2008). Schooling and performance have been 'naturalised' as the focus of these discourses, and reinforced through processes depicted in the genre chain. These pervasive discourses work to tie children to national economies, leisure, schooling and an inherent notion of vulnerability. Such ideas underpin the global policy statements that simultaneously depict children, especially girls, as vulnerable within wider social systems and economies, and position the 'poor child' as the hope for poor countries' development and growth (UNESCO 2000a; McCormick 2012). This section discusses more fully how the policy promotion of just two of the education-related MDGs – focused on universal primary education and girls' schooling – rather than the broader EFA goals, has obscured the different sociocultural contexts of children's lives, and rationalises them as abstract units of human capital serving national growth in competitive, globalised economies.[2]

The promotion of the two MDGs has in many contexts eclipsed the original, broader EFA programme for donors and governments (see also Torres (1999) in Unterhalter (2013)) despite the fact that the continued inequities that face children often relate to the quality, relevance and substance of their education, and to life prospects that lie beyond their access to formal schooling (McCormick 2011, 2012; UNDP 2013). The idea was crystallised in the push over the last decade to bring 'the last 10 per cent' of poor children into the fold of formal schooling, as closely as possible to the age and patterns designated by traditions in donor nations rather than through deliberations within local contexts (UNESCO 2008).[3] However, the quantifiable, time-bound global development agenda of the eight MDGs and narrower interpretation of EFA in line with two of these goals have been widely critiqued for their failure to recognise the lived realities of children, and their education, in highly varying contexts (Crossley and Watson 2003; Abadzi 2004; Alexander 2008; Sanga 2011; Unterhalter 2013).

Comparative analysis of the discursive content of global and national level policy statements also revealed tensions between 'Western' post-industrial norms of childhood and children's lives in varied contexts that are reflected in the mixed, and at times contradictory, policy emphases on formal mass schooling and on non-formal, ongoing education (McCormick 2012). As the statement below shows, despite the focus of EFA on the formal mass schooling sector in practice, the EFA *Dakar Framework* recognises the importance of non-formal on-going education:

> Young people should be given the opportunity for ongoing education . . . Such opportunities should be both meaningful and relevant to their environment and needs, help them become active agents in shaping their future and develop useful work-related skills.
> (UNESCO 2000a, 16)

Here the emphasis on opportunities for 'meaningful' learning highlights another ongoing struggle: to make the curriculum of formal mass schooling relevant for local contexts and the lived realities of children. The EFA *Dakar Framework* pays some attention to multiple forms of education, in recognition of the varying needs of children, and explicitly endorses 'imaginative and diverse approaches to address and actively engage children who are not enrolled in school' (16). Such discourses imply that a sole focus on formal mass schooling is inadequate, despite being seen as the central vehicle for national development in dominant development paradigms. Indeed, this tension is evident in the processes to construct a 'development agenda' beyond the 2015 EFA/MDG deadline, which reiterate the necessity of wider conceptualisations of education, although with continued focus on formal mass schooling (World Bank 2011; Democratic Republic of Timor Leste 2013; DfID 2013; McCormick 2014).

While the *Dakar Framework* explicitly recognises that context-relevant *Education for All* requires equitable policy processes that systematically and substantively incorporate contributions to policy processes from a broad range of people – including young people – and diversified approaches to measurement, this has not been consistently evident in practice (see, for example, Abadzi 2004; McCormick 2011, 2014). This is significant because it is civil society actors who have been the champions and providers of the marginalised education areas of EFA discussed above. However, as Table 7.2 illustrates, the acknowledgement of civil society engagement with the Dakar goals was piecemeal for most countries in the study. Column two of Table 7.2 summarises the limited role of civil society organisations (CSOs) in the construction of the EFA *National Action Plans* (NAP). The columns show the extent to which CSOs were included within the EFANAP for each of the six EFA goals. Document analysis and interviews that are discussed in the following sections revealed consistent civil society activity in all areas, especially in relation to gender; however, as Table 7.2 illustrates, this was not recognised in the EFANAP or by some donors and governments.

The multi-level contexts for these policy contributions and relationships are delineated in the following sections.

Policy contexts for EFA in Southeast Asia and the South Pacific

The genre chain maps aspects of how shared approaches to education policy organisation have been promulgated globally, regionally and nationally through conferences, documents, meetings and workshops. Discourse analysis of national education policy documents was combined with analysis of these policy activities to reveal the ways in which Southeast Asian and South Pacific sub-regions and nations have engaged in this widespread adaptation, adoption and rejection of EFA and the overlapping education MDGs. As illustrated in the genre chain (Table 7.1), the written texts represent an important component that, together with wider processes of their construction and reception, involve a range of activities, actors and agendas.

Regional policy dynamics

Before moving on to consider education policy activities and documentation within national contexts, I outline how children's education is represented in an

Table 7.2 EFANAP acknowledgement and inclusion of CSOs/NGOs against Dakar goals

Country	Inclusion of CSOs in EFANAP construction	Early Childhood Care and Ed.	(Inclusive) universal primary schooling	Quality	Gender	Adult Literacy	Life skills/Life-long learning
Cambodia	Named CSOs included in some aspects	CSOs	Identifies specific NGOs; curriculum	X	Cross-cutting, (no specific CSO)	Identifies specific NGOs	Identifies specific NGOs
Laos	None documented; representative of youth and women's mass organisations on national EFA committee	Community with INGOs	'... mobilise the civil society, local foundations and INGOs to provide scholarships for the poorest children'	X	X	'... strategy is needed ... civil society involvement in combating illiteracy'; 'coordinate literacy' with armed forces social activities	X
Indonesia	One general reference to 'community'; none documented	Community NGOs	X	X	X	X	NGOs, local community management
The Philippines	Named CSOs included in some aspects; used 2000 EFA review to demand inclusion	NGOs	Call for involvement of multiple actors in curriculum	X	X	Identifies specific NGOs	X
Papua New Guinea	One-off community consultation	Community	Churches, community 'in kind'	X	X	NGOs, community	Vocational/ church and 'able orgs'
Vanuatu	Unclear – one-off EFA forum held in 2001	National NGO; community	Vanuatu Society for Disabled People 'important NGO'; NGOs 'inform' primary students	Community level responsibility	X	Non-state; community; 'church-based'	Identifies a specific NGO

Note: 'X' denotes a lack of reference in the *Education for All* National Action Plan (EFANAP). CSO, civil society organisation; INGO, international non-governmental

EFA regional policy statement – the *Asia and Pacific Regional Framework for Action* – in order to map and analyse another important layer of multi-scalar discursive policy activity. The *Asia and Pacific Regional Framework for Action*, released in 2000 by UNESCO, restates the importance of interpreting education in a wider form than schooling. It repeatedly asserts the need to recognise and strengthen both formal and non-formal education (UNESCO 2000a, 57– 62), and identifies as a 'challenge' the 'lack of emphasis on alternative, non-formal approaches to basic education' (57). In addition to engaging in alternative approaches to education, this policy addresses the need to look at formal schooling in broader terms than simply measuring enrolment numbers. It acknowledges increases in primary enrolment in the Asia and Pacific region but notes that 'not enough attention is paid to the retention rate nor the completion of schooling', and that there is therefore a need to recast 'curricula to address the new risks and challenges facing youth in the region' (UNESCO 2000a, 57).

Importantly, the regional framework acknowledges the diverse range of educational approaches that should be considered. It cautions that:

> Care must be taken, however, not to place too much emphasis on child learners at the expense of adult learners . . . Likewise, care should be exercised with official EFA documents, pronouncements and pictures, so as not to convey the false impression that EFA is only about children.
> (UNESCO 2000a, 62)

The emphasis here on deploying the full EFA programme, beyond access to formal schooling, is clear. It also suggests that there is a tendency to elide EFA with access to schooling, along the lines of the MDGs, and so to represent a narrowed approach to education.

This regional policy therefore advocates for principles that are recognised in the wider Dakar/EFA programme, and in this sense also represents a more inclusive approach to childhood and education than the MDGs. In calling for educational policies to take a more holistic approach to children's education, the regional framework also attempts to engage children in decision-making about education, perhaps drawing on the call for participatory approaches embedded in the United Nations Convention on the Rights of the Child (UNCRC) (Mannion 2007). It states that 'children's participation in the Education for All process should be encouraged, considering that childhood is the time when most people begin formal basic education' (UNESCO 2000a, 62). Such an approach to childhood underscores the need for children's voices to be heard, yet, as scholars have argued, this, too, emerges from 'Western' ways of thinking about children (Mannion 2007).

As policy activities are also conducted at sub-regional levels, understanding sub-regional contrasts helps to highlight the ways that more nuanced dynamics play out in contextual and historical aspects of education policy. Sub-regions share climatic and geographical characteristics, histories and practices; indeed some boundaries have been externally imposed, or recently drawn. It is beyond the scope of this chapter to give detailed accounts of this layer of contextual factors, but I will give some examples. Common to the larger, middle-income economies of insular Southeast Asia are issues of scale and inequality in acknowledging and supporting diverse educational needs. The post-conflict situations and politically hierarchical environments of the Mekong Delta nations present significant contextual dynamics that include a lack of equity in participation in, and translation of, policy processes. Collectivist cultural foundations, land ownership dynamics (strongly tied to alternative interpretations of poverty discussed below), linguistic diversity and complex communications and transportation infrastructure are important contextual distinctions that have had impacts on national approaches to EFA policies in the South Pacific and Melanesia. Long histories of South Pacific regional politics, tensions and solidarities have likewise been influential.

National processes, plans and contexts

In the context of the wider EFA initiative that is depicted in the genre chain (Table 7.1), the national EFA processes and action plans were stipulated in the EFA *Dakar Framework* as the core policy tool to realise and transmit EFA goals and norms nationally and, as such, were the focus of close, comparative document analysis. These are in the main modelled on the global *Guidelines for EFA National Action Plans* (a template for process and form) and the *Dakar Framework for Action* (UNESCO 2000a, 2000b). Before discussing the national action plans more closely, I examine Table 7.3 which maps education and development policy and working groups for the six countries by types of education policy actors. According to various education sector actors within the six countries studied, it has been national elites with international groups who have determined educational development policy group composition (see Table 7.3). The composition of and distinctions between groups illustrated here has reinforced existing domestic, regional and global political power dynamics and particular interests, with local CSO representatives included only in some cases, and has in turn been reinforced by international bureaucratic requirements and processes (see Table 7.2). As Table 7.3 and the discussion of specific sub-regional and national contexts below indicate, in all places procedural requirements entailed a degree of government or donor resistance to civil society contributions. This was also evident in the acknowledgement of CSO involvement depicted in Table 7.2. Prescriptive requirements have narrowed the areas of education that the groups have been able to address, diverting their focus away from local and towards global accountability. This has had impacts on the diversity of educational approaches, particularly in terms of outcomes for minority groups and girls' education, as well as non-formal schooling. An emphasis placed on primary schooling – and as a corollary the de-emphasis or absence of adult literacy and other areas – in this documentation, at these fora and by these actors, was found across my analysis of the national-level documentation, policy contexts and interviews.

Table 7.3 Mechanisms for education policy deliberation

Country	Education group			Donor coordination group (and lead); CSO attendance
	National education CSO coalition	Government educational development group		
Cambodia	NGO Education Partnership (NEP)	Joint Technical Working Group, Education (JTWG-Ed); NEP representative		ESWG (WB); NEP representative
Laos	No national coalition (informal INGO network)	Biannual sector working group meetings (executive); bimonthly technical meetings		E(G)SWG; (AusAID/UNICEF); INGO representative, ministry 'liaison'
Indonesia	Indonesia E-Net for Justice	BAPPENAS – inter-departmental development forum		Informal donor working group (intended 6-monthly leadership, in practice AusAID)
The Philippines	Philippines Education Civil Society Network for Justice (E-Net)	Education sub-committee of PDF (Philippines Development Forum); E-net representative		Informal working group (AusAID)
Papua New Guinea	PNG Education Advocacy Network (PEAN)	(National Education Board and Department of Education)		Informal group (UNICEF)
Vanuatu	Vanuatu Education Policy Advocacy Coalition (VEPAC)	None identified (MoE staff attend EPG)		Monthly EPG (annual rotation); CSO attendance after 2013

Note: CSO, civil society organisation; E(G)SWG, Education (Gender) Sector Working Group; EPG, Education Partners Group; ESWG, Education Sector Working Group (World Bank); INGO, international non-governmental organisation; MoE, Ministry of Education; NGO, non-governmental organisation.

The rest of the chapter considers analyses of national policy contexts and historical and socio-political contexts that determine children's education. All six nations have adopted and promoted the EFA and MDG goals to some extent. They have agreed at least rhetorically to their principles in producing EFA National Action Plans and MDG reports, and in this sense have supported the norms around governance, reform and schooling, and have enshrined some of these in their constitutions and in national education laws pertaining particularly to universal primary schooling.

Importantly, the national approaches to EFA planning, policy and content bear a striking degree of similarity across the six countries and sub-regions in this study, in spite of clear cultural, geographical, political and social distinctions (see again Table 7.1 (the genre chain) and Table 7.3 (national policy mechanisms)), thus illustrating EFA and donor influence on the composition and formation of donor and government education sector working groups (McCormick 2011, 2012). In interviews with educational development actors in all six countries, reforms of school systems and of how aid to education was managed and delivered were recurring themes. 'Basic' education was elided with primary schooling in most instances, and occasionally the shift in donor attention to lower secondary was invoked. Interestingly, Cambodian, PNG and Vanuatu EFA plans modify and explicitly reject EFA time frames.

The national plans at once sought to assert national identities and interests, and to reconcile these with the language, norms and processes of the EFA programme. The analysis of multi-level education and development discourses reveals the predominant use of hybrid discourses (for example combining rights-based, justice oriented, instrumentalist aims) in the EFA *National Action Plans* (NAP), and tensions around how elements of EFA discourses are addressed and combined within them. The EFANAP emphasise the promotion of human rights and social justice through contextually relevant education approaches.

The analysis revealed that there were tensions between countries' conformity with globally devised templates – tied to both donor funding and legitimacy – and the reiteration of national priorities. PNG, Vanuatu, Indonesia and the Philippines all heavily emphasised national education and development discourses in their constitutions and EFANAP. Such discursive assertions stem in part from relatively recent independence movements, establishing cohesive citizenries and national identities. An example was the idea of 'integral human development' in PNG, which highlights relevant community-based education for children, established in the constitution and reiterated after independence in the Matane Report (DoE-PNG 1986) and in education plans. It is an approach that explicitly challenges the transferability of methods and targets not suited to the vast range of linguistic and social circumstances which children in PNG experience. Likewise, there was emphasis on *kastom* that includes relationships with land, traditions and spiritual dimensions of education in Vanuatu and, to a lesser extent, Indonesia's national discourse of *Pancasila*, as discussed below.

While Cambodia and Laos invoke their respective Angkorian and Lane Xang dynastic legacies, textual analysis revealed their most recent national constitutions and EFA documentation to be explicitly discursively geared to human resources development and children's formal education for economic competitiveness and growth; a finding that was corroborated in interviews. Such uptake of formal schooling oriented toward developing human resources in national policy and national constitutions exemplifies a global norm endorsed in policy form, and in some of these contexts increasingly in practice.

The following sections derive from the stage of CDA that located children's education in their historical, political and social contexts sub-regionally and nationally, and seek to demonstrate the importance of relevant, nuanced conceptualisations of childhood, education and gender in light of the preceding discussions and other aspects of CDA that have been presented.

The South Pacific/Melanesia: Papua New Guinea and Vanuatu

Education across the islands we know as PNG and Vanuatu had been clan and village-based prior to nineteenth century invasions by various Christian denominations of German, French and British nationality. Children's learning involved acquiring skills relevant to life in the many differing geographical and social contexts (Reta 2010). Distinctions between childhood and adulthood, and transitions between the two, were marked ceremonially and still vary across the islands (Maclean 2004). With missionary incursions came formal literacy training as a 'civilising' tool; this literacy was in the language of whichever moral authority had landed and managed to survive in given areas. Although some churches gave attention to locally relevant skills, such education remained within frameworks that inculcated Christian beliefs and European practices, for example regarding 'hygiene' and 'morality' (Hauck *et al.* 2005).

Long-standing and much publicised law and order problems involving young people in PNG have been tied to urban drift and unemployment after pursuing formal education of limited relevance to predominantly rural contexts. The contradictions inherent in expanding access to 'Westernised' models of schooling, lifestyle and aspirations, but with lack of availability and quality of secondary and higher education to fulfil such hopes, have long been acknowledged (Ahai and Faraclas 1993; Reta 2010; Namorong 2011). Parental disillusionment with formal schooling of poor quality and little relevance resulted in a return to community pre-schooling in 'mother tongues'. However, the issue has been highly politicised, and this perceived failure of schooling has existed in parallel with support for what is seen as the surest way to improved circumstances: 'modern' lifestyles at the individual level, gained through English-language schooling, and integration into the global economy at the national level. The importance of vocational education has been emphasised in PNG and Vanuatu, where access to secondary school is limited by availability and, especially, by expense. A recent sub-regional Melanesian initiative has been the *Alternative Indicators of Well-being* project, piloted in Vanuatu and currently being extended. It asserts the relevance of alternative conceptions and measures of poverty and well-being. This perspective echoes many critiques of the limitations of the MDGs from the Pacific region (Malvatumauri 2012; Democratic Republic of Timor Leste, 2013).

The distinctive history of dual colonisation in Vanuatu has combined with a linguistic diversity paralleled only in PNG to render educational development challenges particularly complex. The politicisation of language use has exacerbated its divisiveness as an issue for education. Education has been an implicit component of debates in terms of linguistic medium and content, compounded by its potential to shore up the power and longevity of the Francophile or Anglophile paradigms. The dual French and English education system has been contentious, and has affected educational aid, assessment, content, governance, resources and training. Alongside concerns about decentralisation and governance, these complex institutional arrangements have been ongoing consequences of the Condominium. The increasing prevalence of the third national language, Bislama, and 115 local languages shape children's experiences and the quality of education and training (Tryon 1998; Early 1999). The daily reality for many *ni-Vanuatu* children and families is a tri-lingual or multi-lingual one, with some siblings in distinct school systems (Early 1999). The growth and spread of the use of Bislama, and its rise as a medium of instruction, has been due to increasing levels of 'urban drift', population growth and resulting inter-marriage. The youth centre and multi-lingual theatre and video productions of the local non-governmental organisation (NGO) *Wan Smol Bag* tackle these and other issues affecting young people and their education, such as 'push-out' (being forced out of school due to limited places), unemployment and HIV, and reach audiences across the islands and regionally.

Cultural, political and social differences between provinces and regions in PNG and Vanuatu represent salient disparities with particular importance for norms around gender equality:

> there is a very significant gap between the relatively high educational performance in matrilineal societies and the much lower performance in most patrilineal societies . . . Girls are often kept at home since it is assumed that they will become homemakers . . . many girls, particularly in the highlands region still get married at an early age.
>
> (Government of PNG 2004, 15)

The gendering practices within communities therefore have significant impact on families' and girls' decisions about schooling. The continuation in some areas of the customary practice of 'bride price' and/or polygamy suggests conflicting norms regarding identity and the roles of girls and women. Having undertaken extensive research in Manus Province in PNG, Gustafsson (1999) underlines that 'models [of gender relations] derived from the Western world do not have the power to explain such cultural differences, nor can they fully account for the implicit meaning of the roles and statuses of men and women in Papua New Guinea society' (1). The high and widespread incidence of domestic violence and violence against children is indicative of challenges that have faced women in areas of PNG and Vanuatu (Vatnabar 2003). According to Gustafsson (1999), the existence – and persistence – of this, and other gender-related issues, can in part be traced to missionary and colonial incursions: 'The modernisation process has brought with it a separation between private and public spheres, and a much stricter line of demarcation between male and female activities' (3).

The lived experiences of *ni-Vanuatu* women are also embedded within wider cultural phenomena, wherein elements of *kastom* (a broad phenomenon taking in customs, traditional beliefs and practices) and Christianity are in tension with contemporary discourses of human – and, in parallel, women's and children's – rights, in spite of these being enshrined in the constitution, and adopted through globalised development rhetoric and strategies, signifying a dissonance in expectations of education. Women, families and communities in most parts of Vanuatu have retained many of those considered 'traditional' roles, especially in rural and remote communities. An NGO reported that communities had expressed hostility and challenged globalised discourses of 'child rights' and girls' rights as compromising those of adults and communities.

Expectations tied to these roles have direct implications for the nature and extent of education for boys and girls. Women are outside the structure of chiefs, as well as outside the structure of the imported political system, there having been only two female parliamentarians (Cox *et al.* 2007). With schooling still focussed on preparing an elite cadre for governing, the lack of political and professional female role models and perceived lack of relevance or prospects can deter girls or their families (Regenvanu 2009). In the formal system, more girls access primary school, but there is a significant drop in attendance for secondary school, tied to expectations of community roles (Government of Vanuatu 2004; Strachan 2004). Both male and female NGO workers reported that some women support the continuation of these structures, and male-dominated patterns are reinforced through styles of government, including donor consultations, although generational and locational differences are emerging. However, the extent to which this is particularly associated with *kastom* in Vanuatu is contested (Piau-Lynch 2007, 5). Difficulties passing the Family Protection Bill again reflect the conflict between informal chief-based structures of resolution and the formal legal system (Cox *et al.* 2007). As in PNG, the role of the churches in education in Vanuatu is strong: Cox *et al.* note that 'the combination of chiefs and churches can be patriarchal and socially conservative' (2007, 48) and has contributed to inter-generational conflicts.

The Mekong Delta: Cambodia and Laos

Even amidst rapid infrastructural development, the militarised recent history of Cambodia and Laos is evident in all aspects of life, from material effects of lives and land lost and damaged, to the extensive psychological and social repercussions of the 1975–1979 genocide, civil war during the 1980s, and extended control under a militaristic state. There are unquantifiable emotional and practical consequences of the fact that within living memory more than three-quarters of the educated were killed, tortured or fled (Dy and Ninomiya 2003). In 2010, over a third of Cambodia's population of more than 14 million were under 18 years of age (UNICEF 2013). Although difficult to identify accurately, Save the Children estimates that approximately 8 per cent of Cambodian children are orphaned. Nee and Healy reflect on ramifications of the recent militarised state control, and norms embedded as a result:

> Within living memory people have lived through a regime where even the value of their lives was not respected by the state. The values of the reciprocal relationships of family and patronage assume more importance than do any broader responsibilities of community or nation.
>
> (2004, 39)

Prescribed family and community roles do continue in some places for women. Buddhist traditions and Pagoda schools have been influential, promoting social norms prohibiting girls' involvement, particularly in rural areas, which again varies according to particular education contexts. Although there have been increases in school access for girls in recent years, education, literacy and schooling rates for girls and women remain behind those of men at all levels in Cambodia and Laos.

Unlike neighbouring Cambodia, Laos' population of around 6.3 million is extremely ethnically diverse. With population growth continuing amongst highland minorities and up-land ethnic groups, there are tensions between these groups and the low-land Lao-T'ai, whose birth rates are falling, but who have traditionally dominated politically and socially (Government of the Lao PDR 2008). Children of ethnic minorities may be forced into schools to learn in the official national language – for many a foreign one – from teachers who may not understand their first or only language (Adams *et al.* 2001). The importance of schooling and language of instruction for building national cohesion, and state authority, was evident in the documentation and policy groupings of both countries (McCormick 2012).

Although Cambodian civil society was excluded from EFA negotiations in various ways related to policy content, information sharing and education policy decision-making processes, its education civil society coalition, the National Education Partnership, has been highly active and recognised institutionally, with scope to influence policy agendas for early childhood and non-formal education. In Laos, however, according to informants, the government did not acknowledge local NGOs. Furthermore, organisations in the international NGO policy group were regarded as 'development agencies' rather than as advocacy-based organisations. This limited the scope for considering diverse education and language approaches for children in minority groups, although tentative recognition of other languages was beginning. Development organisations were aware in their activities of not being critical of government education policies.

Insular Southeast Asia: Indonesia and the Philippines

Indonesia's first education institutions were established when Islam permeated the islands from the late thirteenth century, synthesising with animist and other beliefs (Park and Niyozov 2008). This variety has had lasting implications for education content and delivery. From 1945, Bahasa Indonesia, or Indonesian, became the sole language of formal education, with the exception in nine regions of the first three years of elementary school (Nababan 1991, 115). In contrast, the complex colonial and linguistic trajectories of the Philippines have had lasting effects on education policy processes affecting children. While there are approximately 175 languages in use, the education system officially works in Filipino (Tagalog) and English. In practice, many schools employ some form of bridging lessons or bilingual teaching. Issues of quality and relevance in education have had ongoing importance in both countries for language and political and religious identities.

Debates around Muslim and mainstream (in the Philippines, predominantly Catholic) discrimination in schooling have long existed in both nations. In the Philippines it has been in the conflicted Southern region of Mindanao. The former AusAID and other donors have been concentrated in these poorest areas, where there has been a focus on girls' schooling. In Indonesia, a higher proportion of girls attend *madari*, or Islamic schools, which has been a safer and cheaper option of better quality in some places. However, NGO workers and Indonesian academics reported that there is a potential cultural and gender bias in some such schools (Cipta *et al.* 2009).

The situations of girls and women in Indonesia and the Philippines vary significantly across the countries. For example, within Indonesia vast differences exist between areas governed by Shariah Law in Aceh and large cities like Jakarta and Yogyakarta. Gender parity at primary level was achieved in Indonesia in the 1990s, and in some areas girls' enrolment is higher than boys' at junior secondary level, but declines sharply at secondary level due to prohibitive costs or social expectations. In the Philippines, an important activity has been the civil society education coalition's 'E-net for Justice', which works with young people to raise awareness of EFA in communities for holding government accountable to wider global commitments. Nationally, E-net has successfully campaigned for increased attention through the 'Alternative Learning Systems' stream of education beyond formal schooling. E-net has in addition been integral to multi-scalar advocacy through the regional Asia and South Pacific Association for Basic and Adult Education (ASPBAE) and as a co-chair on the Global Campaign for Education.

Conclusions

Dominant development policy discourses and multi-level education policy processes have sustained particular representations of 'poor' children in aid-receiving countries, and for their education needs. Although young people and civil society are increasingly acknowledged as active agents within some of these processes, their participation, like that of CSOs more broadly, is not yet consistent or institutionalised. In all countries, the common civil society policy promotion of EFA *Dakar Framework* areas beyond primary school access (but that are significant in children's education including early childhood care and education, life-long education and adult literacy) was found to be in tension with donor and state promotion of those MDG goals of primary schooling and gender equality. Contrary to what might have been expected in light of that focus, gender equality is an area where the normative influence of the policy interpretation was mixed in all nations.

The 'poor child' has been represented in policies that have been transferred by donors and governments as at once an economic hope and a figure to be protected through access to systems of schooling based on global, or 'Western', models. I have noted trends, albeit piecemeal, in civil society participation, and that have promoted a wider range of education approaches. These and post-2015 approaches are re-focusing on learning (Barrett, 2011) rather than simply being about access to school. As the original EFA declaration affirmed in 1990, and reaffirmed in the *Dakar Framework* in 2000, these aims of learning and of genuine, widespread participation in processes that determine how learning is best approached, are crucial to relevant education in diverse contexts.

This chapter has considered multilevel discursive policy processes through which representations of 'poor' children, and of their education needs, have been constructed and sustained. A CDA approach provides us with lenses to pose and begin to answer complex policy questions: Who sets agendas and decides on them? Who do policies actually and purportedly represent? And how are policies deployed? By analysing these elements at multiple levels, and making power relations explicit, we can better understand the perceived and practical disjuncture between the goals and application of global policies that affect children and their education. This type of analysis 'denaturalises' how policies for the education of the child are made and promoted. CDA offers a set of questions and tools for understanding the mechanics and power relations between multiple policy actors. Tracing the role of language and representation is an important stage in countering universalising notions of the 'poor child', and allows for more contextualised, nuanced ways to consider global 'education development policy'.

Notes

1 Given the detailed nature of the analysis conducted, including extensive contextual analysis of actors and literatures surveyed, this chapter presents only a partial depiction of the multi-scalar policy process (for fuller details see McCormick 2011, 2012, 2014). Throughout the chapter, comparative summary tables drawn from the multi-scalar CDA represent aspects of the activities and relationships that were analysed and mapped in considering these questions.
2 There are long-standing challenges to such a focus. For South Pacific perspectives see Democratic Republic of Timor Leste 2013, Sanga 2011, Thaman 2003 and McCormick 2014.

3 Improved school access figures for children, and particularly for girls, are seen as indicators of successful development outcomes (OECD 2007; UNESCO 2008; World Bank 2011). Globally, this is driven primarily by the MDG and distorted EFA paradigms, which have conceptualised improved access to schooling in terms of 'catching up' with economically oriented norms of employment and productivity (see also Sriprakash in this volume). Universal primary education was seen to bring about the highest rate of personal and national financial return (Psacharopoulos and Patrinos 2004). However, in a promising development, this idea has more recently been discredited as being oversimplified (Unterhalter 2013; DfID 2013).

References

Abadzi, Helen. 2004. 'Education for All or Just the Smartest Poor?' *Prospects* 34 (3): 271–289. doi: 10.1007/s11125-004-5308-8.

Adams, Don, Geok Hwa Kee, and Lin Lin. 2001. 'Linking Research, Policy, and Strategic Planning to Education Development in Lao People's Democratic Republic.' *Comparative Education Review* 45 (2): 220–241. doi: 0010-4086/2001/4502-0003.

Ahai, Naihuwo, and Nocholas Faraclas. 1993. 'Rights and Expectations in an Age of Debt Crisis: Literacy and Integral Human Development in Papua New Guinea.' In *Knowledge, Culture and Power: International Perspectives on Literacy as Policy and Practice*, edited by Peter Freebody and Anthony R. Welch, 82–101. London: Falmer Press.

Alexander, Robin. 2008. *Education for All, the Quality Imperative and the Problem of Pedagogy*. CREATE Pathways to Access, Research Monograph No. 20. London: CREATE.

Barrett, A. 2011. 'A Millennium Learning Goal for Education Post-2015: A Question of Outcomes or Processes.' *Comparative Education* 47 (1): 119–133.

Blommaert, Jan. 2009. 'Text and Context.' In *Applied Linguistics Methods, A Reader*, edited by Caroline Coffin, Theresa Lillis and Kieran O'Halloran, 182–200. London: Routledge.

Cipta, Andy, Aflina Mustaaina, Ni Loh Gusti Madewanti, and Titi Soentoro. 2009. *The Madrasah Education Development Project (MEDP) in Indonesia*. Jakarta: Solidaritas Perempuan (Women's Solidarity for Human Rights). http://www.forum-adb.org/docs/Madrasah-Education-Development-Project.pdf.

Cox, Marcus, Hannington Alatoa, Linda Kenni, Anna Naupa, Gregory Rawlings, Nikunj Soni, Charles Vatu, George Sokomanu, and Vincent Bulekone. 2007. *The Unfinished State: Drivers of Change in Vanuatu*. Canberra: AusAID.

Crossley, Michael, and Keith Watson. 2003. *Comparative and International Research in Education: Globalisation, Context and Difference*. London: Routledge/Falmer.

Democratic Republic of Timor Leste. 2013. *Key Conclusions from the Roundtable Consultation on Pacific Issues: International Conference on the Post-2015 Development Agenda: 'Development for All: Stop Conflict, Build States and Eradicate Poverty'*. Dili: Government of the Democratic Republic of East Timor.

DfID (Department for International Development). 2013. *Education Position Paper: Improving Learning, Expanding Opportunities*. UK: DfID.

DoE-PNG (Department of Education Papua New Guinea). 1986. *Ministerial Committee Report on a Philosophy of Education*. Port Moresby: DoE-PNG.

Dy, Sideth S., and Akira Ninomiya. 2003. 'Basic Education in Cambodia: The Impact of UNESCO on Policies in the 1990s.' *Education Policy Analysis Archives* 11 (48): 1–20. http://epaa.asu.edu/ojs/article/view/276/402.

Early, Robert. 1999. 'Double Trouble, and Three is a Crowd: Languages in Education and Official Languages in Vanuatu.' *Journal of Multilingual and Multicultural Development* 20 (1): 13–33.

Fairclough, Norman. 2003. *Analysing Discourse: Textual Analysis for Social Research*. London: Routledge.

Government of PNG. 2004. *Millennium Development Goals: Progress Report for Papua New Guinea 2004*. http://planipolis.iiep.unesco.org/upload/Papua%20New%20Guinea/Papua%20New%20Guinea%20MDG.pdf.

Government of the Lao PDR. 2008. *EFA Mid Decade Assessment*. Vientiane: Government of the Lao PDR.

Government of Vanuatu. 2004. *EFA National Plan of Action 2001–2015, Republic of Vanuatu*. Vanuatu: UNESCO.

Gustafsson, Berit. 1999. *Traditions and Modernities in Gender Roles: Transformations in Kinship and Marriage among the M'buke from Manus Province* (Vol. 35). Port Moresby: The National Research Institute.

Hauck, Volker, Angela Mandie-Filer, and Joe Bolger. 2005. *Ringing the Church Bell: The Role of Churches in Governance and Public Performance in Papua New Guinea*. Maastricht: European Centre for Development Policy Management.

Kendall, Nancy. 2008. ' 'Vulnerability' in AIDS-affected States: Rethinking Child Rights, Educational Institutions, and Development Paradigms.' *International Journal of Educational Development* 28 (4): 365–383. doi: 10.1016/j.ijedudev.2007.10.003.

Maclean, Neil. 2004. 'Learning to be a Kanaka: Menace and Mimicry in Papua New Guinea.' *The International Journal of Cultural and Social Practice* 48 (3): 69–89. http://www.academia.edu/4362596/.

Malvatumauri National Council of Chiefs (2012). *Alternative Indicators of Wellbeing for Melanesia: Vanuatu Pilot Study Report 2012*. Port Vila, Vanuatu: Malvatumauri National Council of Chiefs.

Mannion, Greg. 2007. 'Going Spatial, Going Relational: Why 'Listening to Children' and Children's Participation Needs Reframing.' *Discourse: Studies in the Cultural Politics of Education* 28 (3): 405–420. doi: 10.1080/01596300701458970.

McCormick, Alexandra. 2011. 'Some Partners are More Equal than Others: EFA and Civil Society in Papua New Guinea and Vanuatu Education Policy Processes.' *International Education Journal: Comparative Perspectives* 10 (2): 54–70.

McCormick, Alexandra. 2012. 'Whose Education Policies in Aid-receiving Countries? A Critical Discourse Analysis of Normative Transfer through Cambodia and Laos.' *Comparative Education Review* 56 (1): 18–47.

McCormick, Alexandra. 2014. 'Who are the Custodians of Pacific 'Post-2015' Education Futures? Policy Discourses, Education for All and the Millennium Development Goals.' *International Journal of Educational Development* 39: 163–172.

Nababan, P.W.J. 1991. 'Language in Education: The Case of Indonesia.' *International Review of Education* 37 (1): 115–131.

Namorong, Martin. 2011. '*The Political Economy of Everything That's Wrong in PNG.*' Keith Jackson and Friends: PNG Attitude. http://namorong.blogspot.com.au/2011/03/political-economy-of-everything-thats.html (accessed 1 April 2015).

Nee, Meas, and Joan Healy. 2004. *Towards Understanding: Cambodian Villages Beyond War.* North Sydney: Sisters of St. Joseph.
OECD. 2007. *Human Capital: How What You Know Shapes Your Life.* Paris: OECD.
Park, Jaddon, and Sarfaroz Niyozov. 2008. 'Madrasa Education in South Asia and Southeast Asia: Current Issues and Debates.' *Asia Pacific Journal of Education* 28 (4): 323–351.
Piau-Lynch, Andonia. 2007. *Vanuatu: Country Gender Profile.* Tokyo: JICA. http://www.jica.go.jp/english/our_work/thematic_issues/gender/background/pdf/e07van.pdf.
Psacharopoulos, George, and Harry Anthony Patrinos. 2004. 'Human Capital and Rates of Return.' In *International Handbook of Economics of Education*, edited by Geraint Johnes and Jill Johnes, 1–57. Cheltenham: Edward Elgar.
Regenvanu, Ralph. 2009. *The Traditional Economy as a Source of Resilience in Melanesia.* http://www.aidwatch.org.au/sites/aidwatch.org.au/files/Ralph-Brisbane2009LowyInstitute.pdf.
Reta, Medi. 2010. 'Border Crossing Knowledge Systems: A PNG Teacher's Autoethnography.' *The Australian Journal of Indigenous Education* 39 (1): 128–137.
Robinson, Kerry H. 2013. *Innocence, Knowledge and the Construction of Childhood.* Abingdon: Routledge.
Sanga, K. 2011. 'Reframing Pacific Regional Service Delivery: Opportunity Spaces for Together Apart.' *International Education Journal: Comparative Perspectives* 10 (2): 54–70.
Strachan, Jane. 2004. 'Gender and the Formal Education Sector in Vanuatu.' *Development Bulletin* 64: 73–77.
Stromquist, Nelly P. 2007. *The Gender Socialization Process in Schools: A Cross-National Comparison.* New York: UNESCO.
Thaman, K. 2003. *Educational Ideas from Oceania: Selected Readings.* Suva: University of the South Pacific.
Tryon, Darrell. 1998. 'Language, Space and Identity in Vanuatu.' In *Le Voyage Inachevé, à Joël Bonnemaison*, edited by Dominique Guillaud, Maorie Seysset and Annie Walter, 329–335. Paris: Orstom.
UNDP. 2013. *The Rise of the South: Human Progress in a Diverse World (Human Development Report 2013).* New York: UNDP.
UNESCO. 2000a. *The Dakar Framework for Action.* Paris: UNESCO.
UNESCO. 2000b. *Education for All: Preparation of National Plans of Action: Country Guidelines.* Paris: UNESCO.
UNESCO. 2008. *Global Monitoring Report: Education for All by 2015: Will We Make It?* Paris: UNESCO.
UNICEF. 2013. *Education in the Post-2015 Development Agenda: Regional Thematic Consultation in the Asia-Pacific. 28 February and 1 March 2013, Bangkok, Thailand. Outcomes and Recommendations.* UNICEF.
Unterhalter, Elaine. 2013. *Education Targets, Indicators and a Post-2015 Development Agenda: Education for All, the MDGs and Human Development.* London: University of London.
Vatnabar, Margaret G. 2003. 'Gender and Development in Papua New Guinea.' In *Building a Nation in Papua New Guinea: Views of the Post-Independence Generation*, edited by David Kavanamur, Charles Yala and Quinton Clements, 269–282. Canberra: Pandanus Books.

Vavrus, Frances, and Maud Seghers. 2010. 'Critical Discourse Analysis in Comparative Education: A Discursive Study of 'Partnership' in Tanzania's Poverty Reduction Policies.' *Comparative Education Review* 54 (1): 77–102. doi: 10.1086/647972.

World Bank. 2011. *Learning for All: Investing in People's Knowledge and Skills to Promote Development: World Bank Group Education Strategy 2020*. Washington, DC: The World Bank.

8 Modernity and multiple childhoods

Interrogating the education of the rural poor in global India

Arathi Sriprakash

Introduction

There is wide recognition in studies of childhood that the abstract universalism of the 'poor child' in education and development discourses fails to adequately acknowledge, much less address, the diversity of childhood experiences in different contexts. The notion of 'multiple childhoods' has gained much traction in childhood studies, as a way to capture the plurality of children's lived experiences, and to signal the importance of understanding the contexts of those lives for assembling policy and research agendas (James *et al.* 1998; Jenks 2008). As Indian childhood studies scholar Sarada Balagopalan observes in her recent book, the notion of 'multiple childhoods' has produced research 'that over the years denaturalised the assumed universality of concepts like biological age, adult-child differentiation, notions of childcare and children's work, and the affective investments that adults make in children' (Balagopalan 2014, 12). While this is an important project that has eschewed 'a pathological reading of children's lives in the non-west' (12), Balagopalan notes that the liberal tolerance of plurality implied through notions of 'multiple childhoods' has inadvertently de-linked children's lives from the workings of power and 'placed their cultural worlds as largely outside of history, the state and the market' (12). In this chapter, I take up this concern by exploring the limitations of a pluralistic reading of 'multiple childhoods' with respect to education development reforms, particularly in poor rural Indian communities.

The chapter focuses specifically on child-centred education programmes in rural Indian government elementary schools.[1] It examines the implications of a pluralistic figuration of 'the child' for teachers' discursive practices and for the modernist schooling project more broadly. Child-centred reform programmes, promoted by government and non-government development actors, draw on liberal discourses of pluralism by emphasising the importance of valuing rural children's home backgrounds, and treating each child as a unique individual with different and specific interests. However, at the same time, education reforms are establishing what it means to be a child in terms of middle-class, urban and globally oriented ideals of childhood in India. These ideals form the preferred citizen-subject in terms of the nation's recent economic growth, technological advancement and social modernisation. Reform discourses are largely silent on the socio-material conditions of both rural children's lives and of rural schooling practices. I argue that without an explicit and critical interrogation of the social and material contexts of children's lives, specifically relating to issues of modernity and capital, the notion of 'multiple childhoods' risks producing a 'separate but equal' understanding of different – and greatly unequal – childhoods in India (Balagopalan 2014, 12). As I demonstrate in this chapter, a pluralistic perspective on childhood in reform discourses can construct the 'poor child' and their lives as needing to be 'respected but not desired' (Balagopalan 2011, 293). This, I suggest, reinscribes deficit notions of the rural child in teachers' practices that can counter the inclusive and democratic possibilities of child-centred programmes and development more broadly.

The chapter begins with a discussion of the place of the rural 'poor child' in global, modern India. This leads to an examination of the development project occurring in the domain of education; one in which the child-subject is nurtured and developed through modernisation and economic growth. I analyse the ways in which the 'poor child' is constructed through education reform discourses to show how binary hierarchies are established between the rural poor child needing to be reformed, and the urban middle-class child as the preferred citizen-subject. This binary is examined more closely through ethnographic accounts of child-centred education in a rural district of the south Indian state of Karnataka, particularly through the perspectives of teachers. Drawing on Basil Bernstein's notions of 'recontextualisation', I present a sociological analysis of the ways in which teachers reshape reform ideals in their classrooms, and how this reshaping positions the poor rural child and their educational needs.

Urban ideals, global India and the 'poor child'

The confidence of the 'new' global India is seemingly ubiquitous, especially in cosmopolitan metropoles such as Bangalore and Mumbai. On billboards, television and in print media, the nation's aspirations for consumption, economic growth and an international outlook is captured in slogans appealing directly to 'the deserving global Indian', in images of middle-class families consuming modern lifestyle goods, and in corporate cityscapes that represent a prosperous new India. These are the domains for the urban English educated; the presumed bearers of India's modernity. Indeed, since the liberalisation of the economy in 1991, spaces have opened up for new formations of citizenship and a new politics of modernity. These domains are increasingly shaped by neoliberal logics of privatisation and individualisation, but they are also ones which reconstitute particular constructions of the 'traditional'. For example, scholars such as Gopalakrishnan (2006) and Basu (2008) have examined the ways in which Hindu religiosity has been asserted and reconstituted through consumer markets, especially via television, the internet and new media. As Kaviraj (2010, 11) points out, 'modernity does not build institutions in an empty space. It has to *rework* the logic of existing structures which have their own, sometimes surprisingly resilient, justificatory structures' (emphasis added). How the reworking of tradition/modernity occurs in the domain of education provides an illuminating insight into the tensions between urban middle-class ideals and the cultural and social positioning of the rural child living in poverty.

As researchers of Indian modernity have commented, the normative citizen-subject is positioned as male, upper caste, Hindu and English educated (Vasanta 2004; Kumar 2005; Lukose 2009; Kaviraj 2010); a powerful minority in a nation of immense social diversity and inequality. Contemporary discourses of educational development also construct the normative citizen-subject as middle-class and urban: those with available pathways into the global knowledge economy, especially the widely desired industries of technology and communications that have dominated India's recent narrative of economic ascendancy and social modernisation. India's economic growth has been led by the services sector which contributes nearly 50 per cent of GDP, with a small urban elite enjoying increased wealth. However, 90 per cent of India's labour force work in agriculture and the so-called informal sector, and have not had significant increases in wages (Binswanger-Mkhize 2013). Over the last two decades this has produced an even sharper divide between the urban middle classes and the rural poor.

Schooling can be seen to both respond to and drive the formation of the normative citizen-subject. The rapidly and dramatically transforming school market in India is a significant case in point. Fee-charging private schooling, especially with English-medium instruction – a marker of modernity and social mobility – has expanded considerably across both urban and rural areas in the last decade. Recent estimates suggest up to 30 per cent of elementary enrolments across the country are in non-government schools with the proportion much higher at secondary level (DFID 2011). The variation among these private institutions is marked, but it is through the diversity of the private schooling market that new mechanisms for status differentiation are produced across the social spectrum, from the aspirational middle classes to the more established elite. In order to appeal to different sections of the educational market, it is not uncommon to see schools in the private sector promoting the creation of 'global citizens', offering a 'distinct education', or emphasising employment pathways opened up by English instruction to otherwise excluded groups. Meanwhile, the fee-free, vernacular-medium public education system serves the nation's most socially and economically disadvantaged children. As Kaviraj (2010, 163) suggests, this kind of differentiation and educational segmentation has led to a 'quietly effective bifurcation' of the cultural imagining of Indian society, between English-speaking elites (as the desired citizen-subject) and vernacular aspirant groups. The growth of private education in the context of new formations of Indian modernity could be read, then, as a familiar tale of neoliberal forces in education: forces which simultaneously intensify social stratification *and* promise to open up new opportunities for social mobility.

Where does this leave the poor rural child? She is largely absent from cultural narratives of India's economic growth in terms of her linguistic, class and caste locations. The seeming irrelevance of her rural livelihood to the advancement of the nation's knowledge economy further underscores her marginality. Unable to access the spaces of private education, she also fails to live out the fervent aspiration for upward social mobility to which stories of both individual and national progress are attributed. A recognition of 'multiple childhoods' might acknowledge the difference of the rural 'poor child', but to the narrative of global India, this difference is not only undesirable, it runs counter to the ideals of national modernity itself. Being placed so firmly outside normative citizen-subjecthood, the 'poor child' is positioned as a governable subject *in need of reform*. In the following section, I examine the ways in which education policy establishes this particular need in relation to the project of development.

Contemporary education policy agendas for India's rural poor

Many of India's current education development activities are shaped by the priorities of the international *Education for All* campaign outlined in the *Dakar Framework for Action* at the 2000 World Education Forum. As a signatory, India has been committed to the time-bound target of achieving quality universal elementary education by 2015. However, it is important to recognise the ways in which national educational policy discourses also shape the country's priorities for education reform (see arguments made by McCormick in this volume). Indeed, by looking at the multiple policy discourses at work, we can begin to understand the local character of seemingly global discourses of education and development.

The *National Policy on Education 1986* (Government of India 1986) was released in the years leading up to India's economic liberalisation in 1991, and it provides an interesting insight into the ways in which neoliberal discourses and rationales for modernisation come to be reworked, legitimised and strengthened in the domain of education. The *National Policy on Education* explicitly ties the project of schooling to economic development, as section 1.2 of the policy states:

> The country has reached a stage in its economic and technical development when a major effort must be made to derive the maximum benefit from the assets already created and to ensure that the fruits of change reach all sections. Education is the highway to that goal.
>
> (Government of India 1986, 1.2)

This emphasis on education for economic and technical development reflects a now globally familiar understanding of the instrumental purpose of schooling; one that casts the student in human capital terms, and positions their education in relation to macroeconomic gains. In this perspective, issues of equity are addressed by an assumed trickle-down effect of economic growth: that the 'fruits of change reach all sections'.

However, the discourses of modernisation that run through the policy are inflected with caution. For example, reflecting the nation's foundations of Nehruvian socialism, the policy also states its unease towards economic linear expansion:

India's political and social life is passing through a phase, which poses the danger of erosion to long-accepted values. The goals of secularism, socialism, democracy and professional ethics are coming under increasing strain.
(Government of India 1986, 1.11)

Indeed, an interesting reworking of modernist economic rationalism emerges here, which allows for the 'long-accepted' (read, traditional) values of Indian society. This occurs through what Kaviraj (2010) calls 'the logic of existing structures', or as the policy identifies, 'the Indian way of thinking':

In the Indian way of thinking, a human being is a positive asset and a precious national resource, which needs to be cherished, nurtured and developed with tenderness, and care, coupled with dynamism.
(Government of India 1986, 1.10)

Here we start to see the local character of modernist development discourses in Indian education, in which a human capital model of development (in which humans are seen as an 'asset' and 'resource') is entwined with discourses of care and tenderness as well as with postcolonial politics. The policy presents a reworking of colonial discourses that had once positioned India as a childlike and primitive subject of the Empire (Nandy 1983). The postcolonial nation is now arguably constructed as an empowered maternal figure – reminiscent of the *Bharat Mata* or Mother India of the independence movement – charged with nurturing and developing its own child-citizens. The policy goes on to identify specific social groups who become entities for policy intervention; specific subjects for this nurture. As section 5.10 of the *National Policy on Education 1986* (NPE) states, 'The Government will, however, take special steps to cater to the needs of women, rural and tribal students and the deprived sections of society' (Government of India 1986, 5.10). Here, it is not just the child, but all members of these 'deprived' categories who are positioned as immanent subjects. The development of the postcolonial nation, therefore, is linked to the development and reform of these groups, including the rural 'poor child' (Burman 2008).

What is the role of education, particularly for these subjects of reform? The 1986 NPE explicitly emphasises that, as a means of nurturing the nation's children, schooling in India should have 'a warm, welcoming and encouraging approach, in which all concerned share a solicitude for the needs of the child' (Government of India 1986, 5.6). Specifically, the policy advocates the need for 'a child-centred and activity-based process of learning' for primary education (ibid., 5.6). The nurturing of the nation's human capital through education is tied explicitly to a child-centred pedagogic approach; in a sense, child-centred learning becomes a repository for India's reworked modernisation. The approach is positioned in stark contrast to the dominant mode of textbook-based, exam-centred, didactic instruction found across the nation's schools. Child-centred education, then, takes on an instrumental quality; it is the means to reform the (rural poor) child, though little is said in the NPE about how it is to take place in light of the existing structures and socio-material realities of government schooling or disadvantaged children's lives.

The role of child-centred education in India took a turn during the 1990s when the nation's education policy agendas became increasingly influenced by international ambitions linked to *Education for All* campaigns (see discussions in McCormick's chapter in this volume). Child-centred education came to be seen as a way of achieving the universalisation of primary education; an attractive, welcoming and even democratic school environment would help raise enrolment and retention rates, especially in rural areas. By the turn of the century, child-centred education was also seen as an indicator of quality education (Alexander 2008) in both national and international development discourse. The assumed alignment of child-centred education with quality education has been particularly powerful in guiding programme-level interventions in government schooling. Evaluations of government and non-government efforts to improve the quality of schooling came to rely on proxies for child-centred education, such as the use of wall-charts and student grouping, rather than on deeper understandings of 'quality' pedagogic processes – child-centred or otherwise (Alexander 2008).

With the human capital framing of India's education activity, and the aggressive neoliberal reforms that followed the 1986 NPE, the rural child has been cast as in need of 'nurture' through child-centred education, though arguably not primarily for her own empowerment, but for the growth of a national economy that remains unevenly and unjustly structured. The reworking of child-centred education – from its role in 'nurturing' the nation's human capital, to meeting targets for universalising primary education, and to improve the quality of schooling provision – illustrates the multiple discourses at play in India's education reform arena. As the next section explores, this has led to multiple conflicting messages being relayed to teachers working in poor communities about the role of education.

The modern educational project – a case study in Karnataka

Current government educational development reform in India is guided by the national Education for All programme, the Sarva Shiksha Abhiyan (SSA). Reflecting the focus of international Education for All agendas on quality universalisation of elementary education, the SSA was launched under the central Ministry of Human Resource Development in 2001 as an umbrella programme to oversee state-level activities in education. Each state has their own SSA office, and as part of decentralised planning, they manage their own reform activities. The discussions below focus on the reform projects of the south Indian state of Karnataka, to examine how the poor rural child is positioned in state educational programmes, and how these programmes play out in school communities. Indeed, Karnataka provides a particularly unique setting in which to examine the multiple constructions of the child through India's education reform activities.

The state prides itself as being educationally 'forward' compared to other Indian states, in terms of indicators such as access, enrolment and retention in primary schooling. It is also a confident player in the 'new global India'; the state's capital of Bangalore is a cosmopolitan metropolis, home to multinational corporations and technology companies and a growing urban, English-educated middle class. The state's identification with the nation's economic and technological advancement influences the prospective outlook of its education reform programmes. This becomes evident in the ambitions and approaches of the Government of Karnataka's SSA programme.

The 2010 SSA-Karnataka Annual Report outlines the main reform activities carried out in the government elementary schooling sector. Reforms are centred on improving the access, enrolment, retention and quality of government elementary schooling in the state (GoK 2011, 12). The report presents its 'compulsion for reform' in relation to a number of concomitant forces, namely: the commitment to international Education for All agendas; the need to address India's low ranking in the UNDP's Human Development Index; the lessons from the 'East Asia Miracle' in which long-term investment in elementary education has been associated with economic growth in South Korea, Thailand and Japan among other countries; and the public demand for quality universalisation of elementary education to be a fundamental right, as reflected by the 2009 Right to Education Act (GoK 2011, 9). This demonstrates the multiple drivers behind educational reform in Karnataka, from rights-based rationales to national economic growth.

What is notable in the SSA-Karnataka report is the way in which approaches to education reform have been strongly influenced by discourses of global engagement and technological advancement. These are discourses that are prominent in the domains of business and economics, which have now become legitimised in the field of educational development. SSA-Karnataka has made significant investments in computer-assisted learning programmes in over 3000 government elementary schools in order to improve achievement levels and attendance rates in poor communities. These programmes specifically focus on 'rural government school children by providing access to learning through modern technology' (GoK 2011, 177). There is a strong emphasis on public–private partnerships to achieve the state's goals for technological innovation in educational provision, particularly in the rural sector. For example, the report cites a number of privately funded initiatives to provide infrastructure such as computers and projectors, as well as curriculum support material and software.

The rationale for these programmes is repeatedly tied to the imperatives of a middle-class, urban, global economy: they provide the 'opportunity for underprivileged children to enhance their learning through the use of digital technology, also enabling them to participate in the technologically advanced global economy' (GoK 2011, 184). Social class contrasts, as well as urban/rural hierarchies, are made explicit in the aims of these programmes. For example, one initiative sponsored by a non-government community organisation and the multinational Pearson Education company offers computer infrastructure and multimedia resources to schools in order to provide rural students with 'exposure and tools on par with their economically better-off friends in private schools' (GoK 2011, 185). The language of 'friends' invokes a shared (if not level) playing field, but in fact it papers over the realities of deep class and caste social divides.

A recent study of rural parents' perspectives on SSA-Karnataka's Computer Assisted Learning programmes found that 'the computer has an immense symbolic value – separate from its functional value – that is tied to social and economic ascendancy' (Pal *et al.* 2009, 129). In particular, digital literacy was seen as a pathway to urban professions, enabling rural children to leave the agricultural sector and gain greater 'social respect' (Pal *et al.* 2009, 135). The aim of rural schooling in Karnataka is to modernise rural children, but this does little to value and acknowledge rural lives, especially the importance of the agricultural sector. By privileging the domains of the urban Indian elite, and positioning rural knowledge and livelihoods as lacking, such reforms reinscribe urban/rural class and caste hierarchies. As Balagopalan reflects on education reform for the poor in India:

> An urban, bourgeois, class-specific worldview thus gets translated through the discursive work for these education programs – with formal schooling at its heart – into the definition of the ideal "human" self. In the case of these first generation learners, this implies the inherent inferiorisation of their parents' livelihoods as well as their own past and present realities.
>
> (2008, 281)

Certainly, rural children must not be precluded from accessing powerful knowledge (such as computer education). However, the challenge for education policy is to eschew deficit discourses about rural cultures and livelihoods.

The liberal discourses of child-centred education go some way in promoting the idea that every child is unique and equal – offering a potential alternative to the 'poor rural child' as a deficit and homogenous category. These ideals have been taken up by SSA-Karnataka through a major state-wide programme for child-centred education in government primary schools called *Nali Kali*. Teachers across the rural primary sector have been trained in this activity-based method since its introduction in 1997. *Nali Kali* involves the use of stories, games, picture-cards and group work. In the early years of the programme, teachers were required to make their own learning resources based on local contexts and needs – the idea was to promote a locally relevant curriculum which valued the lived experiences and knowledge of rural poor communities. (As the programme was upscaled over the years, standardised material has been produced and distributed to teachers by the state.) Official discourses of the *Nali Kali* programme have constructed rural children as 'creative', 'different', 'equal', 'active' and 'independent', and as children who should have the 'freedom' to learn in 'democratic' and 'participatory' environments (Kaul 2004; see Sriprakash (2012) for a detailed analysis of reform discourses). Reform ideals resonate with liberal notions of 'multiple childhoods' by highlighting plurality and difference, and by positioning rural children as agentic subjects, whose participation in education is to be valued, and whose home backgrounds are to be respected.

Through its reform programmes, the state has relayed to rural primary school teachers in Karnataka multiple and at times discordant messages about the poor child. The rural child is constructed as in need of reform (in particular, to 'modernise' in the image of the urban middle class), and well as being an agentic individual to be valued. We begin to see how discourses of deficit and of valued plurality circulate simultaneously through state education policy. Captured here is the tension of modern schooling identified by Tyler (1993, 52), in which the aim is to both 'set the child free and to form the child more fully'. I turn now to discuss how this tension is negotiated by primary school teachers in Karnataka through their experiences of teaching in contexts of rural poverty.

Educating the rural child

The following discussion of the tensions of schooling for rural children in 'modern' India is based on sociological research conducted in the rural district of Mysore, in Karnataka. Through ethnographic approaches, the study examined the ways in which primary school teachers understood and enacted reform programmes such as *Nali Kali* in the contexts of their under-resourced rural schools. This involved spending 1 year in the district and conducting extensive in-depth interviews with 22 teachers and writing detailed ethnographic accounts of practices in 16 school communities. Interviews were audio-recorded, conducted in a mixture of Kannada and English, and translated and transcribed into English. Pseudonyms for all participants have been used to protect their identities.

The analysis of teachers' discourse and practices draws on Basil Bernstein's sociological theory of 'recontextualisation'. Recontextualisation refers to the ways in which educational discourses are reshaped as they are moved, appropriated and brought into new relationships with other social discourses. It foregrounds the processes through which discourses are relocated and refocused, and traces the social and material forces at play in educational domains. This perspective encourages us to examine how social ideals about the child (for example, as 'different' and 'equal' in child-centred policy discourses) are reshaped – or recontextualised – through social and material lived realities (for example, the contexts of rural schooling). As Bernstein explains:

> As the discourse moves from its original site to its new positioning as a pedagogic discourse, a transformation takes place. The transformation takes place because every time a discourse moves from one position to another, there is a space in which ideology can play.
> (2000, 32)

The lens of recontextualisation helps us to engage with elements of what Kaviraj (2010) describes as the contextual 'reworking' of tradition/modernity in India; the process through which discourses about the poor rural child move and change in the education domain.

The 16 elementary schools included in the ethnographic study were funded and managed by the state government, and ranged in size from small schools of only 50 students in grades 1–5, to large schools of over 400 students in grades 1–7. The schools had basic resources and infrastructure typical of rural government elementary schools in the area: buildings were made of concrete and children generally had access to a small playing field. Free school lunches were provided by the government and were cooked on site. Classrooms were equipped with blackboards, but other learning materials, especially books, were scarce. It was quite usual for one teacher to have up to 50 students in a mixed-aged, mixed-grade class.

The schools were attended mainly by the children of landless agricultural labourers and smallholder farmers from the local villages. According to school records, only a handful of children across the schools had a parent who had completed the first 7 years of elementary education, so many children were on track to be the first generation of school completers in their immediate family. The average adult literacy rate in these communities was just over 50 per cent. Students were predominantly Hindu, and almost half of the students enrolled belonged to marginalised caste and tribe groups. The mushrooming of low-fee private English-medium schools in nearby towns meant that rural families who were able to afford highly desirable English instruction often sought out private education. Therefore, social-class segmentation was occurring within these rural communities through differentiated educational provision. As one teacher put it, 'government school means it is for children who come from poor families'.

In the main, the schools were found to be highly disciplined environments, with hierarchical social relations – especially relating to caste and gender – at times made explicit. Teachers had visible authority in the schools, despite the promotion of 'democratic' learning in the *Nali Kali* child-centred programme. Students would stand to attention when the teacher entered the classroom, and classes would often begin with a *sloka* (a Hindu verse) in reverence of the guru-teacher. Student leaders, identified by teachers as most able, were often from the dominant castes. They were chosen to lead disciplined military style drills during the morning assembly. In class, these students were observed to have greater privileges over the use of space and the teacher's time. They would lead learning activities and, in the teacher's absence, monitor and even discipline other students. Teacher absenteeism was observed to be a persistent issue in these schools, which meant that students were often left on their own for long periods and even whole days at a time.

Teachers' constructions of the rural poor

The significant social distance between teachers and students was emphasised, both explicitly and implicitly, by the teachers who participated in the study. All had been educated themselves in government schools, and some had grown up in rural areas; however, these teachers were now living in urbanised centres near the villages in which they taught, and their own children attended private schools, mostly English-medium. These are markers of upward social mobility which were often invoked by teachers to set themselves apart from the rural children they taught. Thirteen out of the 22 teachers in the study were from dominant or privileged caste groups. During interviews and discussions, the teachers often expressed a mixture of paternalism, romanticism and sympathy for the rural life of their students. For example, discourses of the noble hard-working farmer were often drawn on, and rural people's local knowledge of the land and animals was praised. Villagers were positioned as innocent, having 'simple' needs and resisting materialism – a common vice of 'city people', as one teacher put it.

Teachers described their sympathy for the economic hardships which villagers endured: drought, the challenges of daily-wage labouring and being 'cheated' by those with more power. However, alongside such notions of village life ran a strong deficit discourse of rural communities being 'backward' and *avidyavantha* – 'uneducated'. Class and caste discourses were enmeshed in the view that villagers were ignorant, superstitious and lazy, or that they lacked hygiene, culture, civility, technology, education and discipline. One teacher, Ramesha, described:

> They [rural children] don't have discipline. They are not neat. We have to make children have some discipline when they come to school. They don't wash their clothes or their face, they don't comb their hair, they just come as they are. We are trying to avoid all this.

The deficit views of rural children shored up strong boundaries between the home and the school; the school's explicit function was to discipline and socialise the 'uneducated' rural child, as Ramesha explained, 'we are trying to avoid all this'.

The challenges of teaching in the rural government sector were most often explained in terms of the poor and 'uneducated' backgrounds of rural children. Teachers positioned rural children as in need of attention. As Shivanna describes:

> In villages, more uneducated people are there. Education is a bit less, and poverty is there. So children are not able to study more. Because everybody goes in the morning for labouring, and comes back in the evening, children are not getting much attention at home. So we [teachers] are giving more attention to children, and that is the only thing that remains with children. Children are not getting attention from parents. And even the school is not getting any support from parents.

Shivanna acknowledges the material hardships of rural poverty which contribute to the difficulties faced by families to 'support' the activities of the school. Teachers often explained that parents did not have the material resources to support the school (such as pens and books). A common source of frustration for teachers was that children were not made to attend school regularly and were not provided with basic school equipment and clean uniforms.

This perceived lack of 'support' was compounded by many parents' unfamiliarity with schooling expectations and cultures. As one teacher described, 'parents don't even know to come and ask about their child'. The middle-class cultural codes of modern schooling are often implicit, and can remain hidden to the rural poor who have been historically excluded from formal education. However, such wider perspectives about the relationship between rural communities and school institutions were not always acknowledged. Instead, the perceived poor level of parental engagement in school was often narrowly understood in terms of parents' lack of responsibility, neglect and lack of interest in their children's education. In decontextualising the history and lives of the rural poor, the 'deficits' ascribed to rural children and their families were individualised rather than understood in relation to broader social, political and economic factors.

Indeed, the way the notion of 'interest in education' was used to produce deficit constructions of rural communities was particularly telling of the pervasiveness of middle-class social norms. Consider how Saraswathi, a Year 1 teacher, explains how school success is determined by parental and student 'interest' in education:

> It's not a matter about being uneducated or educated, it is just about interest. They should have interest in their children and in the school. Those who have less interest in learning, whether they are educated or uneducated, such children will be having long absences from school. And the work we give to do at home, they won't do it. Then children will also not have interest [in school].

Here, 'interest' in education is seen to traverse socio-educational boundaries. While this may be so at some level, such notions risk masking the social and material resources behind recognisable forms of 'interest' – resources like 'equipment', 'extra-tuition' and 'doing homework together' which are more easily accessible to the middle classes. For example, many rural families in the district face the pressure of travelling for seasonal work, leading to school absences for many students. However, as Saraswathi's comments suggest, parents who are unable to avoid such seasonal work are charged with a lack of 'interest' in education. Such decontextualised discourses make invisible the middle-class resources that underlie 'good' school engagement and involvement and elide the social-material lived experiences of rural poverty.

For some teachers, the lack of 'interest' in education among rural families was even seen as a type of 'neglect'. This assessment was frequently made in relation to the normative childhood of the urban middle-class and upper castes, as the following comment by Stella Gita suggests:

> Some neglect is there. Nobody will teach them anything at home. For other [urban, middle-class] children, there may be tuitions, or they may teach at home . . . But for these village children, nobody will teach at home, right? What we will teach, they will learn. They'll just take the bag home, that's all.

Such comparisons not only construct urban middle-class childhoods as the ideal, but question the capacity of rural children to succeed in what one teacher called 'the competition era' of global India. At the extreme, some teachers conflated class/caste privilege with intelligence, leading to troubling assessments like this:

> In private school, parents are a bit more intelligent . . . and children will also beintelligent. So they will send them there. But here, in these government schools, children will come here who don't have anything . . . they have nothing in their minds.

From this brief snapshot of teachers' discourses of teaching in rural schools, we begin to see how the poor rural child is positioned as uneducated, neglected, uninterested, undisciplined, unintelligent and empty – with 'nothing in their minds'. These deficit discourses are made speakable through the normative ideal of the urban middle-class upper-caste child – whose childhood is better resourced for schooling, both in terms of material means and social histories of privilege. The cultural distance between the poor rural child and the middle-class urban child articulated by teachers is reminiscent of Steedman's observations of the working classes in London: 'the children of the poor are only a measure of what they lack as children: they are a falling short of a more complicated and richly endowed "real" child' (1986, 127–128). In rural primary schools of Karnataka, teachers' discourses reveal how the rural 'poor child' is seen to fall short of the 'real' child of global India. How then, through such deficit discourses, were teachers reworking – or in Bernstein's terms, recontextualising – liberal notions of child-centred education which seek to emphasise and celebrate the plurality of childhoods?

Recontextualising child-centred education for the rural poor

The teachers I interviewed had been trained in the *Nali Kali* child-centred programme and were familiar with its emphasis on democratic learning environments, activity-based learning, valuing children's backgrounds, and treating each child as an individual. For example, Radhamani explains her role as a *Nali Kali* teacher:

> A teacher should look after the children and should build the relationship with them like her own children. They should be good with children. The child may be poor or rich or whatever. The teacher should love, have faith and patience with the child . . . If the child is telling something to us, we must have patience to listen to them. We should respect the child's opinion.

Many of the ideals of the child-centred programme have been captured in Radhamani's explanation of her role. Teachers were to respect children's opinions, treat children equally, and even teach children with 'love' and 'patience'.

However, the nurture, care and love that were to be shown to the rural child did not always translate into more democratic, participatory or inclusive pedagogies. Most of the *Nali Kali* classrooms observed in the study continued to exhibit strong teacher-led instruction, extensive use of 'copy-writing' (in which students repeatedly write a given word or phrase), and strict discipline including frequent corporal punishment. In particular, the disciplining of children through 'beating' was often seen as a legitimate and effective teaching tool that not only encouraged students to learn, but displayed the commitment of the teacher to their students' success. As one teacher explained, 'if the teacher has love towards the child, and they want the child to learn at any cost, to develop discipline, that is why they will beat'. Here, the child-centred ideal of valuing the individual was recontextualised to defend highly disciplined instruction.

Teachers' understanding of the need to show investment, care and even love for the rural child not only failed to disrupt deficit views of the poor child as undisciplined and uneducated, but in a way *relied* on this deficit construction to legitimise strongly framed pedagogic practices. For example, despite the *Nali Kali* focus on activity-based learning, long lessons involving repeated drills and rote memorisation were commonplace. Such approaches were seen as a more efficient method to relay knowledge, and understood as particularly necessary for rural children because they did not have the opportunity to learn at home. As one teacher explained, she uses drills because 'nobody is there to teach them at home. I have to understand their situation and I have to teach them. If I beat them and if they say "nobody is there to teach us", what can I do?' Child-centred discourses that emphasise individual attention and understanding rural children's 'situations' were being used to reinforce dominant drill-based pedagogies.

Arguably, the child-centred approach encourages teachers to understand their children's 'situations', but this does not go far enough in challenging deficit assumptions about rural childhoods in order to shift teachers' practices. Teachers were recontextualising the aims of the child-centred reform (to set the child free) through the deficit constructions of the rural child (to form the child more fully). This led to the validation of drills, discipline and strongly framed instruction. As Savitha explained:

> In the cities at the age of four years [. . .] they will get them to write. But here, he is five and a half years. The child doesn't even know how to hold the chalk piece. So we get him to write, write, write, and practice . . . that's the reason why we do it . . . So, at least, in that method, let him learn. Let him come to that level.

Through a liberal framework of 'multiple childhoods', the rural child's life is acknowledged but it is far from desired or respected. Moreover, the ideal of a more fully formed urban middle-class child casts the rural child in a game of constant catch up, reinscribing their deficit.

These examples illustrate how social policy ideals about educating the rural child are recontextualised by teachers through discourses of urban/rural, caste and class hierarchies that are arguably being intensified in contemporary contexts of urbanising, globalising India. The modern educational project – to reform the child in the image of the global urban middle class – works through the logic of existing structures and discourses; a deficit view of the rural poor that is enmeshed in a long history of caste and class oppression. By stemming from this logic, even programmes that aim to centre and value the rural child can function to reproduce discourses of inequality and be recontextualised into teaching practices that run counter to the ideals of democratic and participatory schooling.

Conclusion: multiple childhoods and the preferred citizen

> If you see all this, rural children should come forward. Compared to city children, they should not be left behind.
>
> (Sujatha, Year 1 teacher)

The deficit construction of the rural child in India reflects a modernist development agenda which is premised on the need for the rural poor to 'catch up' with urban, middle-class ideals. From policy discourses to teachers' perspectives, the preferred child is the computer-savvy one in the city, embodying the hope and potential of contributing to the global knowledge economy. The notion of multiple childhoods remains a romantic and inadequate concept if it does not pay attention to the social and material realities, the histories and persisting inequalities, of children's lives. Liberal child-centred policy ideals of valuing each individual child that do not address these contexts can not only fail to shift educational practice, but can also reinscribe the distance and exclusion of rural communities from the ideals of modern schooling, and, by extension, from the idea of the preferred citizen-subject.

The significance of this extends far beyond the level of classroom practice. It raises broader questions about the position of the rural child in a national consciousness that has come to privilege the logics of neoliberalism, modernist urban development and economic globalisation, even if reworked through an 'Indian way of thinking'. If the urban middle classes are seen as the normative citizen in education discourses, it is not only because their social and cultural capital positions them as 'good' educational subjects. It is also because their resources allow them access to privatised educational institutions and products that position them as self-managing and self-enterprising over their educational success. As teachers have described, these are the families who are seen to take an 'interest' in education. The rural child living in poverty, without these resources and this access, is positioned as having a 'lack of interest' in education; a difficult and undesirable educational subject, who does not have the capacity to contribute to the education agenda of economic growth and modernisation.

Aihwa Ong (2006, 16) has argued that as the state gives increasing value to self-enterprising subjects as the preferred citizen, 'certain rights and benefits are distributed to marketable talents and denied to those who are judged to lack capacity or potential'. The deficit discourses that are reproduced through education discourses risk rendering the rural 'poor child' invisible and irrelevant to India's development. As Ong describes, such segments of the population are 'excepted from neoliberal criteria and thus rendered excludable as citizens and subjects' (2006, 16). Education development agendas need to push back against this logic by engaging more explicitly and reflexively with the tensions of the modern schooling project in global India. As Indian childhoods scholar Vasanta argues, 'instead of urging the children of the poor to acquire the symbols of childhood that are central to modernity, we should try and expose the representations that negate what is valuable in their lives' (2004, 17). Notions of 'multiple childhoods' and child-centredness that do not go far enough in acknowledging and interrogating the structural and historical inequalities that marginalise the rural poor risk constructing rural communities as not only lacking but as uneducable and irrelevant citizens of a global India.

Note

1 In India, elementary education is generally understood as schooling from Years 1 to 8. However, in the state of Karnataka, the focus of this chapter, elementary education is from Years 1 to 7. There are two stages within elementary education, often referred to as lower primary (Years 1 to 5) and upper primary (Years 6 to 7/8). The research for this chapter focuses on lower primary schooling. Discussions of primary teachers and primary schooling refer to this first stage of the elementary education system.

References

Alexander, Robin. 2008. *Education for All, The Quality Imperative and the Problem of Pedagogy.* London: CREATE.
Balagopalan, Sarada. 2008. 'Memories of Tomorrow: Children, Labor, and the Panacea of Formal Schooling.' *Journal of History of Childhood and Youth* 1 (2): 267–285. doi: 10.1353/hcy.0.0005.
Balagopalan, Sarada. 2011. 'Introduction: Children's Lives and the Indian Context.' *Childhood* 18 (3): 291–297. doi: 10.1177/0907568211413369.
Balagopalan, Sarada. 2014. *Inhabiting 'Childhood': Children, Labour and Schooling in Postcolonial India.* Basingstoke: Palgrave Macmillan.
Basu, Anustap. 2008. 'Hindutva and Informatic Modernization.' *Boundary* 35 (3): 239–250. doi: 10.1215/01903659-2008-018.
Bernstein, Basil B. 2000. *Pedagogy, Symbolic Control, and Identity: Theory, Research, Critique.* Lanham: Rowman & Littlefield.
Binswanger-Mkhize, Hans P. 2013. 'The Stunted Structural Transformation of the Indian Economy.' *Economic and Political Weekly* June 29. http://www.epw.in/review-rural-affairs/stunted-structural-transformation-indian-economy.html.
Burman, Erica. 2008. *Developments: Child, Image, Nation.* London: Routledge.
DFID (Department for International Development). 2011. *Preliminary Study into Low Fee Private Schools and Education.* London: CfBT Education Trust. http://r4d.dfid.gov.uk/pdf/outputs/mis_spc/60912-GyanShalaFinalReport.pdf.
Gopalakrishnan, Shankar. 2006. 'Defining, Constructing, and Policing a 'New India'. Relationship between Neoliberalism and Hindutva.' *Economic Political Weekly* 30 June.
GoK (Government of Karnataka). 2011. *Sarva Shikshana Abhiyana Karnataka Annual Report.* Bangalore: SSA Karnataka.

Government of India. 1986. *National Policy on Education 1986*. New Delhi: Ministry of Human Resource Development.
James, Allison, Chris Jenks, and Alan Prout. 1998. *Theorizing Childhood*. Cambridge: Polity Press.
Jenks, Chris. 2008. 'Constructing Childhood Sociologically.' In *An Introduction to Childhood Studies*, edited by Mary Kehily, 93–111. Maidenhead: Open University Press.
Kaul, Anita. 2004. *Nali Kali: The Joy of Learning*. Paper presented at the National Conference on Enhancing Learning in Elementary Schools, Azim Premji Foundation, Bangalore.
Kaviraj, Sudipta. 2010. *The Imaginary Institution of India: Politics and Ideas*. New York: Columbia University Press.
Kumar, Krishna. 2005. *Political Agenda of Education: A Study of Colonialist and Nationalist Ideas*. New Delhi: Sage.
Lukose, Ritty A. 2009. *Liberalization's Children: Gender, Youth, and Consumer Citizenship in Globalizing India*. Durham: Duke University Press.
Nandy, Ashis. 1983. *The Intimate Enemy: Loss and Recovery of Self under Colonialism*. Oxford: Oxford University Press.
Ong, Aihwa. 2006. *Neoliberalism as Exception: Mutations in Citizenship and Sovereignty*. Durham: Duke University Press.
Pal, Joyojeet, Meera Lakshmanan, and Kentaro Toyama. 2009. "My child will be respected': Parental Perspectives on Computers and Education in Rural India.' *Information System Frontiers* 11: 129–144. doi: 10.1007/s10796-009-9172-1.
Sriprakash, Arathi. 2012. *Pedagogies for Development: The Politics and Practice of Child-Centred Education in India*. Dordrecht: Springer.
Steedman, Carolyn K. 1986. *Landscape for a Good Woman: A Story of Two Lives*. London: Virago.
Tyler, Deborah. 1993. 'Making Better Children.' In *Child and Citizen: Genealogies of Schooling and Subjectivity*, edited by Denise Meredyth and Deborah Tyler, 35–61. Queensland: Griffith University.
Vasanta, Duggirala. 2004. 'Childhood, Work and Schooling: Some Reflections.' *Contemporary Education Dialogue* 2 (1): 5–29. doi: 10.1177/097318490400200102.

9 Picturing education, poverty and childhood from the perspectives of yak herder children in Bhutan

Lucy Hopkins

As Sriprakash's chapter has demonstrated, dominant discourses of education and poverty eradication within the developing world work to tie the construction of the child subject to ideas of national identity, national progress, and modernisation. Such discourses position the educated child subject in terms of a future citizen subject – a modern, urban, white collar worker – whose responsibility it is to 'remake' or 'reform' the nation (Burman 2008). Placed in hierarchical opposition to this ideal subject is the 'poor' child: this child, often positioned as rural and uneducated, is constructed in terms of narratives of lack, deficit and failure.

In this chapter I add to this analysis by examining how discourses of poverty and education are negotiated by children within a migratory yak herding community in the Himalayan Kingdom of Bhutan. The chapter draws on research I conducted in early 2014 in a village school. My research suggests that constructions of education and poverty circulating within development discourses work unnecessarily to establish and reinforce binaries between modernity[1] and tradition; urban and rural life; and mental and menial work; and to construct for children an imagined future subjectivity that is often unattainable yet to which children continue to aspire (Balagopalan 2008). My research has found that rural or 'poor' children who are potentially positioned in terms of deficit and failure by dominant discourses of education and poverty are perfectly capable of rehearsing and articulating the binaries underpinning these discourses. However, when invited to reflect on their own lives and schooling, those same children are simultaneously able to render the relationship between education, poverty, modernity and subjecthood far more complex than is permitted within the binary thinking of dominant development discourses.

Importantly, the chapter makes use of arts-based research methodology in order to make space for children to assert and express their own understandings: the children involved in this research responded to and drew pictures that allowed them to creatively articulate a range of subject positions and to tell specific stories from which they could then extrapolate. Their own and my analysis of the drawings were used to unpick the workings of dominant discourses of education and poverty, and to provide space for alternative conceptualisations. Such methodology weaves cultural studies approaches to text, narrative and visual arts into empirical research in ways that make space for multiple epistemologies and ontologies to emerge (Chase 2008; Cole and Knowles 2008, see also Burman; Gottschall, this volume).

The research context: Bhutan's education system

Bhutan is a Buddhist nation that until recently was mostly closed to the outside world. It is probably most well known globally for its government's desire to foster Gross National Happiness (GNH; Bhutan's unique overarching approach to sustainable development) as a measure to mediate its entry into the modern world.[2]

Modern education was introduced to Bhutan in the 1960s by the Third King as part of a strategy of socioeconomic development and modernisation, coinciding with the gradual opening up of the nation to the world. Prior to this, there were few schools and education had primarily been conducted through a monastic system. As part of the process of modernisation, the Bhutanese government began to engage increasingly with international development discourses and policies: the rapid expansion of the education system from the early 1990s reflected Bhutan's desire to meet *Education for All* targets set by the United Nations (LaPrairie 2014). These goals are also reflected in the provision and structure of schooling: education in Bhutan is free and universal from pre-primary to Class X, after which entry into government schools for Classes XI and XII is dependent on grades (LaPrairie 2014). Until Class XII, education is provided almost entirely within government schools: there are 553 government schools which accommodate more than 176,000 children (Schuelka 2014). These figures reflect Bhutan's achievement of close to 100 per cent school enrolment until Class X (Royal Education Council 2012).

The introduction of formal education to Bhutan has been framed in terms of economic growth and the development of human capital that would allow Bhutanese citizens – and the nation – to participate in the global economy, as well as producing 'cosmopolitan' citizens who were able to look outward to the region, and creating a strong, cohesive national identity (Dorji 2005; Kinga 2005; Phuntsho 2000; Schuelka 2014). Such aims, actively framed to mirror dominant international discourses of education and development (though inflected by the concept of GNH), introduce an entirely different approach to education from the previous monastic system. Schuelka (2014, 20) observes that 'while monastic education emphasises personal enlightenment and life-long reflection, modern education is seen as emphasising the acquirement of skills to be used externally, that is, to be used after school is *completed*'. The modern Bhutanese education system is, therefore, clearly focussed on the creation of the future citizen subject.

The research

The research informing this chapter was underpinned by the notion that attending to children's ways of seeing the world can provide insight into the ways in which children themselves negotiate the positions accorded them by dominant discourses, in this case, discourses about education, poverty, modernity and subjecthood circulating in contemporary Bhutan. Central to this investigation was an interest in how poststructuralist discourse analysis uncovers the ways that social actors make use of multiple – often conflicting – discourses in the constitution of their subjectivities. This has implications both for the methodological approach that I adopted, as well as for the analysis I have undertaken for this chapter.

The research, which was conducted with the permission of the school principal and with signed informed consent forms from participants, involved (audio-recorded) interviews about ideas of education and poverty with four Class VII children from the migratory yak herding community at a village school.[3] Children from this community tend to identify as their homes the very high-altitude pastures where their families live for most of the year. This is in spite of the fact that the children themselves live for most of the school year in the lower-altitude village, sometimes with relatives, sometimes as boarders at the school, sometimes with younger siblings only in a family home built in the village on land given as *kidu* (gift) by the King to ensure children's access to schooling. These are the very children potentially positioned as the rural 'poor' by binary development discourses, in opposition to the ideal future citizen subject.[4]

The children who participated in this study, two girls whose pseudonyms are Kinley and Tashi, and two boys whose pseudonyms are Tshering and Dorji, were aged between 11 and 14 years. Discussions were generated by the children's engagement with two sets of artwork. In the first phase of the research, I invited the children to discuss four drawings of 'education and poverty' done by their classmates for a *Dzonkhag*-wide (administrative district/region) competition in honour of the United Nations International Day for the Eradication of Poverty, on 17 September 2013. In the second phase of the research, I invited each of the children to make drawings themselves while we discussed the children's lives in terms of ideas of education, poverty and yak herding, and in response to questions I posed about the different views of teachers, parents and students to ideas of education and rural life. This paper is informed by an analysis of the discussions that emerged in phase one of the research, and by a detailed examination and analysis of the drawings and discussion I had with one of the children, Tshering, in phase two of the research.

Methodologically, this approach of collecting children's drawings, their interpretations and narratives of their lives allowed for multiple discourses to emerge from their participation in each phase of the research (Davies 2003). Using these two different suites of pictures and discussions surrounding them allowed the children to acknowledge and discuss public discourses about education and poverty, while permitting them to express ideas that run contrary to these public discourses while discussing their own lived experiences. My own analysis of each phase of the research generated for this paper attends to the ways that relations of power play out in terms of the audience for these artworks: while the first suite of drawings used in phase one was intended for viewing by teachers and education officials and therefore called upon the use of school-sanctioned ideas, the second set of drawings generated in phase two was done in response to a more critically inflected interview with the children. The children who were interviewed were able to identify clearly and to discuss these public narratives of education and poverty, while presenting sometimes very different understandings of their own lives. Asking them to draw pictures of their understandings of the views of a range of different influential actors – teachers, parents and students – also made space for the expression of a range of ideas. It also allowed for multiple ways of thinking about their subjective positioning by and in relation to other actors, rather than simply the dominant one.

Poststructuralist understandings of the ways in which social actors take up multiple discourses in the negotiation of their subjectivity (Baxter 2008), then, allow me as researcher to reveal and critique the modernist binaries that are at play within dominant discourses of education and poverty. In addition, such an understanding enables me to explore the ways that children's negotiations of ideas of education, poverty and selfhood draw on multiple often conflicting discourses in ways that undermine the strict modernist hierarchy of education versus poverty.

Mainstream pictures of poverty and education

I begin with an analysis of the discussions that emerged from phase one of the research. In this phase, the four children participants were invited to reflect on the four drawings done by their classmates for a regional competition in honour of the United Nations International Day for the Eradication of Poverty, on 17 September 2013, and chosen as best representing ideas of education and poverty by the teachers at the school. Their selection by the teachers suggests that these drawings illustrate dominant and school-sanctioned ideas of education and poverty, and promote discourses that are considered beneficial or instructive to the children of the school.

One of the fascinating features of this phase of the research is that although the participant children are looking at drawings done by other children, their explanations of the pictures are largely uniform. This speaks to the dominance of particular discourses of education and poverty within the schooling environment.

Each of these pictures creates a hierarchical dichotomy between education and poverty; their attendant representations of each allow me – and the children interviewed – to tease out how these oppositional categories are created and maintained. Thematically, the first drawing is about education, modernity and mobility, which is juxtaposed with poverty, tradition and rural life; the second depicts the straightforward linear trajectory of schooling to work; the third is about the differences between white collar work and farm work, and their attendant links with education and poverty; and the fourth represents the different modes of child subjectivity that accompany ideas of education and poverty. The images elucidate the ways in which such dominant discourses draw on modernist dichotomies between education and poverty, modernity and tradition, good and bad, and particularly, normative childhood and that which lies outside normative

Figure 9.1 Competition drawings of education and poverty

childhood. The children's interpretations also point to the ways in which the child subject is positioned as a future citizen, or as the hope for the family, society and nation.

Education and poverty; modernisation and tradition

My reading of these pictures is that, predictably, they tell a story of the dominant discourses through which education and poverty are constructed. Education, here, is synonymous with modernity, while poverty is seen to be associated with traditional modes of working the land. Roads, aeroplanes, buildings and computers are used as signifiers for education, while poverty is located predominantly within the fields. In a country where the construction of roads to villages remains a major development strategy, the use of transportation as a signifier of modernity is important. Here education is literalised as a route to social and actual mobility. For the children interviewed, such movement outside the country is indeed made possible solely through education which provides opportunities to work, study and travel abroad (see LaPrairie 2014). Importantly, for these children the significance of education's mobilising force is located in the realm of commerce: education, and particularly the English medium education system that is universal across Bhutan (LaPrairie 2014), enables students to, in Tshering's words, 'go to India [and do] whatever they like to do'.

In contrast to the modern, outward focus of education, in these drawings, poverty is located within the traditional world of Bhutan. Poverty is placed in a rural setting – there are no roads leading to the houses in the drawings, and the focus is always on traditional forms of labour. Drawing on ideas of the traditional subsistence farming and pastoral culture, the children's readings of the drawings all identify the 'problem' of poverty as hard (menial) work. Poverty is signified by the need to produce one's own food, a significant reading given Bhutan's relatively recent transition from almost complete subsistence farming to a monetary economy.

Clearly, the dominant discourses of education and poverty represented in these drawings reinscribe modernist binaries by linking education to modernity and poverty to tradition. Such an oppositional positioning is hardly uncommon: as Bhutanese educational anthropologist Dolma Roder (2012, 5) suggests, 'most studies of schools in developing nations see them as places where ideas around modernity and tradition face off, particularly in relation to identity formation'. Here we see this playing out overtly, as education is positioned alongside modernity as transformational, where rural, traditional livelihoods, aligned with poverty, are positioned as stagnant, lacking and difficult. The linking of positive ideals of education to modernisation and monetisation works to privilege commerce over food production, and creates a view of subsistence living *as* poverty. This operates on several levels, as it both obscures the ways in which 'modern' issues of rapid urbanisation and youth unemployment – particularly among educated youth – are also creating situations of poverty in Bhutan (Kinga 2005), and similarly presents an uncomplicated view of rural life in terms of 'tradition', rather than attending to the ways in which rural lives now negotiate between the traditional and the contemporary.

Such an opposition is, of course, both simplistic and problematic, reinscribing as it does ideas of poverty as the natural or inevitable opposite to education. The implications of this are many: while education and modernity are positioned as 'utopian' ideals, 'traditional' life is devalued through its association with poverty. Moreover, the simplistic understanding of education as the route away from/out of poverty without attention to the context of either, as we shall see, engenders a neoliberal, individualistic reading of both education and poverty.

Schooling and success: the deficit model of poverty

Significantly, the drawings – and the children's readings of them – highlight the ways in which dominant discourses of education create a linear and neutralised trajectory of progress through schooling to success, where success is constituted in terms of white collar work. Such a narrative of schooling relies on a sequential understanding of achievement, along with a strong narrative of education as transformative. As Roder (2012, 4) suggests, in Bhutan 'this belief about education's inherent, positive value and instrumental role in "preparing" students for the workplace and the job market is seen everywhere from policy documents to media accounts to casual conversation'. Education is widely conceptualised in terms of an uncomplicated narrative of opportunity with a teleological drive towards employment success. This narrative of progress that accompanies education/modernity is rendered particularly problematic when opposed with poverty, which locates rural life in terms of ideas of deficit and lack.

The neutralisation of this teleological narrative relies on this unquestioned narrative of opportunity that is underpinned by the positioning of the child subject within a neoliberal framework of individualism. Within this frame, education is unquestioningly presented as an opportunity that gives all students the same access to (social) mobility and jobs. As Sarada Balagopalan (2008, 280) suggests in her research on Bengali children's ideas of education, there is an 'underlying ideology that "hard work" and a certain docility on the part of the child would allow him or her to be successful in school and subsequently get a job of relative ease'. Such an unproblematised notion of studying hard as a path to success fails to take into account the ways in which children's contexts and their attendant cultural capital impact on schooling outcomes. Rather, it places the onus on the individual child to ensure their own success.

The idealised view of schooling as transformative and success as individualised becomes particularly problematic in this 'deficit' view, where children's 'failure' to achieve this success is not read in terms of systemic or contextual issues, but rather individual ones. In this neoliberal view, poverty, twinned with educational failure, is disassociated from the contextual and the social, becoming instead a personal and (as I will highlight later) moral problem.

This instrumental vision of schooling in terms of success foregrounds the privileging of white collar work as the only acceptable occupation for school leavers. Researcher Sonam Kinga (2005, 57) suggests that the almost universal desire for employment in the government sector in Bhutan is a hangover from 'the early years of modernisation, [when] education was seen as [the] instrument of joining the civil service'. Aside from being outdated – as employment in the civil service can no longer be assumed as a given for graduates – this discourse of employment success also reinforces the positioning of its opposite, manual labour, as 'less worthy, inferior and requiring no skills' (Balagopalan 2008, 281). Through the focus on white collar work, then, menial work is delegitimised, as are the skills and lifestyle that accompany it.

The distinction between mental and menial work is underscored by the children's use of language in describing these occupations. They use the noun 'job' to signify white collar employment, while manual labour is always described as 'work'. Such a distinction is reflected in the drawings under examination, in which white collar workers are represented as passive and unengaged, their status as employed signified by sitting at a desk. Those workers depicted under the banner of poverty are always *in the process* of labouring – working in the fields, collecting wood or carrying heavy loads. Unsurprisingly, then, for the children, white collar work is associated with leisure, while farm work is seen as 'hard work'.

The privileging of the 'job' over 'work', I argue, signposts the ways in which the linear narrative of education and future employment in the Bhutanese context reinforces a deficit model of rural life. Indeed the 'work' of rural life is positioned by the children in terms of a narrative of failure: according to Kinley, if you don't study hard, 'at last you *cannot* get a job' (my emphasis). The implications of this for children's lived experiences is significant: as the 2006 UNICEF *A Situation Analysis of Children & Women in Bhutan* reports, such a conceptualisation of rural life is reinforced by many children's rejection of parental ways of being and pastoral ways of living (Black and Stalker 2006). Rural life – associated within these drawings unequivocally with poverty (both as 'poorness' and as 'lack') – and its attendant pleasures and benefits are repudiated in favour of the assumed outcome of education.

The schooled child, the future citizen, the normative child

The representation of education and poverty in these student drawings speaks to the ways in which the child is positioned by educational discourses in terms of his/her future citizenship. Across three of the four drawings, the child is represented so emphatically in terms of their future (successful) adult subjectivity that the child itself is almost completely obscured from the picture. I argue that the narrative drive towards a future adult subject – who is defined by their status as a white collar worker – as the model of (educational and subjective) success positions the child in terms of its immanence, while it draws the child subject irrevocably into dialogue with notions of modernisation and nationhood.

Within development education discourses, this subject – this child becoming a future modern citizen – is reified as the saviour of the nation, the future hope of nationhood. As Erica Burman (2008, 1) notes, 'the widespread slogan that "children are our future" highlights the links between individual children, notions of social progress and national welfare that circulate within national and international policy debates'. Burman signals the ways in which such discourses conflate the child subject and the nation, both of which are modelled in terms of progress towards a fixed future state. Children are clearly positioned as the future of the nation, and education as the means through which the nation's future will be secured.[5]

Yet the subject invoked as the ideal child and future adult within these representations is a middle-class, urban one. As Sriprakash argues in her chapter on Indian childhoods (this collection), educational discourses represent the ideal child as future citizen in terms of 'economic growth, technological advancement, and social modernisation' (p. 151). Signifiers of modernisation – computers and desk jobs – stand in for the successful adult subject in these drawings; a far cry from the rural agricultural existence that the majority of Bhutanese people still live. This positioning of the child up against ideals of modernisation – arguably a significant narrative shaping current idea(l)s of nationhood in Bhutan – again reinforces the deficit model of the poor, rural child.

Importantly, discourses of the child as future citizen are underpinned by Western developmental notions of the child as immanent and in process; a subject who is juxtaposed with the complete, rational adult subject (see Hopkins and Sriprakash, this volume). They construct the ideal child in terms of its future possibility: this is not a subject that is legitimated as it is, but is necessarily *becoming*. As a subject in process, this child's own subjectivity is marginalised in favour of the future citizen. Such a construction of the child positions it as simultaneously passive (and thus lacking in any sort of agency), and as a learner for the future, rather than an active participant.[6] What this means for how children themselves negotiate their subjectivities within educational discourses is an interesting question, and one that I take up below, in relation to Tshering's depictions of education.

The drawings analysed for this research suggest that the new ideal modern child subject as it is constructed within educational discourses in Bhutan can indeed be read in terms of Western constructions of childhood which position childhood as a separate space to adulthood, and necessarily as a space of leisure, learning and protection (Jenkins 1998; Holland 2004; Hopkins and Sriprakash, this volume). Within the drawings, the educated child – who is, significantly, located as Western by depictions of his attire in pants and a shirt – has free time, can play, and exists within the space of the home. This child is placed in opposition to the labouring child of poverty, a discursive hierarchy that reveals much about how educational discourses repudiate all forms of child work (see Morganti, Githitho Muriithri, this volume), and sanction a model of childhood underpinned by ideas of play and leisure.

Importantly, the children's readings of these pictures revealed a moral component to the dialectic between the educated child and the uneducated child. While the educated child is positioned as virtuous, the poor child, according to Tashi, compares himself to the 'ideal' child, and, she says, 'he think "I am the worst man in the world" and he is crying'. The location of poverty as a moral issue through a negative comparison with the educated subject reinforces the neoliberal individualisation of the child subject in relation to education: positioning the child in terms of ideas of the 'bad' locates poverty as an intrinsic or inherent quality, but also one that is the responsibility of the subject, rather than a context-based, or socioeconomic issue. According to Tshering's interpretation, the poor child recognises their lack through discourses of 'regret', reaffirming their individual responsibility to 'study hard' and become educated.

Clearly these drawings – and the children's readings of them – highlight the ways that discourses of education and development bring ideas of schooling and poverty into a stark hierarchical dichotomy that privileges education, and its attendant associations with modernity and modernisation, progress and modern citizenship, and even – in the context of a nation guided discursively by ideas of GNH – happiness, over a deficit model of poverty that is closely tied to tradition, 'backwardness' and suffering. Important here too are the ways in which these ideas position the educated child in terms of an urban, middle-class ideal, as the saviour of the nation, a manoeuvre that effectively excludes a majority of the still rural-based populace from engaging in ideas or discourses of nation-building.

Conceptualising education and rural life: contesting hierarchies, complicating binaries

Given that poverty is so heavily tied to ideas of rural life, and the dichotomy between the (educated) urban and the (poor) rural is so closely linked to notions of morality, in this research project I was interested in exploring how the yak herder children at the school under investigation – who are largely positioned outside the urban, middle-class elite – adopt, negotiate and challenge such discourses, and make (alternative) meanings from their own and others' experiences. Making use in particular of Tshering's testimony, together with his own and my analysis of some drawings he did in response to our discussion, in this section, I argue that the yak herder children interviewed engage in complex negotiations of the discourses of education, poverty and childhood that allow them, at some level, to rethink and even avoid the deficit notions of poverty, lack and failure that are attributed to 'traditional' or rural life within dominant discourses. Tshering's testimony about his own life and his drawings largely challenge the hierarchical oppositions created between education and poverty, and paint a picture of a far more ambiguous relationship between ideas of childhood, education and modernisation. Further, they reveal the ways in which students take themselves up as subjects in relation to these dominant discourses (Davies 1993).

Alongside the interviews with the children, I asked them to draw pictures of education and yak herding life. In order to ensure that they would feel able to articulate their own understandings of school and yak herding – rather than those well-known public discourses articulated above – as well as to get a sense of their conceptualisations of the (possibly competing) discourses being drawn on by the important actors in their lives, I asked them to draw three pictures of education: what they thought their teachers think about education, what they themselves think about education, and what their parents think about education. Similarly, I asked the children to draw three pictures of the life of yak herders: what their teachers, they and their parents think about yak herding. Tshering's drawings of education and the lifestyles of yak herding, in particular, reveal a complex understanding of the ways in which different actors' views of children, education and yak herding are shaped and impact on the child subject in various ways.

From the outset, Tshering rejected the unequivocal privileging of education that underpins dominant discourses of schooling. Upon entering the interview room, knowing only that I wished to talk to him about school and yak herding, Tshering leaned into the tape recorder and said:

> In Bhutan, most students don't like to study but family will force them to do, and in [names mountain community], also most students don't like to study but family also force. The students, they like to stay in the house and they watch after yaks, like yak herders, yak herding.

Tshering actively refuses the deficit model of rural life as less valuable than modern education. By drawing on ideas of happiness and desire, he privileges the experiences of yak herding over those of education. His comment also foreshadows his reading of the lack of agency experienced by students in deciding their educational future (an idea on which I will elaborate below in relation to his drawings).

However, Tshering also represents education as integral for the negotiation of the new modern Bhutan. He acknowledges that previously, it was acceptable for people to live in the village with no education; however, in contemporary times, this has become much more difficult:

Tshering: Village life is very hard, madam. It very some . . . some men say this. Old people was not educated. Whatever they like to do is okay. But nowadays, if not educated, we don't know about, when we are going from Trongsa to Bumthang in the bus, they don't know bus inside, bus number and they leave.

Interviewer: So they can't read, so it is difficult for them to get around.

Tshering: Yes madam. And they are . . . fell down. No, they leave on the road.

Interviewer: . . . Oh, they get left behind.

Tshering: Yes madam, left behind. They left.

Here Tshering demonstrates that the changes in Bhutan's society in recent times mean that people who are not able to keep up with the rapid changes in development – which he constitutes in terms of their educational status – will be unable to cope with contemporary life. The relatively 'simple' act of travelling a short distance between two major hubs in central Bhutan, which Tshering uses here as a metaphor for access to modern society, becomes virtually impossible without the literacy and numeracy skills required to catch a bus. Thus for Tshering, while being without education was not a problem in the past – people could do 'whatever they like to do' – now education is imperative. Significantly, education is here aligned with literacy and numeracy as well as a certain cosmopolitanism that being savvy with modern life requires; signifiers which match up with the goals of modern education discussed above. Tshering's example constitutes the subject in terms of the dialectic between modernity and tradition and supports the notion that education is synonymous with modernity, and that village life, or uneducated life, is conceptualised in terms of a deficit, a lack of competence in dealing with the modern world.

Yet Tshering's drawings of education and yak herding demonstrate that he is aware of the constraints of the discourses of education and rural life perpetuated within the schooling system, and within his herding community. His drawing of how he thinks teachers view the mountainous area where he lives illustrates that he sees teachers' views as mimicking the dominant discourses of education and rural life. His drawing shows an idyllic mountain scene, with a small yak herder's cottage, yaks, large flowers, lakes replete with fish and snow-covered peaks.

Picturing education, poverty and childhood 179

Figure 9.2 Tshering's view of what teachers think about yak herding

While these elements of the yak herder's lifestyle were identified by all the children as being reasons why living in the mountains was good or enjoyable, the text of the drawing – 'teacher think study is [more] important than living in [place name]' – draws attention to the ways that Tshering perceives teachers' understandings subvert the notion that natural beauty, cleanliness and community should be desired. Significantly, I read Tshering's drawing as a critique: his statement that this is *what teachers think*, rather than an abstract truth, makes space for him to question this opinion, to subvert the dominant constructions of education and rural life.

In his explanation of the lives of yak herders, Tshering's analysis unsettled the strict hierarchical dichotomy between education/modernity and rural life/poverty by locating yak herding within a monetary economy. Although he talked about yak herding, like the rural/village life represented in the pictures of poverty we were discussing, as a 'difficult' life which requires much hard work, he avoided constituting it in terms of poverty or as 'lacking' by focusing instead on how much money could be made from herding.[7]

> *Tshering:* Yak herding is very difficult madam, but in the winter they sell yak and they earn money. One yak is cost 40,000 [Bhutanese Ngultrum – around £400] something, madam.
>
> *Interviewer:* Yeah, that's a lot of money.

180 *Lucy Hopkins*

> *Tshering:* And most people like yak herding.
>
> *Interviewer:* Why do people like yak herding?
>
> *Tshering:* Because they earn many money, madam.

Although it features the same kinds of 'hard' work as that which is represented as 'poverty' in the previous pictures discussed, the yak herding lifestyle is made acceptable because he can fit it into modern notions of 'success' through its commercial viability.

Yak herding, then, is constructed by Tshering in terms of modernity, rather than as existing outside it. Within the discourse of modernity – premised as it is within Tshering's understanding in terms of a monetary economy – yak herding constitutes an acceptable lifestyle option. Tshering's drawing of what *he* thinks about yak herding further highlights the ways in which Tshering's understandings draw yak herding into the arena of modernity. His drawing shows a boy or a man standing behind a bench that is replete with yak products: cuts of meat, *chugo* (yak cheese, often dried and strung on a 'necklace'), butter and milk. A customer asks the seller 'how much it cost?'. Again, this demonstrates the ways in which Tshering articulates a view of yak herding that is located within the monetary economy, but crucially, he does not locate this transaction within the mountains where the herding community live, but rather within an urban environment: the table sits under streetlights and beside a black-topped road; nearby are two very large apartment buildings. The financial transaction of yak herding – the buying and selling of produce – is here framed as the interface between the

Figure 9.3 Tshering's depiction of what he thinks about yak herding

city and the mountains, and it is this that allows Tshering – within the dominant discourse of modernity – to position yak herding as 'good'. The explanatory text in the drawing says 'yak herding is good because we can earn many money. One yak cost 3500 thousand [sic] something'. Importantly, then, Tshering's legitimation of yak herding does not dislodge the dominance of the discourse of modernisation, but rather adapts notions of herding to fit in with the privileging of money. Moreover, the attribution of moral standards – here signified by 'goodness' – is important, as it works to unsettle the uncritical location of education as 'good' and rural life as 'bad' described in the previous pictures.

Yak herding is thus delinked from ideas of poverty because of its ability to fit into the monetary economy, despite being constructed in terms of the signifiers of 'hard work' and rural life that the children read as standing in for poverty within the representations of dominant discourses of poverty.

Revisioning modernity: thinking anew about education, poverty and the future citizen

Not only do Tshering's drawings represent yak herding in terms of modernity, they also work to critique the uncritical positive association between education and modernity. While he suggests that education is (mostly) 'good', several of his drawings and narratives point to ways in which both ideas of education and ideas of modernity are deserving of more complex interpretations. Particularly telling here is his narrative of the 'bad boy' and of the high stakes of the future citizen subjects.

Figure 9.4 Tshering's view of what parents think about education: the story of the 'bad boy'

Although he acknowledges the links between education, modernity and success, Tshering's drawing and story of the 'bad boy' highlight alternative narratives of modernity and the modern child subject, in which the child, as a product of modernity, is seen as a failed future subject. In his drawing of what parents think about education, Tshering depicts a father, wearing a traditional *gho*, pointing at his son, a boy dressed in western clothes, with long hair. The text says: 'father think my boy study hard but boy is not studying and always he get beat from teacher'. In his explanation of the drawing, Tshering says:

Tshering: This picture is like a story, madam. When he going . . . start going to studying, father say, 'you study hard' and father think also 'my boy is studying hard', but boy is not studying. He get beat from teacher and he is becoming bad boy. And boy is going to town and naughty things, doing, like this, madam. Some father and student, they have problem like this, madam. In Bhutan or [village name] or wherever madam.

Interviewer: Wherever, they have this problem? And this boy, he is not wearing a *gho*, is he? He's wearing pants and shirt.

Tshering: Because he is going to . . . he like to go to town, madam, this boy. And father think, when my boy become class 15 [university graduate], he get job or *lyonpo* [minister], or other job, and boy is not thinking about father, madam. He is thinking her own [sic].

Interviewer: He's thinking about himself? So why does the father want him to be fifteenth graduate?

Tshering: Because father, when father is, when he is fifteenth graduate, he is *lyonpo*, example. He earn money and father is also carry – boy will carry also father, boy will care the father, madam. Father think like this, madam. But boy don't think like this, madam.

While Tshering's narrative reinscribes the construction of the boy who is not educated as 'bad', here this moral judgement is associated not with poverty, but rather with urbanisation. The boy's dress and haircut work as signifiers of modernity (see discussion below) and the idea of the boy liking to 'go to town' is underscored by an emergent but powerful discourse of the 'youth problem' in Bhutan, in which young people – as harbingers of modernity but also as would-be wardens of tradition – are seen to be failing in their role as future citizens by succumbing to 'cultural diffusion'. This term is used widely and often uncritically within Bhutan to name – and explain – any practice undertaken by (young) people that is not seen to be in keeping with Bhutanese tradition. It is unequivocally used in the negative (even by young people themselves), and is positioned in opposition to a static notion of 'culture' that describes the traditional practices of Bhutanese students.[8] Young people who succumb to 'cultural diffusion' are positioned as 'failed' or 'bad' both in moral terms and in relation to discourses of nationhood. Thus, the child is constituted as a failed future citizen *within* the discourse of modernisation; indeed in an almost total about-face from the previously discussed moral positioning of education and poverty, modernisation is seen as the 'corrupting' force.

Paradoxically, while the father's view here seems to correspond with the idea of the educated child as future citizen, Tshering's reasons for the father's desire for an educated son are much more deeply rooted within notions of family and support. These are arguably characteristics that might be associated with 'traditional' life in Bhutan, where urban life is often characterised by worries about the disintegration of family life, community and the risk of 'antisocial behaviours' (see Dorji 2005). As Sriprakash argues, in this collection, such an intertwining of seemingly traditional values with contemporary understandings demonstrates how specious the demarcation of the tradition/modern dichotomy is. However, the boy's self-interest and lack of care for his father in this narrative demonstrates how the 'modern' boy is constituted in opposition to such narratives of family and community.

This powerful counter-discourse about the negative elements of modernity also informs Tshering's ideas about education: despite positioning education as good, Tshering also acknowledges that sometimes alternative narratives of success are possible or preferable. In relation to one of the pictures discussed earlier, Tshering says:

Tshering: I think that this education . . . this picture telling about education is good. People . . . because whenever we get job, we will get. But without education it is also good, madam.

Interviewer: Yes? Tell me why you think it is good.

Tshering: Because, but, some student, madam, when they reach in class ten they cannot get college, madam. They kill themselves and they cannot get good marks in exam. They kill themselves madam.

Interviewer: Yeah, okay, so education can also be really stressful, right?

Tshering: Yes madam. Their father-mother is sad, very sad. Angry with student.

Tshering draws on contemporary conversations about the rising suicide rate among young people in Bhutan[9] to argue that the unquestioned tying of education to ideas of success, 'goodness' and happiness is specious. He details the pressure that discourses of education which link success to white collar work can place on the student, and 'failure' to achieve this narrow version of success – here by not getting the school grades to get into college/university – is a very real possibility.

Yet for Tshering, having education and access to rural life is not a dialectical opposition. When asked if he was happy when he was at home with his family, Tshering replied:

> In the winter vacation, madam. I am happy, because I met with my family, my whole family, my sister, and I met with my yaks. I felt happy and [after] the winter vacation I come back and [get] educated, madam. This, I am happy madam.

Here Tshering is able to reconcile his family life with the life of education, and to privilege both education and rural life in ways that dominant discourses do not.

Education, poverty and the child subject: Tshering's views

Tshering's drawings of ideas of education demonstrate the ways in which he interprets and negotiates the various positionings of the child subject by influential actors. In his drawing of how he thinks teachers view schooling, the teacher is represented as a guiding hand (albeit wielding a stick) in front of a passive class. In this picture the teacher stands at the front of the classroom, beside a blackboard that has letters written on it in Dzongkha. In a speech bubble, she says 'study hard students'. Two children sit at desks in rows, with books in front of them. While the teacher's voice can be heard, the students are silent and faceless.

Figure 9.5 Tshering's view of what teachers think about education

Tshering's explanation of what is happening in the picture suggests that the teacher's view of the teacher–student relationship confirms notions of the child subject as vulnerable and unknowing, and as in need of guidance from the teacher:

Tshering: Teacher, whenever they advise, they advise student to study hard. And student also think and study hard, madam . . .

Interviewer: Okay. And why do you think the teacher says you should 'study hard, students'?

Tshering: Because student, they are small and they don't know. But teacher will advise him, madam. Don't do like this and like this. Do punctuality and like this, advise in the students. Teacher will.

Tshering's constitution of students as 'small' and unknowing is significant here, as it describes the adult–child relationship as a hierarchical relationship of power in which the child is in the process of formation. Further, the location of education in terms of discipline – here signalled by Tshering as punctuality – was enacted by all of the children. This view of discipline *as* education rehearses the positioning of the child subject taken up earlier as immanent and in need of shaping in order to become adult. Arguably, then, Tshering's account of what it means to 'study hard' and become educated is bound up with ideas of the future (modern) subject.

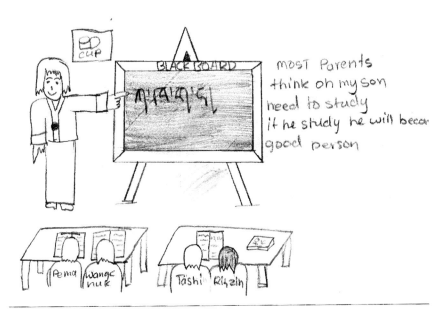

Figure 9.6 Tshering's view of what parents think about yak herding and education

Tshering's perception of his parents' view of education is similarly constituted in terms of the 'becoming' child subject, perhaps demonstrating just how entrenched these dominant discourses are. However, here the future citizen is not depicted simply as someone who is able to get a job, but rather within a discourse of morality, as a (future) 'good person'. In his drawing of how parents think about education, the classroom space is depicted in similar ways to the picture of teachers' views of education: the teacher is at the blackboard, and the students sit behind their desks. The crucial difference, though, is the textual commentary, which reads: 'most parents think oh my son need to study. If he study he will become good person'. Within the context of the children's readings of the initial pictures of education and poverty, where education was constituted as 'good' and poverty as 'bad', this notion of the child subject as a 'good person' is particularly important. Education, it seems, is transformational not only in terms of the outcome of a good job, but also in terms of the (proper) formation of the (morally correct) subject. Yet again, the formation of the 'good' future citizen can be read in terms of neoliberal discourses of individuality: the student is required to study hard to be able to 'become' good, and the possible failure to do so would be seen as a failure to work hard.

However, while Tshering constructs teachers' views of education in terms of a model of the child as immanent, his depiction of his own – or other students' – views of education constructs children as independent agents who resist their disempowered positioning by teachers, albeit agents whose actions are constrained by the context in which they find themselves. In his drawing of how students think about schooling, the teacher instructs the student as in the earlier

Figure 9.7 Tshering's depiction of what he thinks about education

drawing on teachers' perceptions; however, in this drawing the student has both a face and a voice. The teacher tells the student 'cut ur [sic] hair', yet rather than being a passive recipient of this instruction, the student here comments on the teacher's instruction, implicitly rebelling against the teacher's speech: the student thinks, 'This teacher is always telling about hair only'. In a society in which wearing national dress is obligatory in government and (most) private sector work, hairstyle has become an increasingly important signifier of identity, particularly for boys. Indeed, with many boys using their hair to express individuality (ironically through a mimicry of Korean or other international fashions), hairstyles are, in many ways, a site of discursive contest over ideas of modernity versus tradition; individuality versus collectivity; discipline versus waywardness.[10] Hair has become a signifier of morality, and the school a space in which this tussle plays out. Tshering's explanation of his drawing indicates not only that the student in his drawing is resisting his positioning as a passive recipient of teacher instruction, but also that he is represented in terms of his current identity, rather than a future one.

> In that picture, madam, teacher say, madam, this boy, cut your hair. His hair is too long, madam. But this student think, madam, 'oh, this teacher is always telling about hair. We are not a monk' . . . Teacher is advising him, but he is thinking about bad, madam.

Tshering's talk simultaneously acknowledges the desired individuality of the student while recognising how this is constituted as 'bad' within the discourses about discipline and morality within the schooling system. Importantly, then, the fact that the child here *thinks* – using a thought bubble – rather than *speaks* indicates the ways in which the child's agency is contingent on their positioning by the teacher in the classroom. Here Tshering reveals the ways in which the child is positioned by dominant ideas of education as a passive subject, but also how the child rejects such a positioning, albeit in ways that are constrained by their capacity to act within the schooling context.

Conclusion: rethinking children's attitudes in relation to education and development

Ultimately, this chapter has explored how making use of arts-based research methodology to explore children's ways of seeing can reveal the complex, nuanced ways in which children take up, negotiate and reject dominant discourses of education and poverty within their daily lives. In attending to the multiple discourses on which the children draw, the paper argues that the modernist binaries that underpin public discourses of education and poverty are radically reductive, positioning the 'poor' child and the rural child in terms of a deficit model, and setting up an ideal of the educated future subject that is near impossible for most children to achieve. Further, it unpicks the ways in which the twinning of education and modernity – and its focus on progress – is blindly teleological, creating a falsely and unproblematised narrative of (national and subjective) success, that is pitted against rural 'failure'. Tshering's drawings highlight the possibilities for a more nuanced understanding of education, rural life and child subjecthood than these public discourses make possible, revealing how these ideas can be differently negotiated.

The poststructuralist methodological positioning of this paper reveals how multiple, conflicting discourses can be understood and negotiated simultaneously. What we can learn from children's negotiations of such discourses is that it is possible – and even desirable – for conceptualisations of education and poverty and the attendant ideas of the child subject to be more complex, and for policy makers and practitioners in 'development' contexts to expect complexity, rather than relying on oppositions that close down such possibilities. Such an understanding, I argue, is crucial in the rethinking of dominant discourses of development and education, as it allows for more contextualised and nuanced understandings of the child subject's positioning in relation to education and poverty.

Notes

1 My use of the terms 'modernity' and 'modernisation' throughout this paper refer not to the twentieth century understandings of modernism, but rather to the discourses of modernisation that circulate widely in Bhutan (and other 'developing' countries), that are juxtaposed with 'traditional' life. Modernisation is conceptualised in terms of a trajectory of progress toward an intended 'developed' outcome, problematically often one intended to achieve Western notions of development.
2 For more on GNH and education see Phuntsho (2013) and LaPrairie (2014).
3 Interviews were conducted in English, which is the medium of education within all government schools in Bhutan. The students have moderate competence in English and all quotes are transcribed as articulated by the students. See LaPrairie 2014 for a comprehensive analysis of the English medium system in Bhutan.
4 Importantly, as I will demonstrate, while yak herders have never been considered 'poor' by Bhutanese, due to their ability to trade, and now sell, yaks and yak products (primarily milk, cheese and meat), the ways in which the children interviewed discussed their families and their work was aligned with the ways that they talked about rural 'poor' (largely classified as subsistence farmers). While this distinction is important to acknowledge, the opposition that is set up between rural and urban, educated and uneducated within dominant discourses – and indeed within abstract discussions of education and poverty with the children – allows me, here, to align these communities with rurality and 'poverty'. The nuances of this uneasy elision are teased out in this paper.
5 Here I acknowledge that the child has long been positioned as a cipher for the nation within discourses of nationalism and national development. The naturalisation of developmental models of childhood has allowed for this narrative to be transposed onto the nation, and development goals and ideals to be positioned as natural and inevitable, but also as part of a linear trajectory towards a 'mature' or rational (adult) nationhood. See Burman (2008), Nandy (2009) and Hopkins (forthcoming, 2015).
6 See Githitho Muriithri, this collection, for further discussion of these ideas.
7 Despite the fact that the children do describe the work of their parents in similar terms as those that they identified within the drawings as having an association

with ideas of 'poverty' – that is, subsistence labour – none of the children identified their own families as 'poor', choosing to represent them instead as 'normal'. Such a positioning of yak herding outside the narrative of 'poverty' would, arguably, be supported by popular discourse in Bhutan (as there is indeed much money to be made from yaks and yak products); yet given its location within the discourse of rural livelihoods that are rendered distinct from the 'educated life', I am interested here in how this representation of a mode of rural life unsettles the dichotomy between modernity/education and poverty/rural life.

8 For more on anxieties around modernisation and cultural change in relation to youth in Bhutan, see Roder (2012).
9 These conversations have been ongoing in Bhutan in the public sphere: see Dema, 1 November 2013; Tsara, 18 July 2013.
10 While there is not sufficient space here to elaborate, the focus on short hair for boys as a signifier of tradition, discipline and even morality can perhaps be traced back to monastic education that was the main system of education in Bhutan prior to the 1960s. Here we see this reflected in Tshering's assertion that the children 'are not a monk', and therefore should not be subjected to such forms of discipline.

References

Balagopalan, Sarada. 2008. 'Memories of Tomorrow: Children, Labour, and the Panacea of Formal Schooling.' *Journal of the History of Childhood and Youth* 1 (2): 267–285. doi: 10.1353/hcy.0.0005.

Baxter, Judith A. 2008. 'Feminist Post-Structuralist Discourse Analysis: A New Theoretical and Methodological Approach?' In *Gender and Language Research Methodologies*, edited by Kate Harrington, Lia Litosseliti, Helen Sauntson and Jane Sunderland, 243–255. Basingstoke: Palgrave Macmillan.

Black, Maggie, and Peter Stalker. 2006. *A Situation Analysis of Children & Women in Bhutan*. Thimphu, Bhutan: UNICEF.

Burman, Erica. 2008. *Developments: Child, Image, Nation*. Hove, East Sussex: Routledge.

Chase, S. 2008. 'Narrative Inquiry: Multiple Lenses, Approaches, Voices.' In *Collecting and Interpreting Qualitative Materials*, edited by Norman K. Denzin and Y.S. Lincoln, 57–94. Thousand Oaks, CA: Sage.

Cole, A., and J.G. Knowles. 2008. 'Arts-informed Research.' In *Handbook of the Arts in Qualitative Research*, edited by J.G. Knowles and A. Cole, 55–70. Thousand Oaks, CA: Sage.

Davies, Bronwyn. 1993. 'Beyond Dualism and Towards Multiple Subjectivities.' In *Texts of Desire: Essays on Fiction, Femininity, and Schooling*, edited by Linda K. Christian-Smith, 145–172. London: Falmer Press.

Davies, Bronwyn. 2003. *Frogs and Snails and Feminist Tales: Preschool Children and Gender*. Revised edn. Cresswell, NJ: Hampton Press.

Dema, Chencho. 2013. 'Rapidly Rising Suicide Rates Become the Second Biggest Killer after Road Accidents in Bhutan.' *The Bhutanese*, 1 November.

Dorji, Lham. 2005. 'Determinants of School-dropout and Non-enrollment: From the Young People's Perspective.' In *Youth in Bhutan: Education, Employment, Development*, edited by Lham Dorji and Sonam Kinga, 1–33. Thimphu, Bhutan: Centre for Bhutan Studies.

Holland, Patricia. 2004. *Picturing Childhood: The Myth of the Child in Popular Imagery*. New York: I.B. Tauris.

Hopkins, Lucy. Forthcoming. 'Child *as* Nation: Embodying the Nation in Salman Rushdie's *Midnight's Children*.' In *'Childhood' and 'Nation': Global Identities, Local Subjectivities*, edited by Zsuzsanna Millei and Robert J. Imre. New York: Palgrave Macmillan.

Jenkins, Henry, ed. 1998. *The Children's Culture Reader*. New York and London: New York University Press.

Kinga, Sonam. 2005. 'Youth and Unemployment in Bhutan.' In *Youth in Bhutan: Education, Employment, Development*, edited by Lham Dorji and Sonam Kinga, 33–79. Thimphu, Bhutan: Centre for Bhutan Studies.

LaPrairie, Mark. 2014. 'A Case Study of English-Medium Education in Bhutan.' EdD dissertation, University of London.

Nandy, Ashis. 2009. *The Intimate Enemy: Loss and Recovery of Self under Colonialism*. 2nd edn. Oxford: Oxford University Press.

Phuntsho, Karma. 2000. 'On the Two Ways of Learning in Bhutan.' *Journal of Bhutan Studies* 2 (2): 96–126. http://himalaya.socanth.cam.ac.uk/collections/journals/jbs/pdf/JBS_02_02_04.pdf.

Phuntsho, Karma. 2013. *The History of Bhutan*. London: Random House.

Roder, Dolma C. 2012. *'Girls Should Come Up': Gender and Schooling in Contemporary Bhutan*. PhD dissertation, Arizona State University.

Royal Education Council. 2012. *National Education Framework: Shaping Bhutan's Future*. Thimphu, Bhutan: Royal Education Council.

Schuelka, Matthew J. 2014. *Constructing Disability in Bhutan: Schools, Structures, Policies and Global Discourses*. PhD dissertation, University of Minnesota.

Tsara, Ap. 2013. 'Who Says Youth are Happy?' *Bhutan Observer*, 18 July.

Conclusion

10 Revisioning 'development'
Towards a relational understanding of the 'poor child'

Arathi Sriprakash and Lucy Hopkins

When we began conceptualising this book we anticipated that the conclusion would bring together the key perspectives and arguments from each chapter to reflect on how they have enriched our understanding of the lives of poor children and pushed us to think afresh about the projects of development and schooling. And indeed, much of this concluding chapter will be dedicated to that kind of discussion, commenting on the contributions of this volume to the research and policy fields of education and international development. However, before embarking on those observations, we would like first to situate them with respect to our own experiences of reading each chapter – as editors working across disciplinary boundaries, and also as readers engaging with the book at a particular moment in our lives.

We each came to this book with different disciplinary perspectives – Lucy's work has been largely influenced by cultural studies and Arathi has been located in sociology. During the editing process, we discussed how the theories, approaches and analysis of each chapter could help our respective fields – as well as development studies – to engage in different ways with the 'poor child'. This collaborative process of reading allowed us to cut across an analytic distinction that is often set up between our two disciplinary homes: a distinction between discursive representation and materiality. Instead, the multi-sited, multi-disciplinary and multi-method research presented in this collection gave us ways of seeing how the discursive and cultural representation of the 'poor child' is both constituted by, and constitutive of, her lived experience or materiality. For example, children living in contexts of poverty were both resisting and acting in accordance with discourses of childhood that exist in school environments, community practices, and development policy frameworks (see chapters by Morganti, Hopkins, Githitho Muriithi and Medrano). Similarly, we saw how cultural and policy representations of the 'poor child' can be read as sites of contestation which produce particular practices and politics that shape children's lives (see chapters by Burman, Gottschall, Sriprakash and McCormick). As we outline in our concluding discussions, the discursive and the material are brought together analytically in this book as part of what we suggest to be a relational understanding of the 'poor child'.

Both Erica Burman's and Kristina Gottschall's chapters in this volume illuminated the processes and politics of meaning-making through cultural texts that in many ways have inspired us to reflect on our own readings of each contribution. Their analyses pointed to, and set out to challenge, the ways in which there are socially sanctioned modes of reading that can frame what is possible to be known about the 'poor child'. In this book, we set out to shift that frame through a decided interrogation of dominant, socially sanctioned, and universalised ideals about childhood. Our intention: to open out new possibilities for assembling knowledge about childhoods. As readers and editors, our close engagement with each of the chapters brought to life just how partial, contingent and shifting that process of knowing would always be. At times, and in spite of our own project to unsettle universalising notions of childhood, we felt challenged by each author's invitation to consider counter-discourses of the 'poor child'. This brought home how, far from being 'above' those dominant discourses, the understanding we have of our own lives is enmeshed in and given legitimacy by the very discourses we seek to unsettle.

This became a very present issue for us, as during the 2 years in which the book was being prepared, we each became first-time mothers and found ourselves negotiating middle-class Western ideals of childhood in our own lives – while reading, thinking and writing about the very different kinds of childhood discussed in these pages. Some of the foundations of our own parenting – for example, concerning ideals of safety, play and possible futures – were the same middle-class normative foundations we saw as imperative to challenge in this book. We found ourselves negotiating particular desires for our own children, from our positions of privilege, against the ethical and political manoeuvres we were calling for in this book. The chapters compelled us to think carefully, and in relation to our own lives, about what it means to challenge universal notions of the child in an unequal world. As readers, learning about Sabine's and Mama's experiences of work and mobility (in Morganti's chapter), Natalia's and Marcos' experiences of violence and racism (in Medrano's chapter), and even our own encounters with Tshering and his thoughts on work and schooling (in Hopkins' chapter), there were moments when we were reminded how 'normative childhood' (perhaps even that which we imagine for our own children?) is understood in terms of what it is *not* – it is *not* the lives of Sabine, Mama, Natalia, Marcos or Tshering. In this hierarchical dichotomous view, these 'poor children' are, in a sense, *necessary* to the notion of a normative childhood; they perform its 'Other'. As Patricia Holland argues:

> Children from the underdeveloped [sic] world, children who are poor, children who are sick, harmed or disabled pose problems for the dominant image, yet they are, in a curious way, necessary to it.
>
> (2004, 19)

However, each chapter in this book offered a challenge for its readers to rethink oppositional and deficit notions of the 'poor child'. Each of the chapters showed us that a middle-class childhood is not the only version of childhood; that the 'poor child' must be at once included as 'child' while not being subsumed by the normativity of the universal. They highlighted the ways in which children are active and strategic in negotiating their positionings. This is not to deny the effects of poverty on children's lives, but to *situate* children's lives with respect to those very social and historical conditions of inequality. So as readers, learning about the lives, representations, reform and regulation of childhoods in contexts of poverty, we were in many ways engaged in a process of de-centering the self. That is, we were not just 'learning about' the 'poor child', but we were pushed to think *relationally* about childhood and poverty, compelling (re)inspection of our own experiences and practices that come to bear on those lives, and indeed on their representation, reform and regulation.

There are two related points, or lessons if you will, that emerged from our process of reading that we take up in this chapter. The first is the ways in which a relational understanding of childhood and poverty can eschew a deficit view of the 'poor child' by shifting the frame from normative ideals to issues of distribution and justice. Broadly speaking, a relational view is one that takes into account temporal processes, constructions of meaning, social and cultural situatedness, material conditions, and interpretation. As we set out in the introduction, these are the complex 'cultural politics' of childhood in which the discursive and material are brought together analytically. Such an approach does not focus on the 'poor child' as a fixed category (which reaffirms deficit binary thinking), but focuses on tracing the conditions, practices and relations of distribution, recognition and representation that constitute the poor child's world and in fact stretch far beyond it. The second and related point, is that childhood subjectivities are always already multiple, partial and in flux; simultaneously constituted by and constituting of specific relations of power and context. This more complex view of the 'poor child' is central to dismantling the dichotomous understandings of child/adult, rural/urban, race, gender, and even the very location of poverty which shape education, development and indeed everyday life. As we outline in our concluding discussions, addressing these cultural politics of childhood and education are central to revisioning international development research, policy and practice.

Towards a relational understanding of the 'poor child'

The 'poor child' is the subject at the centre of educational development reforms, but how do we *know* that subject? While taking different theoretical and methodological approaches, the chapters in this book have each illustrated how the subject of the 'poor child' can be understood in complex relation to the social, historical and political practices that constitute our world. In doing so, they show there is no fixed ontology of the 'poor child'. By contesting a universal understanding of the 'poor child', however, we do not suggest a relativist position which skirts obligations for social change and social justice. Rather, the challenge for those working in the spheres of development research, policy and practice put forward by each of these chapters is to recognise and respond to the contingencies and relationalities of children's life-worlds. Here we briefly point to some of the ways each of the chapters in this book have contributed to such a relational understanding of the 'poor child'.

We start by considering Angela Githitho Muriithi's historical analysis of the role of labour and schooling in Kenya. Her chapter deftly illuminated how notions of childhood have shifted from a socialised child, to a labouring child, and to a schooled child in Kiratu. Importantly, these shifts are understood with respect to changing political, social and economic conditions which bear out in multiple ways, such as the racialisation of the African child at work, and the positioning of the schooling child as human capital. Githitho Muriithi's contextualising of Kenyan childhoods with respect to precolonial, colonial and postcolonial history compels readers to situate contemporary issues of labour and education, to question the assumed opposition between work and school, and to understand how children in these contexts come to straddle multiple worlds. By illuminating how children in Kiratu negotiate multiple worlds of work and school, Githitho Muriithi's research offers a more complex and situated alternative to the idea of a normative childhood, beyond discourses centred around schooling and play that circulate through global development policies.

The multiplicity of children's experiences, as understood in relation to their social contexts, is central too in Simona Morganti's analysis of mobility and trafficking in Benin. Her work does not diminish the need to urgently address a very real issue of child trafficking, but it is a call for greater nuance in understanding the issue itself. Through sweeping policy statements, legal and public discourse, notions of 'exploitation' and 'trafficking' have been emptied of their meaning: they are not understood in relation to the social practices and conditions of children's lives that in some cases represent negotiated mobility or positive economic participation. Importantly for our understanding of the 'poor child', Morganti's analysis disrupts notions that children are either exploited or agentic; a dichotomous view that legitimises contextually blind discourses of protection and saviour in development activity. Rather, through the accounts of young Beninese girls, we learn how practices of mobility, economic participation, and experiences of violence and exploitation are being constantly negotiated. In this sense, these children's subjectivities are always *in process* rather than being whole, becoming whole, or being wholly known. This highlights the relevance of a processual orientation for development research and policy; one that engages explicitly with the contingencies of their subjects, as much as with the contingencies of their practices and consequences.

The contribution by Luz María Moreno Medrano in this volume also offers an important perspective for education development work, especially to challenge dominant notions of the child subject being inherently vulnerable and passive. By foregrounding participatory and voice-centred approaches, Medrano's research shows how poor migrant children in Mexico are not only reflexive about their life-worlds but are able to strategically negotiate those worlds, often even in the face of extreme adversity. She puts forward a careful and critical account of resilience to demonstrate the ways in which the children in her research make and remake their worlds. Importantly, this resilience is not unhooked from social, historical or economic contexts, but is produced *through* such contexts, and sometimes in ways that disrupt acceptable practice (e.g. stealing). So what Medrano's discussions do, alongside the contributions by Morganti and Githitho Muriithi, is resist creating a new universalist position by simply turning the 'vulnerable poor child' on its head and making claims to its unfettered agency. Agency here is not accompanied by ideas of autonomy, rather it is understood as being contingent on the kinds of power relations that exist around the child. This distinction is significant: it purposefully pushes back against a neoliberal individualisation in which the perceived success or failure to deal with adversity (as a marker of resilience) is attributed to individual characteristics rather than being contingent on conditions of power. Medrano's account is a stark reminder for those working in education and development spheres that the vulnerability associated with the 'poor child' does not reside within an individual, but is a reflection of unequal distribution, recognition and representation that demands collective accountability and action.

The consequences of development discourses that draw on notions of the child as inherently vulnerable, weak or defenceless was powerfully illustrated by Kristina Gottschall in her chapter on Indigenous childhoods and poverty in Australia. Gottschall describes how such discourses are mobilised by government – particularly to characterise 'black childhood' in Australia – to legitimise paternalistic, authoritarian and white intervention in the name of protection. In response, her analysis of the cultural representation of Indigenous childhoods and poverty through Australian cinema highlighted the ways in which films can act as a pedagogic tool. Through cultural engagement, they allow us to rethink the basis of 'what we think we know and how we think we know it' (p. 49). That is, there are multiple representations of the Indigenous child at work in film; Gottschall's analysis discusses Indigenous children as being at risk, vulnerable and sick, as well as capable, good and cohesive. Through film-text, she shows us how new thinking and discourses can emerge about race, gender and poverty in relation to Indigenous childhoods. This brings us back to a processual orientation to development research, policy and practice. It encourages us to ask how our knowledge about the poor child is variously enabled and constrained by discourses, both dominant and counter, and how this knowledge can be used as a basis for change.

Along this line of questioning, Erica Burman's analysis of Save the Children's campaign in the UK 'It shouldn't happen here' unpacks how knowledge about poverty – particularly the location of poverty – is variously contested and legitimised. She shows how the campaign challenges essentialised notions of poverty by foregrounding its relativity, both within and across national contexts. The location of poverty 'here' (in the advanced economy of the UK), as highlighted by the campaign, problematises the binaries between North/South, rich/poor and donors/recipients within development discourse. Burman sees the campaign as challenging the division between 'here' and 'there' which works to underscore questions of distribution and justice in accounts of the 'poor child'. We return to this significant point later in our discussions. The relativity of poverty, how it plays out for example in the lives of the working poor in Britain, importantly orients us towards a relational understanding of the 'poor child'.

By tracing education development policy discourses of childhood at international, regional and sub-regional levels, Alexandra McCormick's contribution provides us with an insight into both the complex workings of international development policy, and the ways in which ideas about childhood and education often get taken up in different national contexts in strikingly similar ways. McCormick shows how the narrow but dominant policy understanding of the schooled child as the central hope for economic growth fails to respond to the socio-historical and political contexts of Southeast Asia and the South Pacific (such as post-conflict instability, language politics and religious diversity, and postcolonial histories). Urging readers to take a processual approach, her critical discourse analysis asks: 'Who controls policy representations? Who is being represented in policies and processes? How are representations of education needs and priorities constructed and deployed?' (p. 129). Importantly, such an analysis orients us towards the politics of representation of the 'global' child, and opens up the space for rethinking child subjectivity in the policy arena.

The consequences of reducing the 'poor child' to human capital for national economic development were also explored in our own chapters, in the contexts of India and Bhutan. In different ways, we critiqued how dominant discourses of development-as-modernisation narrow the project of education so significantly that they can work to reproduce deficit notions of the 'poor child'. A teleological notion of progress in modern educational development discourse can pit the success of the ideal (urban, middle-class) child against the failure of the rural poor child. Arathi Sriprakash's research in India showed how the poor rural child was seen in opposition to the urban middle-class child – the preferred citizen in a global, modern India. This hierarchical positioning became reinscribed through teachers' practices despite the intentions of classroom reforms to value multiple childhoods, including rural livelihoods. The discussions showed that a focus on 'multiple childhoods' in the education development sphere is not enough; such a pluralistic view does not acknowledge the workings of power which produce differentiation and can therefore reinforce inequalities. Here, Sriprakash's chapter signals the importance of a relational view of the child-subject in education development reform, not just a liberal approach that tolerates pluralism.

The commentaries and pictures of young Bhutanese yak herders in Lucy Hopkins' chapter shows just how unproductive modernist binary thinking about education and development can be. With others in this volume, Hopkins illustrates how multiple and at times conflicting subjectivities are negotiated by 'poor children' in their understandings of their lives and education. By listening to children's voices, and taking into account the ways they make and remake their worlds, Hopkins calls for the development project to move beyond its radically reductive figuration of the 'poor child'. Instead of closing down the possibilities for relational and contingent subjectivities, policy makers and practitioners should expect complexity in the ways childhoods are understood. This is to account for, as well as be accountable to, the consequences of education development activity.

In reading our way through each of the chapters in this volume, we see that the 'poor child' cannot be understood as a singular, coherent subject. While each contribution took different theoretical and methodological approaches, we can engage with their discussions along poststructural lines to see how the child subject is multiply constituted and fluid. In this view, the 'poor child' is a subject *in process*. This does not foreclose the possibility for ethical and political response, in the form of pro-poor development activity, education reform or community action. In fact, as Chris Weedon argues: 'the political significance of decentring the subject and abandoning the belief in essential subjectivity is that it opens up subjectivity to change' (1997, 32). By showing how the 'poor child' does not have a fixed ontology, this book underscores how the subjectivities of children living in poverty are constituted by and in relation to others, through local and global contexts. As we signal in the final section of this chapter, this can enable a set of practices for education development policy, research and practice that is relational in its orientation and processual in its approach. Universalism is a discourse based on foreclosure. Instead, by keeping ourselves open to the relationalities and contingencies of the 'poor child', we can move beyond simplistic solutions for misunderstood problems in education and international development.

The problem of poverty

> Between me and the other world there is ever an unasked question: unasked by some through feelings of delicacy; by others through the difficulty of rightly framing it. All, nevertheless, flutter round it [. . .] *How does it feel to be a problem?*
>
> (Du Bois 1903, 1)

The discussions in this book aimed to challenge the normative ideal of childhood that emerges from the image of a middle-class, Western, white, urban, male child. They shook up deficit, dichotomous notions of the 'poor child' that locate her outside of, and problematic to, that ideal. In doing so, and in different ways, the authors in this book shifted the frame from the problem of the 'poor child' to the problem of poverty. They foregrounded the relations of inequality that come to bear on young lives, rather than give legitimacy to a fixed 'ideal' against which one, as Du Bois suggests, gets measured. In a sense, this turns around the question (un)asked of Du Bois, *How does it feel to be a problem?*, to interrogate the ways in which the 'other world', far from being a discrete onlooker, is enmeshed in the problem of poverty.

What we are suggesting here – that the 'poor child' be understood not as a fixed subject for reform, but in shifting relation to politics of poverty and inequality – is not necessarily new. But we argue it has become all the more important to reiterate in a current political context that is witnessing – globally – a decided turning away from collective obligations to social justice, despite evidence of deepening social inequality. For example, as we write this conclusion in Australia, the newly elected conservative government has proposed significant cuts to social welfare, the dismantling of universal health care, and a reduction in international development aid by 10 per cent in real terms. Such an explicit attack on the poor – both in national and international contexts – has been rationalised through the notion that 'the age of entitlement is over'.[1] Implicit in such thinking is that the poor have been undeserving recipients of social support, and 'poverty' is an individual not societal responsibility (see also Phillips 2014). This works to cut the 'other world' free from matters of poverty, as if 'poverty' somehow exists independently of that world. It reflects a persistent tendency of 'exteriorising or exceptionalising poverty, which makes it the product of abnormal or pathological, rather than everyday, social processes' (Mosse 2010, 1158). The relational view of the 'poor child' put forward in this book is an explicit response to that untethering and exteriorising; it has traced the lives, representations and regulation of poor children as a tracing of the relations of social inequality itself.

What is the significance of a relational view of the 'poor child' for how the problem of poverty is understood within research and policy domains? There has been a long debate about the conceptualisation and measurement of poverty in economics and in development studies more broadly. Grusky and Kanbur note a 'third phase' of economics which from the 1990s has been in part 'animated by concerns fundamentally sociological in nature' (2006, 13). During this phase, rational choice models, in which individual preferences are seen as rational, fixed, and given meaning independent of cultural or institutional contexts, were heavily critiqued. Theorisations of adaptive preferences have attempted to overcome some of the fixity and decontextualisation of those rational choice models. Further, the multidimensionality of poverty has been accepted into mainstream development economics, for example through the Human Development Index which is a weighted sum of income, literacy and life expectancy. Although these moves gesture towards the complexity of poverty, it can be argued that they continue to impose an excessively abstract and statistical lens on the social world.

The focus on subjectivity, relationality and contingency in our reading of the 'poor child' in this book poses a challenge for more nuanced and situated approaches to understanding poverty and its consequences. It makes a space for the 'poor child' to be included as a 'child' while simultaneously eschewing the normativity of the universal. Rather than working to 'save' the poor child, this view calls for an approach to childhood and poverty that pays attention to the politics of agency and disempowerment that are embedded in current international development discourses. We conclude this chapter, and our volume, by discussing this challenge in relation to research, policy and practice in education and international development.

'Revisioning' education and international development research, policy and practice

We are writing this at a time of global reflection and debate about the future of international development. The UN has led extensive regional, national and thematic consultations in preparation for the post-2015 development agenda in which issues of childhood traverse key themes including education, inequalities, health and population dynamics (http://www.worldwewant2015.org). Our desire to open up the complexities and contingencies of childhood and poverty have been echoed through many of these global conversations – across myriad case studies, discussion papers and focus groups, particularly through the UN's efforts of 'reaching out to the poor, the marginalised and others whose voices are not usually heard' in its publication *A Million Voices* (UNDG 2013, iii).

However, we also see how the post-2015 consultation process has attempted to rein in the messiness of development to provide simple (or perhaps simplistic) messages about a coherent agenda for international development. Within the education domain, this has led to proclamations such as 'the vision for the post-2015 education agenda calls for a *single harmonized global education framework*' (UNDG 2013, 108, emphasis in original).

This template approach for education – a context-free 'travelling rationality' (Craig and Porter 2006) – is offered despite a simultaneous focus in the post-2015 agenda on 'quality' and 'process', and a contextualised view of education that explicitly seeks to take into account 'increasing economic interdependency, globalisation and technological development; growing pressure on natural resources and increased energy consumption leading to environmental degradation; rapidly changing labour markets; greater interconnectedness; shifting geo-politics; older and more urbanised populations; population growth and "youth bulges"; and growing unemployment and widening inequalities' (UNDG 2013, 108). The tendency towards simplification, categorisation and universality appeals to a desire for development to be a process that is coherent, linear and commensurable, and whose technical success can be easily measured in the face of such complexity and contingency.

Arguably, however, the tensions between contingency, complexity and universality engender an opportunity. As Judith Butler (2004, 339) suggests, universality is an abstraction that remains to be specified: 'it doesn't mean that it cannot be said, but what becomes clear is that it's "empty" when it's said; it only comes to life when it is applied and redeployed in ways that cannot be fully anticipated by anyone who strategically mobilises it'. The discourse of universality implicit in statements like '*single harmonized global education framework*' is, according to Butler, 'driven into crisis again and again by the foreclosures that it makes and that it's forced to rearticulate itself' (2004, 340). For those working in the space of education and international development, there is a task and an opportunity at hand: to keep the discourse of universality open, 'to keep it as a contested site of persistent crisis and not let it be settled' (2004, 340). This 'unsettling' has been precisely the aim of our collection in relation to the 'poor child', and we see it as key to the revisioning of education and international development research, policy and practice more broadly.

Indeed, the relational view of the 'poor child' put forward in this book does very specific political work: in unsettling universal discourses of childhood, education and development, it foregrounds what is at stake ethically if we do not do so. Butler's rereading of Adorno's notion of ethical violence is relevant here: this occurs when an ethical norm – an abstract universality – 'ignores the existing social conditions under which it might be appropriated' (2005, 6). With Adorno, Butler argues that an ethos becomes violent when it 'fails to undergo a reformulation of itself in response to the social and cultural conditions it includes within the scope of its applicability' (2005, 6). In this instance the ethical norm becomes problematic – violent even – because it forecloses the possibility of debate around the status of the universal as normative; its indifference to the context in which it is being enacted is violent because it is imposed without taking the particularity of the social and cultural into consideration.

So our revisioning of development research, policy and practice is as much a matter of ethics as it is a matter of methodology. In our call for a relational and processual approach to understanding the lives of poor children, we draw on the significant contributions of the anthropology of development. Anthropology as a field has had a long history of engagement with international development, and has offered (not uncontested) ways of examining the social processes of 'development' that are 'inevitably transnational, intercultural, and multiscalar and involve the interaction and intermediation of extensive actor networks, with different logics and life-worlds' (Mosse 2013, 228).[2] In gesturing towards a relational and processual approach that can trace these logics and life-worlds, we take Curtis and Spencer's (2012) notion of engaging ethnographically with development as a 'category of practice' that is produced and reproduced as part of people's understandings and experiences of the world. This orients us towards seeing how development 'emerges from, and produces, particular historical circumstances, particular cultural logics, and finally particular subjectivities' (Curtis and Spencer 2012, 179). That is to say, 'development' is not in itself a stable object of critique. Indeed, the proclamation of a *single harmonized global education framework* that is said to have emerged from 'a million voices' (UNDG 2013) is a reminder that development is 'not a coherent set of practices but a set of practices that produces coherence' (Yarrow 2011, 6).

For those working in the development space, tracing the processes through which these practices, circumstances, logics and subjectivities gain their apparent stability and durability in spite of contingency, diffused agency, heterogeneous interests and destabilising elements (Mosse 2013), is to trace how things have come to be, *but also how they can change*. This is the political value of a relational and processual approach; for example, it unsettles the universality of the 'poor child' and follows the conditions, contingencies, practices and consequences of inequality in children's lives. A number of anthropologists of development have taken up this relational and processual orientation, drawing variously on network approaches (cf. Mosse 2005; Li 2007), historical and spatial inquiry (cf. Moore 2005; Subramanian 2009), and tracing practices of governmentality (cf. Englund 2006). In this book we stop short of prescribing specific methods of research or engagement because what we have shown through our multi-disciplinary, multi-method collection is that a relational and processual approach can take a number of forms. Read as a whole, the volume cuts across disciplinary boundaries and instead mobilises multiple methodological approaches to think about the 'poor child' in more complex and nuanced ways. Our intention has been to provide multiple frameworks for interrogating the cultural politics of education, development and childhood. In doing so, we hope this provides a basis for our readers to think critically and reflexively about the problem of poverty and the practices of development in relation to the 'poor child'. This would, in a sense, fulfil the driving desire of this volume to 'de-discipline the child, to view the child from the margins' (p. 15).

Notes

1 This phrase was taken from Australia's then Shadow-Treasurer Joe Hockey's speech entitled 'The end of the age of entitlement' to the Institute of Economic Affairs in London on 17 April 2012. It has been widely repeated by Hockey, now Treasurer, and the current conservative government, to justify cuts to social welfare.
2 The field itself has seen a number of shifts and contestations, for example, relating to its own imperial history, the discursive and cultural turn in the social sciences, the reification of the 'local' and bottom-up participatory approaches, and more recent moves towards historicity and spatiality in anthropologies of development (see Mosse (2013) for a recent review of the field).

References

Butler, Judith. 2004. 'Competing Universalities.' In *The Judith Butler Reader*, edited by S. Salih, 258–277. Oxford: Blackwell Publishing.
Butler, Judith. 2005. *Giving an Account of Oneself.* New York: Fordham University Press.
Craig D., and D. Porter. 2006. *Development Beyond Neoliberalism: Governance, Poverty Reduction and Political Economy.* London: Routledge.
Curtis J., and J. Spencer. 2012. 'Anthropology and the political.' In *The Sage Handbook of Social Anthropology*, Vol. 1, edited by R. Fardon, O. Harris, T. Marchand, M. Nuttall, C. Shore et al., 168–82. Thousand Oaks: Sage.
Du Bois, W.E.B. 1903. *The Souls of Black Folk: Essays and Sketches.* Chicago: A.C. McClurg.
Englund, H. 2006. *Prisoners of Freedom: Human Rights and the African Poor.* Berkeley: University of California Press.
Grusky, David, and Ravi Kanbur. 2006. *Poverty and Inequality.* Stanford: Stanford University Press.
Holland, Patricia. 2004. *Picturing Childhood: The Myth of the Child in Popular Imagery.* New York: I.B. Tauris.
Li, T.M. 2007. 'Practices of assemblage and community forest management.' *Economy and Society* 36: 263–293.
Moore, D. 2005. *Suffering for Territory: Race, Place, and Power in Zimbabwe.* Durham, NC: Duke University Press.
Mosse, David. 2005. *Cultivating Development: An Ethnography of Aid Policy and Practice.* London: Pluto.
Mosse, David. 2010. 'A Relational Approach to Durable Poverty, Inequality and Power.' *The Journal of Development Studies* 46 (7): 1156–1178.

Mosse, David. 2013. 'The Anthropology of International Development.' *Annual Review of Anthropology* 42: 227–246.
Phillips, Ruth. 2014. 'Welfare.' In *2014–15 Budget Response from Academic Stand Against Poverty, Oceania*. Sydney: University of Sydney.
Subramanian, A. 2009. *Shorelines: Space and Rights in South India*. Stanford: Stanford University Press.
UNDG. 2013. *A Million Voices: The World We Want. A Sustainable Future with Dignity for All*. United Nations Development Group.
Weedon, Chris. 1997. *Feminist Practice and Poststructuralist Theory*. 2nd edn. Oxford: Oxford University Press.
Yarrow, T. 2011. *Development Beyond Politics: Aid, Activism and NGOs in Ghana*. Basingstoke: Palgrave Macmillan.

Index

abstract child subject 7, 8
adaptation skills 108–109
Adorno, Theodor 5, 202
adult-child relationship 10, 185
Africa 32, 34, 35, 196; child mobility 87; child trafficking 84, 89; colonial exploitation of labour 72; formal education in 73
agency 14, 178, 197, 200
aid agencies 26, 33, 38n4, 129
Aitken, Stuart 13
Althusser, Louis 28
anthropology 202, 203n2
Ariès, Philippe 66–67, 78, 80n3
arts-based research methodology 168–169, 170, 187
Asia and Pacific Regional Framework for Action 137
AusAID *see* Australian Agency for International Development
austerity measures 26, 37, 38
Australia 15, 43–61, 197, 199–200
Australian Agency for International Development (AusAID) 128, 145
autonomy 114, 115, 117, 120, 121, 197

Baird, Barbara 6, 8, 13–14
Balagopalan, Sarada 11–12, 13, 104, 151, 158, 174
Basu, Anustap 152
'becoming' child subject 9, 11, 55, 176, 186
Beneath Clouds (2002) 44, 51, 53, 55–56, 57
Benin 16, 84–101, 196

Bernstein, Basil 152, 159, 163
best interests 11
Bhabha, Homi 17n1
Bhutan 16–17, 168–190, 198
'black child' subject 48, 53, 55, 197
Blommaert, Jan 130
Boswell, Christina 102, 121
Bourdillon, M. 81n15
Boyden, Jo 67, 97
Burley, Hansel 106
Burman, Erica 7–10, 12, 15, 23–42, 43, 175, 193–194, 197
Butler, Judith 5, 25, 201–202

Cambodia 128, 136, 139, 140–141, 143–144
Canals-Cerdá, José 65
capitalism 70, 72
caste 153, 158, 160, 161, 162, 163, 164–165
CDA *see* critical discourse analysis
charity 24–25, 29, 34, 36, 37
child-centred education 151, 152, 155–156, 158, 163–164, 165, 166
child labour: abolitionist and child centred discourses 67; ILO Convention 98n4; impact on schooling 65; Kenya 66, 70–73, 74, 75–76, 77–78, 79–80, 196; Mexico 115; migrant children in Benin 85, 86, 87, 91–97; repudiated by educational discourses 176; use of the term 68–69; Western perspective 121; *see also* work
Child Poverty Act (2010) 26
'child saving' discourses 11, 13

child trafficking 84–101, 196
childhood: Australian films 49–57; challenging the concept of 103–105; child labour and education 65, 66; developmental approaches to 67, 176, 188n5; discourses of 9, 23, 25, 26, 33, 104, 121; images of 36; Indigenous child subjects 44–45, 48; Kenya 69–80, 196; as living social practice 67–68; Mexico 104; multiple childhoods 104, 151–152, 154, 158, 164–166, 195, 198; nature and 7–8; popular films 46; racialisation of 72; relational view 195–199, 200, 201–202; South Pacific 141; universalism 194; as Western invention 66–67; *see also* normative childhood; 'poor child'
Christianity 143
citizenship 152, 153, 175, 176
civil society organisations (CSOs) 127, 133, 135, 138, 139, 146
class 8, 14, 23, 37; India 157–158, 160, 161, 163, 164–165; popular films 46, 47; *see also* middle class; working class
Coalition government (UK) 26, 37
collectivism 138
Collins, Felicity 50
colonialism 4, 10, 49; India 155; Kenya 70–73, 79; Mexico 103, 104–105, 118
coming-of-age films 49–50
community support 108
computer-assisted learning 157–158
corporal punishment 112–113, 164
Cox, Marcus 143
creativity 111
Crilly, Shane 46
crime 76
critical discourse analysis (CDA) 128–130, 141, 146
CSOs *see* civil society organisations
cultural analysis 45, 49, 56
cultural diffusion 182–183
cultural politics 6, 15, 44, 195, 203
cultural relativism 14, 17n3, 68
cultural studies 15, 16, 168–169, 193

culture 8; construction of identities 103; popular films 45, 46; resilience 117
Curtis, J. 202
customs 143

Daily Mail 31, 32–35, 36, 37
Dakar Framework 134–135, 138, 146, 154
Davis, Therese 50
De Mause, Lloyd 80n3
deconstruction 24, 26
deficit model of the child 10, 104, 168; Bhutan 174, 175, 177; dominant discourses 187; India 16, 159, 161, 162, 163, 164–165; Indigenous child subjects 55, 56; relational view of childhood 195; resilience 105–106
Department for International Development 36
Dermody, Sue 51
development 5, 10, 17; anthropology of 202; Bhutan 169; discourses 6–7, 8–13, 169, 188, 200; India 152, 155; multiple subjectivities 198; NGO campaigns 35; politicisation of 37; post-2015 development agenda 200–201; practices of 202, 203
developmental approaches to childhood 67, 176, 188n5
developmental assets 106, 108–109
disasters 33, 36, 74
discipline 164, 185, 187, 189n10
discourse analysis 15, 24, 135; critical 128–130, 141, 146; multiple discourses in negotiation of subjectivity 170, 171
discrimination 107, 109, 110, 118, 119, 145
divorce 106
djoko 86
domestic violence 142–143
domestic workers 85, 91–92, 93, 94–96
drill-based pedagogies 164
drug trafficking 77
Du Bois, W.E.B. 199

E-net for Justice 145
earn and learn schools 81n15

East Asia 157
economic growth 175, 198; Bhutan 169; India 151–152, 153, 154, 157
economic struggles 110, 111, 112
education: child labour and 65–66, 72, 77–78, 79; children's drawings in Bhutan 168, 170, 171–176, 177–180, 181–187; dominant discourses 12, 16, 168, 169–170, 173, 177, 178, 186, 187–188; educational expansion in Bhutan 169; India 151–152, 153, 154–165, 166; Kenya 66, 70, 73–74, 75, 77–78; Mexico 116, 117; middle-class subject 11; modernist binaries 171, 173, 187–188; parental 107–108; politics of interpretation 47; post-2015 development agenda 201
Education for All (EFA) 78–79, 127–128, 130–135, 147n3; *Asia and Pacific Regional Framework for Action* 137; Bhutan 169; Cambodia 144; *Dakar Framework* 134–135, 138, 146, 154; genre chain 129–130, 131–133; India 154, 156; National Action Plans 129, 135, 136, 140; national processes 138–141; Philippines 145
elementary education *see* primary education
elites 153
equality 6, 14, 15
Erny, Pierre 70
essentialism 14, 103
ethical violence 202
ethnicity 5, 144; *see also* race
ethnocentrism 32, 68
ethnography 105
European colonialism 72
European Union (EU) 27
Evans, Gary W. 76
exploitation: child labour 65, 72, 80, 115; definition of 98n7; migrant children in Benin 85–86, 90, 92, 93, 95, 97, 196

family: construction of identities 103; family breakdown in Kenya 76, 78; migrant children in Benin 86–87, 88, 91, 93, 94–95; modernity in Bhutan 183; nuclear family 87; as protective factor 108, 109, 117, 119; *see also* parents
famine 33
feminist theory 24, 45, 46–47
films 43–44, 45–47, 49–57, 197
forced labour 71–72
fostering 86, 90, 91, 95
Foucauldian analysis 24
FPE *see* Free Primary Education
Fraser, Nancy 17n2
Free Primary Education (FPE) 66, 74, 79
Frones, Ivar 67–68

Gallasch, Keith 51
gender 8, 14, 23, 195; Education for All National Action Plans 136; gender equality 127, 146; India 160; Indigenous child subjects 44, 45, 50, 197; migrant girls in Benin 85, 88, 91–92, 93–96; popular films 46, 47; South Pacific 142–143; *see also* girls; masculinity; women
genre chains 129–130, 131–133, 135
Gillard, Garry 50
girls: civil society organisations 138; migrant girls in Benin 85, 88, 91–92, 93–96; Millennium Development Goals 127, 134; South Pacific 142–143; Southeast Asia 144, 145
Giroux, Henry 47
Gonick, Marnina 50
Gopalakrishnan, Shankar 152
Gordon, Kimberley A. 106
Gordon, Linda 11
Gottschall, Kristina 15, 43–61, 193–194, 197
Greene, Sheila 121
Gronemeyer, Marianne 37
Grusky, David 200
Guardian 32
Gustafsson, Berit 143

hairstyles 187, 189n10
Heady, Christopher 65
health issues 31
Healy, Joan 144

Index

Hill, Malcolm 121
Hinduism 152, 153, 160
Hobbs, Sandy 68
Hockey, Joe 203n1
Hodge, Robert 28
Holland, Patricia 194
home 87
Hopkins, Lucy 3–19, 168–190, 193–204
housing 107, 109, 111–112
human capital 134, 198; Bhutan 169; India 154, 155, 156; Kenya 66, 73–74, 79, 196
human resources development 140–141
human rights 89, 140, 143
hunger 75

identity 6, 103, 115, 119, 121, 173, 187; *see also* subjectivity
ILO *see* International Labour Organization
immanence 8–11, 175, 176, 185, 186
immigrants 27, 30, 37, 103; *see also* migration
income 107
India 3–4, 16, 36, 72, 151–167, 198
Indigeneity 46
Indigenous Australians 43–61, 197
Indigenous Mexicans 105, 117–119
individualism 37, 67, 173, 174, 197
Indonesia 128, 136, 139, 140, 145
inequalities 106, 134, 197, 198; India 152, 165, 166; indigenous communities 118; policy 127–128; politics of poverty 199–200; popular films 45; post-2015 development agenda 201; Save the Children UK campaign 33, 34, 37; Southeast Asia 138; subjecthood 47
innocence 8–9, 11–13, 17n4, 48, 55, 104, 120
intelligence 163
interdisciplinarity 5, 14–15, 193, 202–203
International Labour Organization (ILO) 77, 98n4
interpellation 28
interpretation, politics of 45–47
the Intervention (2007) 48–49
Islam 145

James, Adrian 68, 69, 78
James, Allison 67, 68, 69, 78
Jenkins, Henry 4
Jennings, Karen 46

Kanbur, Ravi 200
Karnataka 156–165
kastom 140, 143
Kaviraj, Sudipta 152–153, 155, 159
Kayongo-Male, Diane 70
Kelada, Odette 49
Kellett, Mary 121
Kenya 16, 66, 69–80, 196
Kenyatta, Jomo 69–70
Kinga, Sonam 174
Kiratu 66, 69–80
Kress, Gunther 28

'labouring child' 66, 70–73, 74, 77, 78, 79–80
land alienation 70, 71, 75, 80n8
land rights 47, 71
Langton, Marcia 46
language: critical discourse analysis 128–129, 146; Indonesia 145; Laos 144; Philippines 145; Save the Children UK campaign 33, 35, 37; South Pacific 141, 142
Laos 128, 136, 139, 140–141, 143–144
learning 45, 47, 146
Leonard, Madeleine 104
Lieten, Georges Kristoffel 68
life expectancy 43
life-long learning 127, 136, 146
literacy 127, 136, 138, 141, 146, 160, 178
'lost child' trope 51
Lovell, Melissa 57n3
Lusted, David 47

malnutrition 75
Mannion, G. 84–85
Marsh, Pauline 50
masculinity 3, 4, 47–48; development discourses 9; Indigenous Australians 53–54, 57
materiality 193
maturity 67

Index 209

McCormick, Alexandra 16, 127–150, 198
McKee, Alan 45, 46
MDGs *see* Millennium Development Goals
media 26, 32–35, 36
Medrano, Luz María Stella Moreno 16, 102–123, 194, 196–197
Mekong Delta 138, 143–144
Melanesia 138, 141–143
metaphors 46
Mexico 16, 102–123, 196–197
Meyer, Anneke 8, 48
middle class 3, 4, 47–48, 103, 176, 199; children as future citizens 11; development discourses 9; future adult subject 175; imposition of middle-class values 121; India 151, 152–153, 157, 162–163, 164–165; 'middle-class colonisation' 120; Western ideals of childhood 194
migration: Benin 84, 85–86, 87, 88, 89–90, 96–97; Mexico 103, 115; protective factors 108; *see also* immigrants
Miliband, David 37
Millennium Development Goals (MDGs) 127–129, 134, 137, 140, 141–142, 146, 147n3
missionaries 73, 141, 143
mobility 84, 85–86, 87, 89–90, 96–97, 196
modal verbs 28
modernisation 168, 176, 198; Bhutan 169, 172, 174, 175, 183, 188n1; future adult subject 175; India 151–152, 154, 159
modernity 187–188; Bhutan 169–170, 171–173, 174, 179, 180–183, 188n1, 189n7; dialectic with tradition 168, 173, 176, 178, 183, 187; India 152–153, 154, 155, 159, 165, 166
morality 176, 177, 181, 182–183, 186, 187
Moreton-Robinson, Aileen 46–47, 51
Morganti, Simona 16, 84–101, 194, 196
mortality rates 43
Mosse, David 200, 202
multi-scalar policy discourses 128–130

multiple childhoods 104, 151–152, 154, 158, 164–166, 195, 198
Muriithi, Angela Githitho 16, 65–83, 196
Murray, Douglas 32–35
Myers, William E. 67

Nali Kali programme 158, 159, 160, 163–164
NAPs *see* National Action Plans
narrative approaches 102, 121
National Action Plans (NAPs) 129, 135, 136, 140
national identity 169
nationhood 175, 176, 183, 188n5
nature 7–8
Nee, Meas 144
neglect 52, 55, 106, 162
neo-colonialism 85
neoliberalism: discourses of individualism 37, 173, 174, 186, 197; India 152, 153, 156, 165–166
NGOs *see* non-governmental organisations
Nieuwenhuys, Olga 4, 7, 14
Njeru, Enos Hudson 70
non-governmental organisations (NGOs) 35, 85; Cambodia 144; child labour 65; child trafficking 84, 86, 88, 93, 96–97; Education for All National Action Plans 136; South Pacific 143
normative childhood 1, 4–5, 6–8, 47–48, 194, 199; challenging 121; children's drawings in Bhutan 171–172; Education for All 128; India 162, 163; Indigenous Australian children in film 52, 55; play 12–13; Western concepts of childhood 8–9; *see also* universalism
nuclear family 87

OECD *see* Organisation for Economic Cooperation and Development
Ong, Aihwa 165–166
O'Regan, Tom 50
Organisation for Economic Cooperation and Development (OECD) 130
'Other' 3, 4, 194

210 Index

overseas aid 36
Overton, John 71
Oxfam 38n4

Pal, Joyojeet 158
Palmer, Dave 50
Papua New Guinea 128, 136, 139, 140, 141–143
parents: children's drawings in Bhutan 186; children's resilience in Mexico 110, 112–113, 115–116, 117–118, 119; India 161–162, 163; lack of education 107–108; migrant children in Benin 86–87, 91, 93, 94–95; *see also* family
participation 137
paternalism 48, 161, 197
patriarchy 143
pedagogy 164
Pedraza-Gomez, Zandra 72
Penn, Helen 78–79
people-smuggling 89
personal characteristics 108–109
Philippines 128, 136, 139, 140, 145
place 29, 45, 46, 47
play 11, 12–13
pluralism 151, 152, 158, 198
policy 35, 102, 127–150, 200–202; child labour and education in Kenya 78–80; critical discourse analysis 128–130, 146; discourses 127–128, 145–146, 193, 198; education policy in India 154–156, 164–165; genre chains 129–130, 131–133, 135; narrative approach 121; national processes 138–141; regional dynamics 135–138; Save the Children UK campaign 31–32; sub-regional contexts 137–138
politics: critical discourse analysis 128–129; Save the Children UK campaign 34–35; *see also* cultural politics
politics of interpretation 45–47
'poor child' 3, 5, 23, 120–121, 168, 194–195, 203; Indian rural poor child 152, 153–154, 155–156, 158, 159–165, 166; Indigenous 44; policy discourses 127–128, 134, 145–146, 193; reimagining the 13–15; relational view 195–199, 200, 201–202; resilience 106; *see also* childhood; deficit model of the child; poverty
popular films 43–44, 45–47, 49–57, 197
postcolonialism 10, 17n1, 24, 45, 105, 120; contemporary cinema 46–47, 50; India 155
poststructuralism 14, 45, 46–47, 170, 171, 188, 199
'potentiality' 73–74, 76
poverty 6, 107, 195; Australia 43, 44, 57n1; child labour 65; children's drawings in Bhutan 168, 170, 171–176, 177, 179–181, 186, 188n7; dominant discourses 168, 169–170, 173, 177, 181, 187–188; Indian rural poor child 152, 153–154, 155–156, 158, 159–165, 166; Indigenous child subjects 44, 45, 52, 53, 56, 57, 197; Kenya 72, 73, 74–76, 78, 79; Mexico 103, 104, 111, 114, 120; modernist binaries 171, 173, 187–188; problem of 199–200, 203; relationality of 15; relative 31, 34, 35–36, 38; rurality and 188n4; Save the Children UK campaign 23, 24, 26–38, 197; South Pacific 141; Western discourses 104; *see also* 'poor child'
power 12, 121, 197; adult-child relationship 185; children's drawings 170–171; critical discourse analysis 128–129, 146; multiple childhoods 151, 195
primary (elementary) education 127, 136, 138, 140, 147n3; *Asia and Pacific Regional Framework for Action* 137; Bhutan 169; gender equality 145; India 153, 154, 156, 157, 160, 166n1; Kenya 66, 74, 79; Millennium Development Goals 134, 146
private schools 153, 160, 161, 163
processual approach 196, 198, 199, 202
progress 10, 168, 176, 187–188, 198
proletarianisation 71, 73, 80n5
prostitution 77
protectionism 11–12, 67, 79, 103–104; child trafficking 85, 97; Education

for All 78; Indigenous child subjects 48, 54, 197; migrant children 88
protective factors 106, 108, 109, 112–113, 117, 119, 120
Prout, Alan 9, 67
psychology 67, 106

Quijano, A. 72

Rabbit Proof Fence (2002) 49
race 8, 14, 23, 195; 'black child' subject 48, 53, 55; colonial exploitation of labour 72; Indigenous child subjects 44, 45, 197; popular films 46, 47, 52; racial divide 51; Save the Children UK campaign 29–30
racism 30, 107, 117; Indigenous child subjects 44, 52, 56; Mexico 105
rationalism 155
rationality 67, 200
recontextualisation 152, 159, 163–165
reflexivity 121
relational view of childhood 195–199, 200, 201–202
relative poverty 31, 34, 35–36, 38
relativism 14, 17n3, 68, 114, 195
representation 15–16, 36, 193, 195, 198
resilience 102–103, 104, 105–120, 121, 196–197
Ridao-Cano, Cristóbal 65
Rigg, Julie 54
risk factors 106, 107–108, 109
Robinson, Kerry 7
Roder, Dolma 173, 174
role models 108
rural life: children's views in Bhutan 175, 177–179, 181, 184, 188, 189n7; Indian rural poor child 152, 153–154, 155–156, 158, 159–165, 166
Ryan-Fazileau, Susan 51

Salesian Sisters 93, 98n10
Samson and Delilah (2009) 44, 51, 52–53, 56, 57
Sarva Shiksha Abhiyan (SSA) 156–158
Save the Children UK 23, 24–38, 197
'schooled child' 66, 73–74, 78, 79–80, 196, 198

schools 11–13; Bhutan 169, 170–171; India 16, 153, 159–165; Kenya 77; Mexico 102, 116, 117, 120; modernity versus tradition 173; protective factors 108; *see also* education
Schuelka, Matthew J. 169
Scotland 30
Seccombe, Karen 107
secondary education: India 153; Indonesia 145; Kenya 78; Zimbabwe 81n15
self-esteem 106
Sen, Ivan 44, 50–51, 54, 55
sexism 107
sexual abuse 48–49, 85–86, 113
single parents 76
social mobility 153, 154, 161, 172
social semiotics 26
social support 106, 107, 108
social workers 93–94
'socialised child' 66, 69–70, 74, 78, 79
sociology 15, 106, 193
South Africa 36
South Pacific 16, 127, 128, 130, 135–143, 198
Southeast Asia 16, 127, 128, 130, 135–141, 143–145, 198
Spencer, J. 202
Sriprakash, Arathi 3–19, 151–167, 168, 175, 183, 193–204
SSA *see* Sarva Shiksha Abhiyan
Stacey, Jackie 9
Steedman, Carolyn K. 163
stereotypes 46
Stichter, Sharon B. 80n5
subjectivity 5, 14, 168, 199, 200; future adult subject 175, 176, 185; Indigenous Australians 49; multiple discourses in negotiation of subjectivity 170, 171; multiple subjectivities 195, 198; of need 35–36; policy arena 198; popular films 45; textual representations 15–16
suicide 183

Taylor, Affrica 7
teachers 159–165, 179, 184–185, 186–187, 198

technology 157
teenage pregnancy 106
texts 15–16, 24, 25, 193–194; policy 130, 135; politics of interpretation 45–47
Thornton, Warwick 44, 50–51
Toomelah (2011) 44, 51, 52, 53–55, 57
tradition 168, 173, 176, 178, 183, 187
truth 36
Tyler, Deborah 159

UK *see* United Kingdom
UKIP *see* United Kingdom Independence Party
UN *see* United Nations
UNCRC *see* United Nations Convention on the Rights of the Child
UNESCO *see* United Nations Educational, Social and Cultural Organisation
UNICEF *see* United Nations Children's Fund
United Kingdom (UK) 15, 23, 26–38, 43, 197
United Kingdom Independence Party (UKIP) 27, 37
United Nations (UN) 127, 169, 200–201
United Nations Children's Fund (UNICEF) 26, 31, 89, 91, 93, 175
United Nations Convention on the Rights of the Child (UNCRC) 7, 11, 65, 78, 98n1, 137
United Nations Educational, Social and Cultural Organisation (UNESCO) 66, 130, 131, 132, 134, 137
universalism 5, 7, 14, 17n3, 199; abstract 151; Butler on universality 201–202; universal child subject 3, 5, 6–8, 13, 14, 47–48; universal view of childhood 67, 68, 194
urbanisation 103, 173, 182

Vanuatu 128, 136, 139, 140, 141–143
Vasanta, Duggirala 166
vidomègons 85, 90–92, 93, 95
violence: ethical 202; Indigenous child subjects 52; intra-familial 109, 110, 112–113; Kenya 76; migrant children in Benin 87, 92, 94–95, 96, 196; as risk factor 106; South Pacific 142–143
vocational education 141
voices, children's 84–85, 103, 114, 121
vulnerability 9, 103, 120, 197; childhood innocence 11–12; developmental approach to childhood 67; Education for All 78; Indigenous child subject 45, 48, 50, 52, 53, 57; Kenya 79; migrant children 86, 88, 94; policy discourses 127, 134; teacher-student relationship 185; universal child subject 14; Western concepts of childhood 55, 104

Wales 30
Walji, Parveen 70
Wallace, Jo-Ann 10
Weedon, Chris 199
welfare provision 26, 37, 200
Western culture 10, 104, 176
White, Ben 67
white collar work 173, 174–175, 183
whiteness 3–5, 9, 30, 47–48
Whitham, Graham 39n10
women: India 155; labour in colonial Kenya 71; South Pacific 142–143; Southeast Asia 144, 145; *see also* gender; girls
Woodhead, Jacinda 50–51
work 12, 65–66; child poverty 31; children's drawings in Bhutan 171, 173–175, 179–181, 183, 188n7; India 153, 162; Kenya 70–73, 75–76, 77–78, 79–80, 196; Mexico 112, 114, 115, 116, 120; migrant children in Benin 85, 86, 87, 91–97; non-Western conceptions of childhood 67; *see also* child labour
working class 30, 121
working poor 24, 30, 31, 33, 36, 37, 39n9, 43
World Bank 36, 130

yak herding 177–181, 188n4, 189n7
Yarrow, T. 202

Zimbabwe 81n15